Jaguar Books on Latin America

Series Editors

WILLIAM H. BEEZLEY, Neville (
American Studies, Texas Christian University
COLIN M. MACLACHLAN, Professor and Chair, Department
of History, Tulane University

Volumes Published

John E. Kicza, ed., *The Indian in Latin American History: Resistance,
Resilience, and Acculturation* (1993). Cloth ISBN 0-8420-2421-2
Paper ISBN 0-8420-2425-5

Susan E. Place, ed., *Tropical Rainforests: Latin American Nature and
Society in Transition* (1993). Cloth ISBN 0-8420-2423-9
Paper ISBN 0-8420-2427-1

Paul W. Drake, ed., *Money Doctors, Foreign Debts, and Economic
Reforms in Latin America from the 1890s to the Present* (1994).
Cloth ISBN 0-8420-2434-4   Paper ISBN 0-8420-2435-2

John A. Britton, ed., *Molding the Hearts and Minds: Education,
Communications, and Social Change in Latin America* (1994).
Cloth ISBN 0-8420-2489-1   Paper ISBN 0-8420-2490-5

Darién J. Davis, ed., *Slavery and Beyond: The African Impact on Latin
America and the Caribbean* (1995). Cloth ISBN 0-8420-2484-0
Paper ISBN 0-8420-2485-9

David J. Weber and Jane M. Rausch, eds., *Where Cultures Meet: Frontiers
in Latin American History* (1994). Cloth ISBN 0-8420-2477-8
Paper ISBN 0-8420-2478-6

Gertrude M. Yeager, ed., *Confronting Change, Challenging Tradition:
Women in Latin American History* (1994). Cloth ISBN 0-8420-2479-4
Paper ISBN 0-8420-2480-8

Linda Alexander Rodríguez, ed., *Rank and Privilege: The Military and
Society in Latin America* (1994). Cloth ISBN 0-8420-2432-8
Paper ISBN 0-8420-2433-6

Gilbert M. Joseph and Mark D. Szuchman, eds., *I Saw a City Invincible:
Urban Portraits of Latin America* (1996). Cloth ISBN 0-8420-2495-6
Paper ISBN 0-8420-2496-4

Roderic Ai Camp, ed., *Democracy in Latin America: Patterns and Cycles* (1996). Cloth ISBN 0-8420-2512-X   Paper ISBN 0-8420-2513-8

Oscar J. Martínez, ed., *U.S.-Mexico Borderlands: Historical and Contemporary Perspectives* (1996). Cloth ISBN 0-8420-2446-8 Paper ISBN 0-8420-2447-6

William O. Walker III, ed., *Drugs in the Western Hemisphere: An Odyssey of Cultures in Conflict* (1996). Cloth ISBN 0-8420-2422-0 Paper ISBN 0-8420-2426-3

I Saw
a
City
Invincible

I Saw
a
City
Invincible

Urban Portraits of Latin America

Gilbert M. Joseph and Mark D. Szuchman
Editors

Jaguar Books on Latin America
Number 9

A Scholarly Resources Inc. Imprint
Wilmington, Delaware

© 1996 by Scholarly Resources Inc.
All rights reserved
First published 1996
Printed and bound in the United States of America

Scholarly Resources Inc.
104 Greenhill Avenue
Wilmington, DE 19805-1897

Library of Congress Cataloging-in-Publication Data

I saw a city invincible : urban portraits of Latin America / Gilbert M.
   Joseph and Mark D. Szuchman, editors.
       p.   cm. — (Jaguar books in Latin America : no. 9)
   Includes bibliographical references.
   ISBN 0-8420-2495-6 (cloth : alk. paper) — ISBN 0-8420-2496-4
(pbk. : alk. paper)
     1. Cities and towns—Latin America—History. 2. Capitals
(Cities)—Latin America—History. 3. Urbanization—Latin America—
History. I. Joseph, G. M. (Gilbert Michael), 1947–   . II. Szuchman,
Mark D., 1948–   . III. Series.
HT127.5.I22   1995
307.76'4'098—dc20   95-820
                                                                              CIP

∞ The paper used in this publication meets the minimum requirements
of the American National Standard for permanence of paper for printed
library materials, Z39.48, 1984.

To Richard M. Morse

Acknowledgments

A number of individuals have lent valuable support to this volume at critical stages. Most of all, the editors gratefully acknowledge the encouragement and inspiration provided by Richard Morse, the dean of Latin American urbanists. Professor Morse initially suggested the need for such an anthology in his Yale graduate seminars in Latin American urban history in the early 1970s, one of which kindled Gil Joseph's interest in the project. In a real sense, the present volume represents an engagement with an important segment of Morse's work on the Latin American city. It gives us great pleasure to dedicate this book to him.

Several of Joseph's colleagues in Morse's old graduate seminar—Darrell Levi, Joan Bak, Ann Twinam, and Bainbridge Cowell, Jr.—played crucial roles in the early stages of the project, which began as a joint enterprise. These colleagues helped to select passages in the works by Bernabé Cobo, Juan Agustín García, Luis dos Santos Vilhena, Miguel Samper, Joaquín Capelo, Juan Alvarez, and Gilberto Leite de Barros and to research biographical information on these authors. Their contributions are individually acknowledged in the appropriate chapters. Professor Levi's advice was particularly useful in preparing the first two selections on Brazil and in thinking about some of the larger themes of the collection. In each case, teaching and research obligations called these colleagues away from the project in the mid-1970s, yet their initial efforts made the editors' task that much easier. To Jorge Hardoy of the Universidad Torcuato di Tella, Buenos Aires, we also express our appreciation for several important, orienting suggestions during the project's initial stages.

More recently, we have benefited from the translation skills of Sharon Kellum and Gerald Curtis, the extensive research assistance of Timothy Henderson, the timely word processing of Elena Maubrey, and the editorial guidance of Linda Pote Musumeci. We also are indebted to Bob Levine for kindly making available the oral histories of Carolina Maria de Jesus's children, excerpts of which appear in Chapter 10. Finally, we express our thanks to Bill Beezley, our Jaguar series editor, who, in his inimitable fashion, persuaded Joseph to rekindle an old intellectual flame and resurrect a project that has never been more timely.

Contents

Preface, **xi**

1 MARK D. SZUCHMAN, The City as Vision—The Development of Urban Culture in Latin America, **1**

2 Tenochtitlán and Mexico City under Aztec and Spanish Rule, **33**

  JACQUES SOUSTELLE, Daily Life of the Aztecs on the Eve of the Spanish Conquest, **35**

  CHARLES GIBSON, The Aztecs under Spanish Rule, **47**

3 BERNABÉ COBO, Viceregal Lima in the Seventeenth Century, **59**

4 JUAN AGUSTÍN GARCÍA, Colonial Buenos Aires, **71**

5 LUIS DOS SANTOS VILHENA, Bahia in the Late Colonial Period, **85**

6 MIGUEL SAMPER, Bogotá in the Nineteenth Century, **103**

7 JOAQUÍN CAPELO, Lima in the Nineteenth Century, **119**

8 JUAN ALVAREZ, Buenos Aires in the Early Twentieth Century, **133**

9 GILBERTO LEITE DE BARROS, The Transformation of São Paulo, **149**

10 CAROLINA MARIA DE JESUS, Another São Paulo, **165**

11 JONATHAN KANDELL, Mexico's Megalopolis, **181**

Suggested Readings, **203**

Preface

Walt Whitman's *I Dream'd in a Dream* speaks of the power of a community of citizens whose solidarities would erect a bastion impervious to any attack, moral or otherwise. The history of Latin America's cities has not always evoked images of great solidarity on the part of its residents, yet it is a history of retained supremacy throughout five hundred years of urban existence in the Western Hemisphere.

Spaniards, who in many ways had become the Romans of Europe's medieval and early modern ages, equated civilization with urban existence. Committed to notions of medieval nobility that they would appropriate in an environment safe from the certain contempt of a true European aristocracy, the early Spanish conquerors of the New World rapidly established themselves as urban lords and, in the process, sought to erect barriers between themselves and the masses of Indians that surrounded their enclaves. Thus, the Latin American city was virtually coterminous with the Columbian encounter. With its precocious establishment came the privileged attributes: the locus of political authority, the hub of ecclesiastical activity, the nerve center of commerce and finance, and the essential venue for conspicuous consumption. Ever since the colonial era, the city has remained the premier form of human association in Latin America.

The essays collected in this volume represent some of the most enduring reflections on the Latin American city by commentators who, far from being detached observers, were themselves formed in this urban milieu. Public officials and political activists, journalists, *pensadores* social commentators, and "protest writers," they comprised an important component of their contemporaries' world, in most cases as members of an intelligentsia that was not above self-criticism. Of our eleven authors, all but three are native Latin Americans, and these three either grew up in the region's cities or spent a sizable portion of their careers there. Their writings provide us with critical analyses of a broad historical experience, beginning with the conquest of the Aztecs' Tenochtitlán in the early sixteenth century, continuing with imperial Spain's Hapsburg and Bourbon periods, moving through Latin America's nineteenth-century *belle époque*, when the region's sophisticated metropolises rivaled their western European counterparts, and ending with the "future shock" of today's megalopolises.

The novelty and importance of this collection derive from an unsettling paradox. While we have significant historical treatments of the Latin American city, the voices and accounts of the Latin American urban contemporaries themselves have rarely been gathered to be heard apart from the au courant scholars who have ably analyzed, quantified, and interpreted urban life. Moreover, academic advances have exacted a price. Modern social science and humanist scholarship has tended to be reductionist or integrationist; it has atomized familiar units into small components or else it has assured us that no unit is understandable if it is not inserted into vast global configurations.

The city has been a notable victim of analytical and interpretive decomposition at the hands of spatial ecology, location theory, interest group theory, small group theory, sectoral analysis, demographic analysis, diffusionist and dependency theories, and world systems analysis—not to mention excessive postmodern deconstruction. But to the people who live in a city, or to the planners and administrators who must cope with it, the city remains very much a "real" entity, composed of complex, interacting parts yet always more than the sum of those parts. This comprehensive view came more naturally to bygone observers of Latin American cities. At times, it comes naturally to present-day observers who turn their attention to the past. This volume assembles a series of such synoptic urban portraits, not merely for their historical interest but as therapy for our fragmented perception of the urban phenomena that currently surround us.

In preparing this anthology, we also attempt to meet a long-standing pedagogical need. The works of Bernabé Cobo, Juan Agustín García, Luis dos Santos Vilhena, Miguel Samper, Joaquín Capelo, Juan Alvarez, and Gilberto Leite de Barros are neither well known nor immediately available to students outside their countries of publication. By translating and bringing these classics together—albeit in abridged form—in a common edition, we hope they will find the wider audience they deserve.

The selections gathered here emphasize Latin American cities of the first rank: Mexico City, Lima, Buenos Aires, Salvador da Bahia, Bogotá, and São Paulo. While they display a healthy geographical distribution, they do not adequately represent regional capitals or secondary cities, nor do they include all functional types (for example, a "mining city," a "port city," and so forth). On the other hand, several—Mexico City, Lima, Buenos Aires, and São Paulo—are represented more than once. This should afford distinct advantages, permitting the reader to trace continuity and change over long periods of time, while exposing him or her to contrasting approaches and literary styles.

Of course, it is not our purpose to catalog the entire Latin American urban spectrum. Rather, we intend to showcase a highly select collection of urban portraits, each unique yet having something in common when viewed as a group. We might regard these individual studies as "family portraits" and think in terms of a Latin American "family of cities." But the similarities that emerge in these accounts can be likened to family resemblances only if we remember, in the words of Richard Morse, that "resemblance is not identity, nor do family members live out identical careers."[*] That the careers are not identical is due to structural differences—geographic, demographic, economic, political—found in each urban situation and highlighted by our authors. Still, the reader is sure to find a haunting resemblance between Samper's stagnant, bureaucratic Bogotá of the late 1860s (Chapter 6) and the decadent Lima portrayed by Capelo several decades later (Chapter 7). Reading between the lines, one may also spot a more subtle likeness in the disparate careers of Lima (as portrayed in Chapters 3 and 7) and São Paulo (Chapter 9)—a likeness not readily evident from an examination of the respective indicators of economic change, technological capability, or social mobility, but perhaps lying in durable cultural patterns deeply embedded in the urban fabric.

The portraits in our gallery capture both the broad contours and the daily transactions of Latin American city life, from the dynamic era of the conquistadores to the deafening bustle of today's crowds. The collection provides a unique opportunity to "hear" Latin American culture in the voices of the protagonists coming out of the urban core. These voices will be subject to differing interpretations, just as the role of the city in Latin American history and society is complex and multifaceted. Nonetheless, the reader will quickly grasp that the problems of economic inequity, social and ethnic conflict, inadequate physical resources, administrative inefficiency, and inept social planning—all of which still afflict the region's cities—are of centuries-old dimensions. The historical development of the Latin American city can be ignored by more present-minded scholars and urban planners only at the risk of oversimplification and lack of understanding. It is our hope that this volume will help to minimize that risk.

[*]Richard M. Morse, *Lima en 1900: Estudio crítico y antología* (Lima: Instituto de Estudios Peruanos, 1973), 42–43.

1

The City as Vision—The Development of Urban Culture in Latin America

Mark D. Szuchman

No other people have paid more attention over the ages to their urban dimensions than the Latin Americans. This preoccupation crosses nearly every genre of discourse, ranging from the self-conscious styles of academic scholars to the more freely expressed and popular forms of minstrels, street poets, folklorists, and essayists. Where Amerindian populations had held a powerful demographic presence and a significant cultural weight, their cities delineated the cultural outlines of urban Latin America. By contrast, areas that were largely devoid of indigenous societies at the time of European contact left open the physical and cultural spaces that would be filled by Europeans' perspectives on civilization. From the earliest Spanish contact with the Indies, from the time of Christopher Columbus, the frame of reference for any notion or thing considered worthy was urban in nature. Even in the realm of medieval lore, where myth and religion blended into popular belief systems, the city loomed large. Thus, we find legends, such as that of the Seven Enchanted Cities, to have been associated with the Indies. Believed to have been created by seven Portuguese bishops who had fled the Arab invasion of the Iberian peninsula, this tale of urban life appears among the first proposed examples of utopia.

The Spaniards placed particularly strong emphasis on the city, giving it an all-encompassing role that included administration, the reproduction of capital, ecclesiastical management, and responsibility for virtually all cultural activities. Of all the peoples that Rome had brought within its domain, the Iberians most closely imitated their conquerors in the significance they assigned to the city. In turn, Iberians reconstituted this prominence in the Indies, heightening it, in fact, in all matters social and cultural. In the economic realm, however, the city was limited to serving as a marketplace for the purposes of exchange and distribution, not for production, which would remain the preserve of the countryside.

Although their goals in the Indies varied in the details, the early settlers generally came seeking wealth, attracted by tales of riches, some real, most imagined. Their hopes of realizing their aspirations were intensified by a Spain that, for many, remained inhospitable to their material well-being and indifferent to the idea of significant social mobility. Although social and economic structures in Spain did not offer citizens much hope for material improvement, their limitations did not occasion ideological deviation or religious dissidence. The fall of Muslim Granada into Christian hands in 1492 signaled the culmination of a program of cultural and religious homogeneity sponsored by the Catholic monarchs, Ferdinand and Isabella. The subsequent expulsion of Jews and suppression of Muslims completed the process of establishing the widely shared consensus on political and religious tenets that united ruler and ruled. Thus, the conditions that attracted emigrants from Iberia to the Indies, or "pull factors," were material in nature and consistent with the material and nonideological "push factors."

The timing of the Spaniards' contact with the Indies had a lasting effect on subsequent cultural patterns and belief systems. Unlike the era of settlement by British dissenters in the seventeenth century, the late fifteenth and early sixteenth centuries were not periods in which the nature of government, religion, or social relations was in question. The Spaniards came with absolute certainty of both the social propriety of their ways and the religious righteousness that justified their goals and means. Furthermore, these sentiments endured centuries after the initial settlement, in effect perpetuating a European presence deep within—and spread throughout—the Western Hemisphere. Not surprisingly, it was the Spanish philosopher José Ortega y Gasset who defined the psychological condition of colonialism as a consequence of a people whose entire culture had originated elsewhere.[1]

The Age of Foundations

The Spaniards could hardly hide their contempt for the Amerindians' lifestyles and value systems. Although they marveled at their major cities, such as the Aztecs' Tenochtitlán, their appreciation was limited largely to admiration of the physical grandeur. Indeed, Spaniards measured themselves against Indians on the basis of the latter's deficiencies, not their achievements. Thus, for Francisco Pizarro and his men, the conquest of the Incas was "rendered greater not because the Indians are such worthy opponents but because they are so 'bestial,' " according to Francisco de

Jerez, who was present at the battle of Cajamarca.[2] The Indians' traditional concerns for the land were not equally shared by the Spaniards, whose status considerations depended on other factors, many of which were urban in orientation. Thus, the early conquerors of Peru, who owned fine homes in the city and profited from productive grants of Indian labor and tribute (encomiendas) both there and in the countryside, had little reason to yearn for huge estates to satisfy status pretensions.[3] To be sure, commercial agriculture could offer handsome profits, yet there is no evidence of land accumulation or large estates.[4]

The Spaniards marveled at the great urban centers of the most powerful Amerindian empires, those of the Aztecs and the Incas. Thus, Bernal Díaz del Castillo, who chronicled his participation in the conquest of the Aztecs, led by Hernán Cortés in 1519, writes about the central marketplace of the capital city of Tenochtitlán with all the excitement of a discoverer of wondrous treasures:

> We were astounded at the great number of people and the quantities of merchandise, and at the orderliness and good arrangements that prevailed, for we had never seen such a thing before. The chieftains who accompanied us pointed everything out. Every kind of merchandise was kept separate and had its fixed place . . . with the dealers in gold, silver, and precious stones, feathers, cloaks, and embroidered goods, and male and female slaves to be sold in that market.[5]

The impression left on the Spaniards was all the more striking after they saw the metropolitan expanse that served as the hub of the Aztec confederation. Standing atop one of the pyramids, which served as religious and bureaucratic nuclei, Montezuma presented his urban domain. Díaz del Castillo later recalled:

> So we stood there looking. . . . We saw the three causeways that led into Mexico: the causeway of Iztapalapa by which we had entered four days before, and that of Tacuba . . . and that of Tepeaquilla. We saw the fresh water which came from Chapultepec to supply the city, and the bridges that were constructed at intervals on the causeways so that the water could flow in and out from one part of the lake to another. We saw a great number of canoes, some coming with provisions and others returning with cargo and merchandise; and we saw too that one could not pass from one house to another of that great city and the other cities that were built on the water except over wooden drawbridges or by canoe. We saw *cues* [pyramids] and shrines in these cities that looked like gleaming white towers and castles: a marvelous sight.[6]

The French anthropologist Jacques Soustelle described in detail, and with a great deal of respect, the life-style and environment of Tenochtitlán's dwellers (Chapter 2). He relied considerably on the reports that Cortés sent to Charles V, in which he richly commented upon numerous aspects of Aztec civilization. Much more the conqueror and politician than Bernal Díaz, Cortés portrayed the Aztec capital as a vast matrix of political, social, and economic development. His descriptions and analyses were portrayed in a manner that drew favorable comparisons with the development of western Europeans. Cortés wanted his king to envision the high level of sophistication and achievement of his new subjects, which was on a par with anything he might find in Europe, and thereby aggrandized the achievement of his own conquest.

In both the Aztec and the Inca empires, politics and religion fused into a seamless administrative apparatus. Political and juridical decisions were taken in accordance with astrological indications and religious representations. Indian high clergy had consultative functions and served the political nobility in an advisory capacity. In analyzing the Aztecs' junction of religion and politics within their urban space, Soustelle captured one of the basic similarities with the devoutly Christian conquerors of the early sixteenth century. Describing Tenochtitlán's major plaza, Soustelle writes: "This great central square is splendid enough today, with its cathedral and the presidential palace; but what a prodigious effect it must have had upon the beholder in the Tenochtitlán of Motecuhzoma. State and religion combined their highest manifestations in this one place. . . . The upward sweep of the temples and the long tranquility of the palaces joined there, as if to unite both the hopes of men and the divine providence in the maintenance of the established order."

The expanse of Tenochtitlán that Cortés and his men had gazed upon and marveled at contained one of the world's largest populations, matching or surpassing the populations of Paris, Venice, Milan and Naples, and far beyond what any city in Spain could offer.[7] They sensed this enormous potential immediately, and all their Roman-Iberian traditions told them—with absolute certainty—of the still greater urban magnificence that they would construct in the form of Mexico City.

The certainty of their moves, their confidence in their strategies, and the optimism with which they envisioned their futures shaped a dramatically special moment in the expansion of Mediterranean and urban Europe. Much has been written about the characteristics of both Amerindians and Spaniards to account for the victorious outcome by handfuls of European men over Amerindian forces so vastly superior in numbers.[8] The confidence with which they carried out their mission stands out as one of the Spaniards' special characteristics. Of greater interest to us, however, is the continuing presence of that confidence beyond the phase of military and religious conquest and its subtle demonstration throughout the late sixteenth and early seventeenth centuries, the formative years of the Spanish-American experience.

The Spaniards' view that all matter, including people, fits within a linear and hierarchical world, according to principles of natural law, was manifested in the physical layout of their cities. In this regard, Spanish urban centers contrasted sharply with the Indians' approach to urban design. Spanish cities were laid out according to a *traza* (plan), which was followed faithfully to the extent allowed by the local topography. Streets were laid out linearly, intersections met at right angles; the resulting grid pattern represented their sense of perfect order and the neat placement of people within a well-defined space. Charles Gibson points to the differences found within Mexico City between the Spaniards' quarters in the center and the outlying Indian neighborhoods (barrios) (Chapter 2):

> Inside the city, the first Spaniards began by marking off the central portion, an area of some thirteen blocks in each direction, as the zone of white occupation. The region immediately surrounding this *traza* then comprised the colonial Indian communit[ies]. . . . Each of the four [communities] was L-shaped at one of the four corners of the interior *traza*, and each necessarily gave up a portion of its territory to the Spanish center. The *traza* was symmetrically laid out with streets flanking rectangular blocks. Though some modifications in its size and internal form were made, its orderly plan always contrasted with the irregular disposition of streets in the Indian wards, and its monumental public and private buildings stood in equally sharp contrast to the Indians' adobe houses.

The Spaniards' intention of keeping the races apart dissolved in the reality of daily urban contact. As Gibson points out, city life promoted contact among peoples and the resultant mixing of the races. Despite all evidence to the contrary, the Spaniards did not easily surrender their notions regarding the immutability of the world order. Thus, at the core of their belief system rested a sense of the universality of their cultural mission. Their belief in the constancy across time and space of the principles of natural law on which they rested their moral and political codes of conduct meant that the world was neatly divided into those who followed the Spaniards' ways and those who needed to be forced into submission.[9] The Catholic kings, Ferdinand and Isabella, joined the fundamentals of morality, Christianity, and Spanish civilization into a seamless cultural complex that defined all alternatives as heretical, odious, and unacceptable. Later on, the Christian Humanism propagated by Erasmus found very little space to maneuver in Counter-Reformation Spain. Indeed, in the middle of the sixteenth century, the Catholic Church and Spanish society in general left only a minimal space for dissidence.[10]

With absolute belief in the supremacy of their ways over all others', the Spaniards constructed a cultural edifice that shut out all disallowed or inexplicable beliefs and behaviors. In principle, their politics was the politics of conformity, their religion one of subservience to authority, their view of themselves a reflection of satisfaction, and their institutions overwhelming. Thus, Spaniards of the fifteenth century did not admit to the cultural or spiritual potentialities of other peoples. Not surprisingly, they transferred their entire sweep of mental and material values to the Western Hemisphere. So much so, in fact, that some scholars would agree with Anthony Pagden that generations later—and unlike their Italian or Dutch counterparts—Spanish subjects in America "had no culture and no history fully independent of what had once been for all of them their 'mother country.' "[11]

The Middle Period

Historians divide the period of the Spaniards' conquest of the New World into two parts: the Caribbean period and the mainland phase. The Caribbean, or Antillean, period lasted from 1492 to approximately 1520. This was an era of experimentation, blunder, and learning. One of the greatest ironies of world history is that the Spaniards—a people with relatively little overseas experience and ill equipped to carry out large-scale expeditionary waves—managed to accumulate the richest and most far-flung empire known to Europe. Without much firsthand experience overseas on which to base their expectations, the Spaniards were confident of finding great nations, large cities, and vast material cultures. All this was far beyond what they encountered in the Caribbean. In the process, they demanded labor and other services that exceeded the capacity of the islands' native peoples. In the end, the region's Indians succumbed to their mistreatment and to deadly European diseases. By the early sixteenth century, the Indians of the Caribbean had virtually disappeared.

Eager to explore further, command larger human and material resources, and establish a more meaningful empire, the Spaniards had been frequently venturing eastward from the Antilles, reconnoitering the coastal areas of Central America, the Yucatán peninsula, and further north. These probings also entailed contacts with the indigenous peoples, sometimes taking them back to the Caribbean islands as slaves, at other times learning from them about greater nations and riches some distance away. By the second decade of the sixteenth century, equipped with a generation's worth of accumulated information, part fact and part wishful thinking, the Spaniards were poised to launch themselves from the Caribbean to the mainland. By 1521 they had conquered the Aztecs and by 1532 they had brought down the Incas. Over the next fifty years the Spaniards would fill in and expand their presence, conquering and settling areas throughout much of the Indies.

The Spaniards moved their conquest from the Caribbean to the mainland and consolidated at a remarkable speed their domination over the vast space that would become the Spanish Empire. The conquest phase was largely completed by the 1580s, and, by the start of the seventeenth century, virtually every urban settlement that would have any lasting significance had been created. Within these new spaces, habits of mind and administration persisted well into the postconquest era. The years spanning the seventeenth through much of the nineteenth centuries, known as the "middle period" of Latin American history, witnessed the reconstitution of the racial, administrative, and judicial proclivities of the conquest age, always adjusting for the shifts—often subtle ones—that took place over time.

Not long ago, historians tended to ignore or take very little notice of this period, which begins with the completion of the conquest and traverses the era of significant administrative reforms of the late eighteenth century. More recently, however, the middle period has received much greater attention. Scholars have come to realize that discernibly American patterns slowly developed during this long span of time. Recent research has reflected this understanding by focusing on the evolution of Spanish, Indian, and African interactions, the development of regional economies, the adaptation of European norms to the American reality, the role of ranching and mining, the mechanisms of commercial exchange, and other issues. Going far beyond the previous investigations of imperial politics, recent research has probed into the actual conduct of the postconquest peoples of different regions of Latin America, the overwhelming majority of whom conducted their lives without any direct contact with Europe or Europeans.[12]

We have learned much from this literature. Among the most important lessons are, first, the slow yet profound fracturing of the worldview fifteenth-century Spaniards had instilled; and second, the regionalization of contacts and exchanges with lasting consequences for political and administrative coherence, an unimaginable concept in the sixteenth century. In the end, the perfectly structured world in which all that was known had a predefined place simply could not be sustained. From the three races familiar to the Spaniards—white, Indian, black—many racial hues were formed; from the singularity and orthodoxy of Roman Catholicism emanated multiple interpretations of Scripture and varied religious practices; from an envisioned linearity of political authority there developed numerous and conflicting political loyalties; and from a simple and direct commerce between centers of production in Europe and the Indies, new internal markets arose for the sustenance of regional populations. By the last third of the eighteenth century, Latin America was a vastly different—and internally differentiated—place than the conquerors could have ever envisioned.

Spanish law in the Indies had originally constructed the notion of two "estates" or "republics," one consisting of Indians and the other of whites. Such compartmentalization of peoples and races, however, could never be maintained. In the end, the circulation and contacts of both peoples resulted in the mixing of races. These mestizos, who along with whites, pure Indians, and, in some regions, blacks roamed the countryside and the cities, raised concerns among the authorities. A seemingly endless cycle of attempted control followed by failure took place: ordinances restricting contact and movement, followed by longer lists of racial categories, followed by more restrictive ordinances. Ultimately, no ordinance could counter the reality of racial mixture or the tendency for people to migrate as needed. The historian Charles Gibson describes the careful detail with which the Spaniards laid out the districts within Mexico City, built on the ruins of Tenochtitlán after its fall to the forces of Cortés (Chapter 2). The city was to consist of areas that separated the races, neighborhoods for the exclusive use of Indians, with others established for the residential segregation of the Spaniards. "The regulations spoke," writes Gibson, "as had preceding regulations, of a separation of Indian peoples in the city for ecclesiastical and tribute purposes. But the new system, once established, did nothing further to separate Indians from other inhabitants."

The Spaniards did not count the culture and belief systems of Indians as valuable components of their realms. Disdained as much by legislation as by neglect, the general disregard for the Amerindians can be gleaned from the sketches of the city of Lima written in the first third of the seventeenth century by Bernabé Cobo. His descriptions are striking for the relative absence of mention of the indigenous world (Chapter 3). Cobo's depiction of a maturing Lima is characterized by pride of achievement and the ebullient optimism of an even brighter future. Cobo cannot "foresee the end or limit to Lima's growth in the future." But his Lima is a Christian Lima, its architecture that of a European city, and its commerce consists of a European material culture sustained by the foodstuffs of the Americas. In sum, colonial Lima epitomizes the reconstitution of the European world centered in Latin America's cities.

Cobo was writing about Lima at the same time that Father Antonio Vázquez de Espinosa was traveling throughout the Spanish Indies, noting the diversity contained in its vastness. Vázquez de Espinosa reported that neither the demographic density nor the concentration of material wealth found in urban centers such as Mexico City and Lima was found elsewhere in Spanish America.[13] Thus, while the term "city" was commonly assigned to population centers, many of them would not warrant much more than the term "village" in our modern parlance. Yet, despite differences in order of magnitude, they were remarkably similar in matters of administrative domain and even in physical characteristics. They concentrated administrative, political, economic, and religious functions within their spaces.[14] The cities of the Indies functioned as vessels of Spanish culture; moreover, they acted as leading edges, transmitting important elements of this culture into the rural areas.[15]

Cobo describes Lima's central plaza with unrestrained enthusiasm: the seat of viceregal government forms the "largest and most luxurious structure in this kingdom." Cobo's comfort and his confidence in Lima is sustained in no small measure by the triumph of civil authority over a militarized and bloody past. It is not a minor point, albeit one delivered en passant, that Cobo makes when describing the presence of the gallows in the central plaza during Pizarro's time. His mention of their removal by subsequent viceroys, intent on reestablishing peace among the Spanish factions that took up arms against each other soon after the conquest, fits well with his confident view of Lima's destiny.

Toward the end of the eighteenth century, the public mind-set and the administrative philosophies emanating from Spain began to diverge. In the process, new and multiple interests and identities appeared, sometimes pitting authorities against subjects, regions against regions, officials against each other, customs against innovations. All this took place in the context of a set of material and demographic conditions that bespoke growth and development.

The Age of Reform

During the eighteenth century, the frequency and volume of movement among the peoples of Ibero-America took a sharp, upward turn. After approximately one hundred years of declining population (especially among Indians), the consequence primarily of disease, the number of people in the Indies surged in this century. The larger cities felt the results of the growing pressure on the land caused by the increase. As the demands by families who lived in rural areas for food and employment outstripped the regional resources, younger members of households sought opportunities elsewhere, especially in the greater urban centers. In the Mexican district of Celaya, for example, over one-third of the households contained no young men between the ages of 15 and 19, the result of an out-migration pattern that was being replicated throughout much of Mexico. By 1821, Guadalajara's household sizes had been diminished as a consequence of an out-migration rate of over 50 percent by young men and women, aged 15 to 20.[16] By the late eighteenth century, a great part of the population of Spanish America was on the move, and the likeliest destinations were the larger cities. The consequences for the system of social control were not necessarily violent, but always tense for the elites and the authorities, who equated unfettered mobility with anarchy. Concern with the movement of people, usually rural dwellers, Indians, mestizos, and the lower classes, was common among officials who saw it as a consequence of low moral standing and not of social and economic policies.[17]

In Mexico, the urban setting tended to be less violent in comparison to the countryside, even while political activity in the cities remained vibrant. It has been argued that the considerable cityward migration undermined the propensity for collective action—at least in the short run—owing to the social atomization engendered in the urban environment.[18] The process of late eighteenth- and nineteenth-century migration from regions that were either poor or undergoing pauperization was widely felt in Spanish America. At the other end of the hemisphere, migration within the Río de la Plata region of Argentina moved populations from some of the stagnant provinces of the interior to the ones with greater economic potential. Thus, by 1810 significant numbers of migrants from the provinces of Catamarca, Santiago del Estero, La Rioja, and San Juan had found their way into the cities of Córdoba and Buenos Aires.[19]

The eighteenth century also witnessed a significant expansion in the influence wielded by intellectual and economic circles, invariably located in the cities. By the century's second half, enlightened groups of intellectuals and promoters of the material well-being of different regions were busy discussing and planning the latest ideas for modernizing everything from the economy to the educational and administrative systems. Booster associations, along the lines of those formed by the French Encyclopedists, sprang up throughout Spanish America promoting the economy, creating lending libraries, facilitating fast-evolving liberal trade policies, and, in some cases, substituting for a lethargic royal administration and enhancing the quality of life. For example, in 1792 economic liberals in the city of Havana founded the Sociedad Económica de Amigos del País. It was headed by Francisco Arango, a well-to-do and influential sugar planter. This "Economic Society," modeled after others that had been established in western Europe and Spanish America, had all the appearances of a private club yet performed with great effectiveness in influencing government policy for the benefit of the merchants and sugar planters who were its members.[20] Such organizations were instrumental in advancing infrastructural projects and improving educational facilities. They expanded the information available for the region's economic development.

While renewal was in the air during the second half of the eighteenth century, the period was also accompanied by unrest. Rebellions by Indians, especially in the Andean zones, were a source of deep concern for the authorities and for the white population. Towns and cities were not immune to conflicts engendered by changes brought about by the authorities, as areas in which the lives of most people directly, such as had barely been touched, now experienced the presence of the state through tax collection and an expanded bureaucracy.[21]

Several of the movements of resistance to those late eighteenth-century measures were centered in cities. One of the era's better-known urban protest movements was the *comuneros'* revolt of 1781 in New Granada (the northwestern part of South America, comprised of the area including present-day Panama, Colombia, Venezuela, and Ecuador). Widespread and involving over twenty thousand insurgents at its height, the rebellion combined petty and local grievances on the part of many who felt that their *comunas* (communities) were losing autonomy. A generalized sense that fundamental change was being imposed without consultation with the populace drove many to resist policies enacted in faraway Spain. Local traditions and privileges, dating to no particular legislation but rather to customary practices under the more relaxed oversight of the Hapsburg Crown, were now under attack by efficiency-minded Bourbon technocrats. The resistance by the *comuneros* of New Granada to the Bourbon authorities did not, however, reflect a desire for independence. Far from being a radical departure in the direction of nation-building, the regional revolt represented a desire for the retention of traditional bonds between subject and Crown. Rather than a forward movement in the direction of independence, these rebels sought to put into practice a backward-looking understanding of the pact between ruler and ruled that had provided the foundation for society in Europe's late medieval era.[22]

In fact, urban rebellions had begun in New Granada in the 1760s, almost two decades before the *comuneros'* revolt. It was then that the city of Quito was rocked by a series of incidents that tested the royal authorities' will and ability to impose new taxing practices and rates. The resistance that took place in 1765 became known as the "rebellion of the barrios," a name that accurately associated wide-ranging protests with a concern for the maintenance of local traditions. The rebellion coalesced different social and ethnic sectors of the community into resisting Bourbon reforms of the excise system, especially the elimination of tax farming and a more effective collection of sales taxes (*alcabala*) and duties on locally made brandy (aguardiente). Since ecclesiastical orders also would have been forbidden to produce aguardiente, the gathering resistance also included the clerics of the region, who ultimately brokered the restoration of peace and order. In the end, the rebellion of the barrios followed the pattern of most urban disturbances during this era: it was territorially circumscribed to the issues raised by local protesters—no overarching ideologies bridged distant lands to forge a social movement.

In Brazil, the second half of the eighteenth century also brought a heightened concern with the social disorder that coincided with increased wealth and urban growth. Apprehension combined with justifiable pride comes through in Luis dos Santos Vilhena's portrait of the city of Bahia at the turn of the nineteenth century (Chapter 5). Santos Vilhena describes the "grandeur" of Bahia but worries about uncontrolled urban growth, with the "construction of buildings wherever anyone wished, without any thought for the future." By century's end, Brazilian cities were demonstrating some of the same characteristics discerned in the Spanish-American areas. The growth of population meant an increasingly complicated set of decisions for municipal authorities. Economic growth failed to eradicate extreme poverty, and this was illustrated by the opulence that marked homes and public buildings while a floating population of indigents languished in public areas. In Bahia, the social order was felt to be fragile. "I do not consider it agreeable to political and economic dictates to allow the city to fill up with the three kinds of beggars: whites, mulattoes, and Negroes," writes Santos Vilhena, consciously underplaying his own grave concerns. "Moreover, it does not appear to be a very discreet policy to tolerate crowds of Negroes of both sexes in the streets and public squares of the city."

The Bourbons' fiscal and administrative reforms benefited some areas while they presented serious challenges to others. The reforms' double-edged quality could be seen in their effects on an influential group in any major city, the merchants in control of the import-export trade. The liberalization of trade policies in the late 1770s had presented expanded opportunities for merchants in cities such as Veracruz, Santiago de Chile, and Buenos Aires that had been on the fringe of economic activities. For merchants' groups in the older, more populous viceregal capitals, such as Mexico City and Lima, the new policies had resulted in a challenge, in the form of dangerous competition. The creation of a merchants' guild (*consulado*) in the city of Veracruz meant that provincial trade routes, previously neglected or bypassed, were now increasingly used, a trend stimulated by a new network of merchants who sometimes bypassed their counterparts in Mexico City.[23] These developments had far-reaching consequences, extending beyond the colonial period. The first Mexican railway, for example, which was begun in 1837, followed the route that had been designed in the 1790s by the *consulado* of Mexico City, linking the capital with the cities of Orizaba and Córdoba, until it reached its destination in Veracruz.[24]

Similar dynamics took place in South America. The designation and expansion of new trade outlets in Chile began to erode the position held by Lima's merchants, traditionally dominant in South America's commerce. By contrast, the city of Santiago took on greater importance and expanded its regional influence.[25] It is important to note that these measures did not usually result from agitation originating from within mercantile circles in the colonies; on the contrary, administrative and fiscal changes were based on the economic ideas of Charles III's ministers and were decreed by the authorities in Spain, often against the wishes of the local traders.[26]

The city of Buenos Aires, too, benefited from the Bourbon reforms, most frequently at the expense of cities in the interior, which fell into an economic malaise. One of the most poignant and representative images evoking the dead weight of past glories was drawn by the Argentine intellectual, Domingo Sarmiento. He described a ritual his mother witnessed with regularity at the end of the eighteenth century while growing up in the interior city of San Juan, lying at the foot of the Andes Mountains.

> Once or twice a year an unusual chore took place at home. The large entrance doors, held up by enormous bronze bolts, were closed, and the two interior courtyards were separated from each other in order to prevent the family youngsters from viewing. And then, my mother used to tell me, the negress Rosa, Spanish-speaking and exceedingly curious, would tell her in bizarre whisperings, "today there is *sunning!*" Swiftly, she would place a hand-held ladder against a window that looked out over the patio, and lifted my then-childlike mother, who would carefully raise her head in order to see what was happening below. What a great impression is made seeing things in the flesh, my mother would tell me: the courtyard would be covered with hides on which a thick layer of blackened silver coins was laid out to remove the mildew. And later, two old slaves, custodians of the treasure, walked around from one hide to another, and removed the coins, which made loud sounds.[27]

The decay of the interior's economic and productive systems—the "mildewing" of some of the venerable colonial cities of the Spanish-American hinterland—would be accelerated over the course of the nineteenth century. By contrast, the reforms were highly beneficial to other cities, especially those which were brought fully into the realm of free trade based on goods produced by industrial Europe.

Buenos Aires represented one of the clearest examples of cities invigorated by the transatlantic commerce of the late eighteenth century.

Designated as the capital of the new viceroyalty of the Río de la Plata in 1776, Buenos Aires became one of the most dynamic cities of South America and underwent a number of improvements. In the central square, the Recova, a long arcade that cut the plaza in half and contained all manner of merchants' stalls, was built. The Recova reflected the Bourbon era's emphasis on commercial development and the activation of investment capital. Like many other Spanish-American cities, Buenos Aires also built an *alameda* (an extensive park with walking grounds) along the river. *Alamedas* provided testimony to the growing importance of the outdoors in the citizenry's recreational activities. Meantime, central plazas were also beautified. By the start of the nineteenth century, the city was not only the place to be but also the place to be seen.

This energetic pace of life contrasted sharply with the more languid forms of social and commercial exchange of previous times. Writing in 1900, Juan Agustín García noted that the sluggishness of pre-eighteenth-century Buenos Aires was caused by the area's meager resources, the undependable nature of contraband trade, and the capriciousness of local officials, who were impervious to ideas of progress (Chapter 4). For García, the basic ingredient of change was capital. Yet, along with greater opportunities for trade and finance, the other mainstay of the age of enlightened despotism was greater political oversight. Thus, García is correct when he points to a troublesome contradiction peculiar to the era: while Buenos Aires developed significantly in wealth and population, the political influence wielded by its cabildo (town council) declined in the face of newly appointed royal officials. This basic incongruity of economic development in the face of increasingly limited political autonomy raised the level of frustration among some local leaders and propelled them to contemplate new political relationships.

Thus, one of the most striking ironies of the Bourbon period was that its liberalization of trade and rationalization of administration brought to the fore a degree of dissension not previously seen. As Richard Morse has pointed out, in the context of the Spanish monarchical authoritarian tradition, the introduction of liberal ideas had a destabilizing effect in that these concepts tended to undermine the legitimacy of traditional authoritarian modes but failed to create a sufficiently accepted basis for authority.[28] In the case of most of Spanish America, the political and intellectual debates regarding the validity and efficacy of traditional systems as compared with innovative ones took place in the newly dynamic cities.

Urban areas had always been the repositories of intellectual accomplishments. Universities, learned circles, discussion groups, and printing presses had all been monopolized by cities, which, in Spanish America, had always constituted the first centers for the circulation of information from Europe. It is no wonder, then, that the transmission of ideas circulating in the early nineteenth century and the political debates that ensued from such ideas would make of the cities reservoirs of doubts about continued union with Spain. The venues for such discussions were the same as before: literary societies, economic improvement associations, Encyclopedist reading and discussion groups, and university circles.

By the start of the nineteenth century, municipal governments in Spanish America had become the principal scene of local, American authority, in part as a consequence of some of the reforms introduced by the Bourbon Crown, which deliberately re-hispanicized institutions through the device of political appointments. Starting in the 1760s and 1770s, the Crown embarked on a policy of appointing Spaniards to political posts. This was the consequence of discovering the extent to which creoles, or American-born individuals, had been able to dominate judicial, fiscal, and other administrative posts and councils. By the early 1800s the *audiencias* (regional political bodies responsible for a combined set of judicial, legislative, and even some executive functions) had largely been returned to *peninsulares* beholden to Spain and its royal authorities, thereby reducing the creoles' policymaking space to the cabildos.[29] Moreover, the most important and powerful *audiencias* had jurisdiction over the same districts as the most powerful cabildos, that is, the viceregal capitals. It was not long before political maneuverings in such areas reflected animosities between Americans and Spaniards, creoles and *peninsulares*.

As soon as Spanish-American cities received the news of the forced abdication of Ferdinand VII in 1808 and the appointment of Joseph Bonaparte to the throne by his brother Napoleon, Spanish and creole forces began devising strategies and lining up allies as they positioned themselves to fill the sudden political vacuum across the breadth of Spanish America's urban landscape. In the process, the city became the principal point of reference for political "parties," a term normally used to mean factions or personal retinues, rather than formal institutions of political allegiances. The critical mass of interest groups, along with their leaders and spokesmen, were to be found in the cities, and often only in the cities. Yet, the nominal allegiances among politicians proved insufficient to settle differences among contending parties, whose contests for domination of the political space required more than civilian negotiations. In the end, military prowess became an essential component of politics. The militarization of politics would radically alter the traditional importance of the city in the determination of political direction.

The Challenge of the Countryside and Urban Recovery

Negotiations and machinations continued among the traditional political players who debated the course of action after Napoleon's removal of Ferdinand VII. These discussions often touched on new, and for the empire, dangerous subjects, including alternative structures of government and the determination of policies closer to home and away from distant Spain.

As the news of Ferdinand's captivity spread, capital cities such as Mexico City and Buenos Aires tried to fill the perceived political vacuum by extending their direct control. Some scholars have argued that this period witnessed the rise of an urban imperialism, as major cities attempted to govern their respective hinterlands. In any event, regions were thrown into bitter battles over a protracted period of turmoil as they vied with each other to hold centralized power and dominate vital resources.[30]

The countryside suffered much more than the city the consequences of the militarization that accompanied political crises in the nineteenth century. Ideologies were debated and plans were proposed in major urban centers, sometimes with the bitterest discourse available to intellectual antagonists. Their principal weapons were rhetorical, aided by such instruments as pasquinades, newspaper articles, editorials, and decrees. "Political society," as the term was used for the participants in the debates, was centered in the city. The countryside presented a sharp contrast.

The political discourse that originated in the cities eventually reached the rural zone. There it was circulated, interpreted by the political chiefs and brokers of the rural communities or by crude village intellectuals, and eventually translated into action as men were drafted and armies mobilized. Meeting places in rural areas often amounted to nothing more than the humble abodes of community leaders, or, frequently, ramshackle structures that may have served as combination bar and general goods stores. In Argentina, these establishments, known as *pulperías*, reflected the urban centers' loss of control over information and resources. A keen analyst of the manner in which information circulated in the countryside notes the power of these informal processes: in the late 1820s "a 'war of public opinion'—in the words of the press—broke out. It was waged mainly in the *pulperías* and small villages. The weapon of choice in this war was the word or, as the press characterized it, the 'inflammatory rumor.' The principal broadcasters were the *pulpería* owners and their 'anarchist' regular patrons, men of the countryside who used these establishments as their primary places to socialize and keep up with current events. In the villages, store owners were joined by residents, including parish priests, who also 'incited rebellion' through their homilies."[31]

As the experience of shaping nations in much of Latin America involved costly military approaches, the urban gentry began to associate political restiveness with rural backwardness. Thus, José Manuel Beruti, a chronicler of urban life in Buenos Aires at the start of the nineteenth century, would characterize meetings to discuss issues of political importance as "clubs" in which individuals "of talent" and "wise men" gave speeches and exchanged views on issues related to the public welfare.[32] When the armies that had been defending the interests of many of these individuals were defeated in 1820 by forces from the poorer interior provinces, Beruti entered in his diary on October 2, 1820, that "the fatherland, fragmented by contending sides [was] at risk of becoming the victim of petty, insolent, and armed plebeians wishing to bring down the decent people, ruin them and make them their equals in quality and misery."[33]

The start of the nineteenth century thus saw an increasingly clearer vision of contending cultures, based on distinctions between cities and the interior. Despite experiences with urban disturbances, the countryside—largely a calm setting during most of the colonial era—came to be known as the principal region of discontent and rebelliousness.[34] In Mexico, for example, urban passivity coincided with widespread rural insurrection in the early 1800s; popular rebellions were based largely on rural grievances and often failed to engage the interests or sympathy of the urban classes.[35]

Cities in Latin America, which had always attracted migrants from the interior, would, in the course of the nineteenth century, experience an acceleration of internal migratory flows. City-bound migrants generally moved from the poorer regions to those in which they expected to realize a better life. Frequently, they were people of color; virtually always they came from humble origins. They found employment in the casual labor market as servants, journeymen, and contract or ad hoc laborers, alternating between periods of unemployment and ephemeral jobs. Their condition, however, also placed them at risk of vagrancy; indeed, the very act of migrating, the physical detachment from one's area of birth, was associated with dangerous transiency and idleness.[36] Miguel Samper's depiction of Bogotá reflects the vision of urban anarchy by a member of the city's gentry (Chapter 6):

> Parasitism is so developed here that deciding whether to answer a greeting is today a matter to ponder carefully. And paying one of those Castilian compliments, such as "I am at your service," or "Command me," constitutes a real threat to one's pocketbook. Little by little, those smiling and open countenances characteristic of our climate, our race,

and our traditional and daily habits are disappearing because each smile
is a stimulus and each stimulus brings a bloodletting.

Joaquín Capelo's depiction of casual laborers illustrates the existence of this growing sector in Lima at the close of the nineteenth century
and extends Samper's concerns regarding Bogotá (Chapter 7). He places
the growing population of itinerant workers in the category of *servicios
menores*, which he refers to as the type of employment that produced no
material goods, but rather sustained the already existing sources of wealth,
largely in the area of personal services. Capelo does not hide his disdain
for the individuals who floated around Lima and other cities of Latin
America, moving from one job to another. His frame of reference is quite
narrow. "The minor services, however humble the status of the job may
be," writes Capelo, "nevertheless have a positive value: *one earns a living*; the bum and the criminal steal it. The most humble servant is infinitely superior to the idler, the thief, and the murderer." The city as
observed by Samper and Capelo contained some disturbing elements that
sharply contrasted with earlier views of universal truths and feelings of
optimistic certainty.

Cities, especially capital cities, regained their prominence in the last
third of the nineteenth century. In areas where the colonial power had
dissipated as different regions competed for supremacy, political authority once again found its center in the old capitals of the colonial administrative jurisdictions, particularly the viceroyalties and *audiencias*. This
return to an urban-predominant order was inevitable in light of the pre-
eminent position that cities had enjoyed since the sixteenth century. The
reemergence of cities, however, was expedited by the economic conditions that were developing elsewhere, particularly in Europe; technological innovations and new political environments also accelerated the urban
recovery.

As political power was recentralized and its effectiveness consolidated, the results could be seen in the hinterlands as cities became the
repositories of the new authority. The fear for the loss of social control
that underlay the visions of Samper and Capelo were not lost on government officials in the last quarter of the nineteenth century. Measures of
control were applied, with special emphasis in the countryside. In Brazil,
for example, the harsh drought that affected the northeast in the late 1870s
aggravated the situation of thousands of *retirantes*, poverty-stricken
residents of the region who were recruited to work on inefficient
government-sponsored projects. Fraud and exploitation, however, made
a mockery of relief efforts. Codifying sentiments long felt by elites in
Latin America, the failure of these projects provided leaders with the evidence that the poor were the victims of their own moral shortcomings.

Only compulsory labor laws—to be sure, legally distinct from slavery—coupled with the inculcation of the morally virtuous aspects of work would solve the problem of indigence.[37]

In the end, however, such methods fell far short of bringing about their intended outcomes: compulsory measures, though often accompanied by harsh treatment, seldom succeeded in binding the peasantry to the land. Despite regulations to limit geographic mobility, population movement, especially cityward migration, had been and would remain an historical reality.[38] Thus, the economic dimensions of the countryside and its administration bore consequences for cities, where growth was enhanced by people seeking greater opportunities. For example, Santiago, Chile's capital city, grew at an annual average rate of over 4 percent between 1885 and 1895, mainly as the result of migration within Chile, rather than natural population increase or immigration from abroad.[39] Chilean cityward migrants had the same incentives for their relocation as other Latin Americans. The limitations of the countryside combined with the growing industrial base of cities to offer the right combination of inducements.

The economic dimensions that underlay the growing domination of Latin American cities is illustrated in the case of São Paulo by Gilberto Leite de Barros (Chapter 9). One of the key elements in the process was an entrepreneurial spirit found among many residents, who expanded the frontiers of agricultural exploitation and trade well beyond urban confines (although they remained dependent on the urban markets for consumption). Leite de Barros notes that farming and mule trading provided unusually great opportunities for economic mobility: for the first time, "farming came to symbolize a stable profession which enhanced a man's position . . . cloth[ing] him in nobility and dignity . . . [and obliging] him to become a traditional patriarch." For his part, the mule trader significantly facilitated the circulation of capital and goods.[40]

The domination of Brazil's southern region by the city of São Paulo is a further demonstration of the dynamic relationship that existed between the growing export-oriented production of the hinterlands and the expanded administrative and economic capacity of the city. That relationship became a feature of late nineteenth-century Latin America. Leite de Barros could not have put it more succinctly: "The surge of progress that took place in the middle of the nineteenth century due to the cultivation of coffee on the Paulista plateau hastened the expansion of the city of São Paulo."

Even if the wars for independence in much of Spanish America shifted the base of military—and some political—operations away from the primary cities, agricultural regions never won an outright victory. Due to

the failure to establish a durable rural order, political authorities located
in central cities now became the incontestable articulators of national
destinies. European diplomatic and financial observers, especially those
of Great Britain and France, along with their counterparts from the United
States, found the political and intellectual leaders located in the major
cities to be the most approachable potential partners. They also proved to
be the most amenable respondents to proposals for foreign economic
projects. With the help of ample credit lines and equipped with investments of unprecedented dimensions, political and military leaders centered in the national capitals were able to acquire railroads and repeating
rifles, string telegraph lines and mobilize armies, and secure capital and
gain social control. By the early 1900s the upward spiral of economic
growth and the centralization of authority were complete. The regional
strongmen had given way to even more powerful personalities, more co-
hesively tied to a matrix of investors—both national and foreign—and
professional military officers. Large-scale gains were reported in exports
to the United States and western Europe. This was the age of Latin
America's primary export boom: an industrial world, hungry for food to
nourish its growing populations and for raw materials to use in its manufacturing ventures, found in Latin America bread and ore, cereals and
nitrates, meats, and return on capital. And at the center of decision making and resource distribution were the Latin American cities and their
elites.

Cities began to grow dramatically in size and opulence. Elites built
homes of palatial dimensions, and the straight-line model of street design
relaxed into imitations of Paris's undulating boulevards and designated
green spaces. The use of public space increased and more people engaged
in outdoor activities.[41] The poor continued to live in humble structures,
which now included a new residential form: the *conventillo*. As urban
population densities increased, so did pressure to optimize the utilization
of space. The result was the subdivision of old colonial structures and the
consequent rise of the tenement. Thus, wealth and poverty continued to
coexist in sharp contrast. Certainly, Latin America's population did not
become primarily urban; indeed, a majority of each country's population
at the end of World War I still lived in rural areas. Moreover, even the
most crowded cities, Buenos Aires, Rio de Janeiro, and Mexico City, were
not nearly as large as Paris, New York, or London.[42] But two interrelated
trends clearly had been established and would only be reinforced over the
course of the twentieth century. First, capital cities far outdistanced all
other locations in the concentration of demographic and financial resources. Thus, even if in the 1890s Guatemala City, with its 72,000 people,
was dwarfed by Buenos Aires and its 664,000 residents, the two cities

shared a common economic and political dominance over their respective nations. Second, the capital cities' dominance by the start of the 1900s attracted streams of migrants, which have grown uninterruptedly throughout this century and which were made up of people engaged in both internal and international movement. Thus, the preeminence gained during the era of the export boom paved the way for what ultimately turned into a macrocephalic condition: the concentration in one city of population, financial, and political resources out of all proportion to their distribution throughout the rest of the country. Moreover, the degree of social and economic development became closely associated with the extent of urbanization. Thus, Latin American nations with advanced economies, such as Mexico, Brazil, and Argentina, displayed the highest urban concentrations.

In the first decades of the 1900s some observers were already noting these patterns with dismay. In 1918, Juan Alvarez observed that "Buenos Aires costs the Argentine republic dearly" (Chapter 8). He commented on the inefficiency that resulted from one city dominating and demanding so much in the way of investment, infrastructure, labor, and development from the rest of the country. Some economists, too, worried about the *nature* of the commercial relationship with the countries of western Europe and the United States, seeing the dangers of an overemphasis on primary production to the exclusion of industrial development. In 1918, while Juan Alvarez worried about the costs being exerted on the nation by the city of Buenos Aires, the Argentine economist Alejandro Bunge and his colleagues sounded a warning about the prevailing model—stagnation would result from the overspecialization on cattle and crops on the pampas. Only the sponsorship of diversification by the state, especially in the industrial sector, could prevent the worst effects of a skewed economic relationship with the industrial world.[43] By the end of World War II, there was enough consensus on the need of the state to sustain industrial development to codify the theories into import-substitution programs that would further develop principal cities, not only as centers of consumption but also as major focal points of production.[44]

The Leviathan

Nationalism combined with practical considerations, including the satisfaction of growing and diverse political constituencies in the cities, and economic development theories to create significant opportunities to build industrial programs. The roots of such development in the larger Latin American economies had been planted during the Great Depression, when the virtual absence of foreign capital investments increased the possibilities for national entrepreneurs to gain shares in the domestic manufacturing environment. This process was accelerated during World War II, when Latin America benefited from large volumes of commodity exports at high prices. Furthermore, the war extended the period of opportunity for domestic entrepreneurs insofar as neither capital investments nor imported manufactured goods could be found easily.

As administered by state-sponsored economic planning boards, each nation's program of import substitution became the leading edge of economic development. In Mexico, for example, the government embarked on a system of direct control of imports, thereby protecting national manufacturing from foreign competition.[45] Mexico's metropolitan areas, especially Mexico City and Monterrey, were poised to take advantage of these conditions. People flocked to these areas as at no time before as industrial development encouraged the continuance of the migratory traditions of the nation's hinterland. In 1940 the city of Monterrey contained 186,000 people and Mexico City was home to 1.5 million individuals. The next two decades saw Monterrey's population grow by an astounding 91 and 95 percent, respectively. Mexico City's population grew 85 percent between 1940 and 1950 and another 70 percent between 1950 and 1960. Net internal migration accounted for the overwhelming majority of this growth: no more than 30 percent of the males living in Monterrey in the mid-1960s had been born in the city.[46] The story is repeated with varying degrees of demographic growth: Rio de Janeiro, São Paulo, Caracas, Bogotá, Santiago, Buenos Aires, Lima—these and other cities had grown by the 1970s into immense administrative, social, and cultural webs, internally complex and externally tied to the rest of their respective nations through the networks woven by the migrants themselves.

Sociologists and anthropologists began to discover the highly dynamic nature of Latin America's rural-urban migration process. They also began to analyze the intimate relationship between the characteristics of migration and the information flow that crisscrosses the spaces between Latin America's rural communities and metropolitan areas. Furthermore, they discovered that migrants' social relationships and structures of exchange once inside the major cities are often nothing more than the reconstitution of the linkages and exchanges that existed in their small towns of origin. These social ties within the big cities are not only expressions of the migrants' continued attachment to their communal roots but are also essential for their urban survival.[47]

Cities in Latin America tell a story of dynamism and tremendous growth. Although there is nothing new about the dominance of capital cities in Latin America, or about their determination of what goes on (or fails to) in the most remote regions of their countries, the pace and challenge of their growth have increased dramatically in the second half of the twentieth century. Historians, sociologists, anthropologists, and journalists have analyzed the patterns of, and the consequences arising from, the migration that accounts for much of the urban growth of twentieth-century Latin America. Unfortunately, we have precious few accounts of the experiences of migrants written in their own words. One exception is the diary of Carolina Maria de Jesus, an impoverished Brazilian who, as a young woman, moved with her daughter from the state of Minas Gerais to the thriving metropolis of São Paulo (Chapter 10). Blessed with an unusual gift for writing, she kept a journal, which was published in 1960 and subsequently translated into several languages.[48] *Child of the Dark*, the English-language version, depicts the travails of those who, attracted by the city's presumed opportunities, barely managed their subsistence within the labyrinths of their slums. Through her descriptions of daily life in metropolitan Brazil, the reader gains insight into the difficulties of survival. The diary opened the eyes of countless Brazilians to the instances of violence, alcoholism, disease, and hunger that characterized the daily lives of thousands of people a short distance from their own neighborhoods.

Growth, complexity, and even personal struggle have also enhanced cultural richness. The Brazilian samba, a rich blend of poverty and music, is one of the most exciting sounds of the city. In the book *Samba*, Alma Guillermoprieto reveals that in Rio de Janeiro poor blacks combine musical traditions from the slave-holding days of the nineteenth century with modern survival strategies centered around samba schools, where they socialize and express their African roots.[49] Public dancing during festivals is a common feature of Latin America's urban landscape. It is also one of the most inclusive activities in societies that for so long and in subtle ways have segregated the rich from the poor. Dancing in Rio is as essential a part of urban life as it is a vibrant expression of popular culture. In this regard, the massive numbers of migrants who have settled into Latin America's cities have significantly changed the cultural landscape.

The incorporation of popular traditions into the public spheres of culture is testimony to the dynamic changes brought about by the growth of the popular sector in Latin America's cities. Gone are the days of the prohibition of milling around by the poor or the restrictions against public dancing. During the second half of the nineteenth century, carnival celebrants in the Argentine cities of Salta and Corrientes had been restricted "by unspoken convention" to the unpaved portions of the plazas. In contrast, by the midtwentieth century, workers in industrial cities in the same country used common spaces for festive behavior, deliberately shattering the conventional boundaries, established by the elites, to regulate public behavior.[50]

As metropolitan areas have turned into demographic giants, they have become increasingly difficult to administer. Perhaps the clearest example of unrestrained Latin American urban growth is Mexico City, home today to approximately twenty million people, or nearly one-quarter of the nation's population. With an average of more than five thousand people per square kilometer, Mexico City contains the greatest population density in the world. To judge by recent trends, further growth is assured: by the year 2000, nearly thirty million people will call Mexico City home. Jonathan Kandell portrayed this urban behemoth in his 1988 "biography" of the city (Chapter 11). Kandell grew up in Mexico City and covered the beat for the *New York Times* in the 1980s. His account demonstrates how people continue to arrive, despite the city's inability to absorb them. In his treatment of Roberto Jara, an ordinary migrant, one gains an appreciation of the multiple dimensions that figure in the pull of the city and the push of the countryside. The reader is given a lively tour of the Federal District since the 1940s when it grew from a charming city of 1.5 million souls—a city where "the air was clear"—to a baffling, smog-ridden megalopolis. Kandell employs personal conflicts and dramatic episodes to portray sharply contrasting images of the city—its attractions and its nightmares. Readers will have to decide which visions resonate more; quite likely, as is the case with much of Latin America, the exuberant and the adverse will meld into inextricable contradictions.

Conclusions

Latin Americans have historically imagined the city in positive ways, that is, they have recognized it as the locus of a particular type of civilization that endows its members with a more comprehensive existence. This is not a perspective shared by all cultures. The British tradition, for example, has viewed the city as a venue for corruption, a space fraught with dangers for the young and the innocent; peace and safety are found, by contrast, in the countryside. These views hold that the city erodes, rather than endows, civilized existence. We can see expressions of these notions in the literature of English writers such as Charles Dickens, beginning with the Industrial Revolution. In the United States, the city has been similarly regarded as a place where freedom and moral development are compromised.[51] It is not surprising, therefore, that in both England and the United States, the university—that most comprehensive center of higher learning—was established in the pastoral purity of the countryside. In Latin America, education, particularly higher-level education, was a privilege accorded exclusively to the city.

The positive nature assigned to the city in historical Latin America was derived as much from what the city contained as from what the countryside lacked. By denying so many of its assets to the rural areas over the centuries, the Latin American city has pulled in millions of people who found little choice in the matter. In the process, it has shattered families, traditions, and small communities, which, in turn, have had to be reconstituted in the face of considerable odds and in an incomparably more impersonal environment. In parts of Latin America today, cities are no longer held in the same high regard; the weight and power of municipal authorities have been weakened significantly in cities where crime and overcrowding have made human life a cheap—and disposable—commodity. Police have given up on many barrios in Mexico City, Bogotá, Lima, Rio de Janeiro, and elsewhere, where their own safety is not guaranteed. It is one of the supreme ironies that urban areas with concentrations of poverty-stricken folk and people of color are today effectively forbidden to public safety officers, the elites' instruments of power and authority. This represents a reversal of the conditions created in the sixteenth century by the Spaniards, who delineated the Indians' barrios in order to maintain them apart. Today these areas have become, in effect, autonomous urban regions where citizens' groups have filled the vacuum left by the authorities. As a result, self-sufficient communities have arisen from within the boundaries of major cities in a demonstration, once again, of the resilience of urban life in Latin America.[52]

The expansion of Latin American cities into suburban regions, beyond the jurisdictional boundaries set by urban administrators, has embraced both slums and middle-class areas. If the *favelas* on the outskirts of São Paulo formed the backdrop of Carolina Maria de Jesus's existence, the districts of Copacabana, Ipanema, and Leblón absorbed the middle class's expansion out of the center of Rio de Janeiro. The same process of territorial expansion on the part of the middle class took place in other areas, such as Providencia and Tobalaba in Santiago, San Angel and Pedregal in Mexico City, Pocitos and Carrasco in Montevideo, Chapinero and Chicó in Bogotá.[53] At the same time, the middle class was buffeted by the highly inflationary era of the 1970s and 1980s. The exceptional growth of Latin America's foreign debt during the 1980s placed an enormous financial burden on large segments of the middle class. Its survival in many cases depended on speculation in the urban real estate market, which, in turn, spurred further construction. Today, the Latin American city provides a landscape of sharp contrasts: high-rise structures share the urban core with crumbling tenements, while rings of

American-style suburbs randomly synchronize with "towns" consisting of precariously built housing.

The city has been a feature of Latin America for over five hundred years. Even as its culture changes, indeed, *because* of its adaptability to change, its contrasts and its diversity will continue. Our own vision of the city will surely change as well. In the process, the lenses through which we analyze urban culture, social relationships, and economic exchanges will need continued adjustment, refracting the past and its actors.

Notes

1. José Ortega y Gasset, *La revolución de las masas* (Madrid: Espasa Calpe, 1937).

2. Patricia Seed, " 'Failing to Marvel': Atahualpa's Encounter with the Word," *Latin American Research Review* 26, no. 1 (1991): 15.

3. Steve J. Stern, "The Rise and Fall of Indian-White Alliances: A Regional View of 'Conquest' History," *Hispanic American Historical Review* 61 (August 1981): 472.

4. Ibid., 473.

5. Bernal Díaz del Castillo, *The Conquest of New Spain*, trans. with an introduction by J. M. Cohen (New York: Penguin Books, 1963), 232.

6. Ibid., 234–35.

7. Michael C. Meyer and William L. Sherman, *The Course of Mexican History*, 4th ed. (New York: Oxford University Press, 1991), 87.

8. For a detailed view of the lives of the men who conquered the Incas, see James Lockhart, *The Men of Cajamarca: A Social and Biographical Study of the First Conquerors of Peru* (Austin: University of Texas Press, 1972). The most comprehensive review of the preconquest Incas is provided by Garcilaso de la Vega, *Royal Commentaries of the Incas and General History of Peru* (Austin: University of Texas Press, 1966).

9. Peggy K. Liss, *Mexico under Spain, 1521–1556* (Chicago: University of Chicago Press, 1975), 4.

10. Teodoro Hampe-Martínez, "The Diffusion of Books and Ideas in Colonial Peru: A Study of Private Libraries (XVI and XVII Centuries)," *Hispanic American Historical Review* 73 (May 1993): 211–33.

11. Anthony Pagden, *Spanish Imperialism and the Political Imagination* (New Haven: Yale University Press, 1990), 91–92.

12. The titles are too numerous to list here, but a representative sample of topics would include the following works: Peter Bakewell, *Silver Entrepreneurship in Seventeenth-Century Potosí: The Life and Times of Antonio López de Quiroga* (Albuquerque: University of New Mexico Press, 1988); Stephanie Blank, "Patrons, Clients, and Kin in Seventeenth-Century Caracas: A Methodological Essay in Colonial Spanish-American Social History," *Hispanic American Historical Review* 54 (May 1974): 260–84; Richard Boyer, "Mexico in the Seventeenth Century: Transition of a Colonial Society," *Hispanic American Historical Review* 57 (August 1977): 455–78; David A. Brading, *The First America: The*

Spanish Monarchy, Creole Patriots, and the Liberal State, 1492–1867 (New York: Cambridge University Press, 1991); Lolita Gutiérrez Brockington, *The Leverage of Labor: Managing the Cortés Haciendas in Tehuantepec, 1588–1688* (Durham: Duke University Press, 1989); Fred Bronner, "Peruvian Encomenderos in 1630: Elite Circulation and Consolidation," *Hispanic American Historical Review* 57 (November 1977): 633–59; Thomas Calvo, "The Warmth of the Hearth: Seventeenth-Century Guadalajara Families," in *Sexuality and Marriage in Colonial Latin America,* ed. Asunción Lavrin (Lincoln: University of Nebraska Press, 1989), 287–312; François Chevalier, *Land and Society in Colonial Mexico* (Berkeley: University of California Press, 1970); Jeffrey A. Cole, "An Abolitionism Born of Frustration: The Conde de Lemos and the Potosí Mita, 1667–1673," *Hispanic American Historical Review* 63 (May 1983): 307–33; José Cuello, "The Persistence of Indian Slavery and Encomienda in the Northeast of Colonial Mexico, 1577–1723," *Journal of Social History* 21 (Summer 1988): 683–700; Nicholas Cushner, *Jesuit Ranches and the Agrarian Development of Colonial Argentina, 1650–1767* (Albany: State University of New York Press, 1983); Brian Evans, "Migration Processes in Upper Peru in the Seventeenth Century," in *Migration in Colonial Spanish America,* ed. David J. Robinson (Cambridge, England: Cambridge University Press, 1990), 62–85; Valerie Fraser, *The Architecture of Conquest: Building in the Viceroyalty of Peru, 1535–1635* (Cambridge, England: Cambridge University Press, 1990); J. I. Israel, *Race, Class, and Politics in Colonial Mexico, 1610–1670* (London: Oxford University Press, 1975); Elsa Malvido, "Migration Patterns of the Novices of the Order of San Francisco in Mexico City, 1649–1749," in *Migration in Colonial Spanish America,* ed. David J. Robinson (Cambridge, England: Cambridge University Press, 1990), 181–92; Cheryl English Martin, "Popular Speech and Social Order in Northern Mexico, 1650–1830," *Comparative Studies in Society and History* 32 (January 1990): 305–24; Muriel Nazzari, "Parents and Daughters: Change in the Practice of Dowry in São Paulo (1600–1770)," *Hispanic American Historical Review* 70 (November 1990): 639–65; John L. Phelan, *The Kingdom of Quito in the Seventeenth Century: Bureaucratic Politics in the Spanish Empire* (Madison: University of Wisconsin Press, 1967); David J. Robinson, ed., *Migration in Colonial Spanish America* (Cambridge, England: Cambridge University Press, 1990); Eduardo Saguier, "The Contradictory Nature of the Spanish American Colonial State and the Origin of Self-Government in the Río de la Plata Region: The Case of Buenos Aires in the Early Seventeenth Century," *Revista de Historia de América* 97 (1984): 23–44; Patricia Seed, *To Love, Honor, and Obey in Colonial Mexico: Conflicts Over Marriage Choice, 1574–1821* (Stanford: Stanford University Press, 1988); Susan A. Soeiro, "The Social and Economic Role of the Convent: Women and Nuns in Colonial Bahia, 1677–1800," *Hispanic American Historical Review* 54 (May 1974): 209–32; Steve J. Stern, *Peru's Indian Peoples and the Challenge of Spanish Conquest: Huamanga to 1640* (Madison: University of Wisconsin Press, 1982); Mark D. Szuchman, ed., *The Middle Period in Latin American History: Beliefs and Attitudes, 17th–19th Centuries* (Boulder, CO: Lynne Rienner Publishers, 1989); Eric Van Young, "Mexican Rural History Since Chevalier: The Historiography of the Colonial Hacienda," *Latin American Research Review* 28, no. 3 (1983): 5–62; and Ann M. Wightman, *Indigenous Migration and Social Change: The* Forasteros *of Cuzco, 1570–1720* (Durham: Duke University Press, 1990).

13. For descriptions of Mexico City and Lima, see Antonio Vázquez de Espinosa, *Description of the Indies (c. 1620)*, trans. Charles Upson Clark (Washington, DC: Smithsonian Institution Press, 1968), 148–72 and 427–74, respectively.

14. Nicolás Sánchez Albornoz, *The Population of Latin America: A History*, trans. W. A. R. Richardson (Berkeley: University of California Press, 1974), 80–81.

15. Jorge E. Hardoy and Carmen Aranovich, "Urban Scales and Functions in Spanish America Toward the Year 1600: First Conclusions," *Latin American Research Review* 5 (Fall 1970): 57–110.

16. Catherine E. Doenges, "Patterns of Domestic Life in Colonial Mexico: Views from the Household," *Latin American Population History Bulletin* 19 (Spring 1991): 29.

17. William P. McGreevey, *An Economic History of Colombia, 1845–1930* (Cambridge: Cambridge University Press, 1971), 60–61.

18. Eric Van Young, "Islands in the Storm: Quiet Cities and Violent Countrysides in the Mexican Independence Era," *Past and Present* 118 (February 1988): 147.

19. Mark D. Szuchman, "Household Structure and Political Crisis: Buenos Aires, 1810–1860," *Latin American Research Review* 21, no. 3 (1986): 55–93; Susan M. Socolow, "Buenos Aires at the Time of Independence," in *Buenos Aires, 400 Years*, ed. Stanley R. Ross and Thomas F. McGann (Austin: University of Texas Press, 1982), 18–39; Ernesto J. A. Maeder, *Evolución demográfica argentina de 1810 a 1869* (Buenos Aires: Editorial Universitaria de Buenos Aires, 1969); Emilio Ravignani, *Territorio y población, padrón de la campaña de Buenos Aires (1778). Padrones complementarios de la ciudad de Buenos Aires (1806, 1807, 1809, 1810)* (Buenos Aires: Compañía de Billetes de Banco, 1919); Dora Estela Celton, "Censo de la ciudad de Córdoba del año 1840. Estudio demográfico" (Ph.D. thesis, Universidad de Córdoba, 1971); and Alfredo E. Lattes, "La migración como factor de cambio de población en la Argentina," *Documento de Trabajo* No. 76 (Buenos Aires: Instituto Torcuato di Tella, 1972).

20. Hugh Thomas, *Cuba: The Pursuit of Freedom* (New York: Harper and Row, 1971), 75; and Robert J. Shafer, *Economic Societies in the Spanish World, 1763–1821* (Syracuse: Syracuse University Press, 1958), 45.

21. For a view of the effects of economic and administrative conditions on Indian communities, see Leon G. Campbell, "Recent Research on Andean Peasant Revolts, 1750–1830," *Latin American Research Review* 14 (1979): 3–50; idem, "The Historiography of the Peruvian Guerrilla Movement," *Latin American Research Review* 8 (1973): 45–70; Friedrich Katz, ed., *Riot, Rebellion, and Revolution: Rural Social Conflict in Mexico* (Princeton: Princeton University Press, 1988); Jane Loy, "The Forgotten *Comuneros*: The 1781 Revolt in the Llanos of Casanare," *Hispanic American Historical Review* 61 (May 1981): 235–57; Margarita Menegus Bornemann, "Economía y comunidades indígenas. El efecto de la supresión del sistema de reparto de mercancías en la intendencia de México, 1786–1810," *Mexican Studies* 5 (Summer 1989): 201–19; Wightman, *Indigenous Migration*; Anthony McFarlane, "The 'Rebellion of the Barrios': Urban Insurrection in Bourbon Quito," *Hispanic American Historical Review* 69 (May 1989): 283–330; and idem, "Civil Disorders and Popular Protests in Late Colonial New Granada," *Hispanic American Historical Review* 64 (February 1984): 17–54.

22. For a thorough study of the *comuneros* revolt, see John L. Phelan, *The People and the King: The* Comunero *Revolt in Colombia, 1781* (Madison: University of Wisconsin Press, 1978).

23. David A. Brading, *Miners and Merchants in Bourbon Mexico, 1763–1810* (Cambridge: Cambridge University Press, 1971), 114–19.

24. Margarita Urias, "Militares y comerciantes en México, 1830–1846," in *Orígenes y desarrollo de la burguesía en América Latina, 1700–1955*, coord. Enrique Florescano (Mexico City: Editorial Nueva Imágen, 1985), 102.

25. Jacques A. Barbier, *Reform and Politics in Bourbon Chile, 1755–1796* (Ottawa: University of Ottawa Press, 1980), 27–36.

26. Claudio Véliz, *The Centralist Tradition of Latin America* (Princeton: Princeton University Press, 1980), 126.

27. Domingo F. Sarmiento, *Recuerdos de provincia* (Buenos Aires: Editorial Sopena, 1938), 78.

28. Richard M. Morse, "Toward a Theory of Spanish American Politics," *Journal of the History of Ideas* 15 (1954): 71–93; and idem, "The Heritage of Latin America," in *The Founding of New Societies: Studies in the History of the United States, Latin America, South Africa, Canada, and Australia*, Louis Hartz et al. (New York: Harcourt, Brace, and Jovanovich, 1964), 123–77.

29. For the effects of these changes in the affairs of the viceroyalty of Peru, see John R. Fisher, "The Intendant System and the Cabildos of Peru, 1784–1810," *Hispanic American Historical Review* 49 (August 1969): 430–53; and John R. Fisher, *Government and Society in Colonial Peru* (London: Athlone Press, 1970).

30. Nettie Lee Benson, ed., *Mexico and the Spanish Cortes, 1810–1822: Eight Essays* (Austin: University of Texas Press, 1966), 209.

31. Pilar González Bernaldo, "Social Imagery and Its Political Implications in a Rural Conflict: The Uprising of 1828–29," in *Revolution and Restoration: The Rearrangement of Power in Argentina, 1776–1860*, ed. Mark D. Szuchman and Jonathan C. Brown (Lincoln: University of Nebraska Press, 1994), 185. For the effectiveness of countryside gathering places, see, among others, the narrative of Colonel Prudencio Arnold, *Un soldado argentino* (Buenos Aires: EUDEBA, 1970), 26–28. The power of priests to mobilize the masses was considerable. Evidence abounds that the clergy was effective in recruiting men for armed struggles throughout Latin America. In a letter dated December 21, 1828, the Argentine political leader J. M. Díaz Vélez wrote to General Juan Lavalle advising him to replace a troublesome priest and warning him to take heed of such matters: "Do not tell me, my friend, that priests are not important, for they very much are." Archivo General de la Nación VII-1-3-6, fol. 80–81. For the Mexican case, see Hugh M. Hamill, *The Hidalgo Revolt* (Gainesville: University of Florida Press, 1966); and Wilbert H. Timmons, *Morelos: Priest, Soldier, Statesman of Mexico* (El Paso: Texas Western College Press, 1963).

32. José Manuel Beruti, *Memorias curiosas, Biblioteca de Mayo* (Buenos Aires: Senado de la Nación, 1960), IV:3784, 3822.

33. Ibid., IV:3933.

34. John Tutino argues that the rural passivity of the Mexican colonial era resulted from Crown policies aimed at maintaining Indian village communities as counterweights to Spanish and Mexican landowners. See John Tutino, "Agrarian Social Change and Peasant Rebellion in Nineteenth-Century Mexico: The Example of Chalco," in *Riot, Rebellion, and Revolution: Rural Social Con-*

flict in Mexico, ed. Friedrich Katz (Princeton: Princeton University Press, 1987), 95–140.

35. Eric Van Young, "Islands in the Storm," 130–55.

36. Ricardo D. Salvatore, "Labor Control and Discrimination: The Contratista System in Mendoza, Argentina, 1880–1920," *Agricultural History* 60 (Summer 1986): 52–80.

37. Gerald Greenfield, "The Great Drought and Elite Discourse in Imperial Brazil," *Hispanic American Historical Review* 72 (August 1992): 375–400.

38. See Arnold J. Bauer, "Rural Workers in Spanish America: Problems of Peonage and Oppression," *Hispanic American Historical Review* 59 (February 1979): 34–63; Ricardo D. Salvatore and Jonathan C. Brown, "Trade and Proletarianization in the Late Colonial Banda Oriental: Evidence from the Estancia de las Vacas, 1791–1805," *Hispanic American Historical Review* 67 (August 1987): 431–59.

39. Peter DeShazo, *Urban Workers and Labor Unions in Chile, 1902–1927* (Madison: University of Wisconsin Press, 1983), 4.

40. A similar process of entrepreneurship was under way in the Argentine coastal regions, beginning in the 1860s, when agriculture and pastoral production was increased by the incorporation of underutilized land, large-scale immigrant labor, the importation of capital, and the creation of new commercial and transportation networks. Thus, capitalist enterprise extended into areas that had not yet been active in commercialization and production and satisfied new demands; see Leandro H. Gutiérrez and Juan Suriano, "Between Rise and Fall: Self-Employed Workers in Buenos Aires, 1850–1880," in *Essays in Argentine Labour History, 1870–1930*, ed. Jeremy Adelman (London: Macmillan and Company, 1992).

41. The relationship of urban landscape in Latin America with evolving economic and political domains was explored in a series of papers presented at the Latin American Studies Association Congress in Los Angeles in September 1992. See Barbara Tannenbaum, "A Capital City by Design: Mexico City in the Porfiriato, 1876–1910"; Mark D. Szuchman, "Architecture and Political Transition in Urban Argentina: From Ancien Régime to Liberalism"; James Holton, "Regulating Labor and Domesticating Dangerous Classes: Urban Planning and Home Ownership in São Paulo"; and David Myers, "Imagining Democracy: Caracas and the Consolidation of the Punto Fijo Regime."

42. Sánchez Albornoz, *The Population of Latin America*, 180.

43. Juan Carlos Korol and Hilda Sábato, "Incomplete Industrialization: An Argentine Obsession," *Latin American Research Review* 25, no. 1 (1990): 8–9.

44. Ibid., 11.

45. Jorge Balán, Harley L. Browning, and Elizabeth Jelin, *Men in a Developing Society: Geographic Mobility in Monterrey, Mexico* (Austin: University of Texas Press, 1973), 42.

46. Ibid., 61–62.

47. Larissa Lomnitz, "Migration and Network in Latin America," in *Current Perspectives in Latin American Urban Research*, ed. Alejandro Portes and Harley L. Browning (Austin: University of Texas Press, 1976), 133–50, shows these patterns for Mexico City. Repeated instances of migration back and forth from the hinterlands to major cities have been shown by urban sociologists; see Alejandro Portes and John Walton, *Urban Latin America: The Political Condition from Above and Below* (Austin: University of Texas Press, 1976).

48. For a study of the work's genesis and impact, see Robert M. Levine, "The Cautionary Tale of Carolina Maria de Jesus," *Latin American Research Review* 29, no. 1 (1994): 55–83.

49. Alma Guillermoprieto, *Samba* (New York: Alfred A. Knopf, 1990).

50. James R. Scobie, *Secondary Cities of Argentina: The Social History of Corrientes, Salta, and Mendoza, 1850–1910* (Stanford: Stanford University Press, 1988), 83–84; and Daniel James, "October 17th and 18th, 1945: Mass Protest, Peronism, and the Argentine Working Class," *Journal of Social History* 21 (Spring 1988): 441–61. James refers to E. P. Thompson's notions of popular ridicule against symbols of authority; see Thompson, "Eighteenth-Century English Society: Class Struggle without Class," *Social History* 3, no. 2 (May 1978): 133–65.

51. For a view of the city in the American mind, see Morton White and Lucia White, *The Intellectual versus the City: From Thomas Jefferson to Frank Lloyd Wright* (Cambridge, MA: Harvard University Press, 1962).

52. Robert Gay, "Neighborhood Associations and Political Change in Rio de Janeiro," *Latin American Research Review* 25, no. 1 (1990): 102–18; and Alejandro Portes, "Latin American Urbanization in the Years of the Crisis," *Latin American Research Review* 24, no. 3 (1989): 7–44.

53. José Luis Romero, *Latinoamérica: Las ciudades y las ideas* (Mexico City: Siglo XXI Editores, 1976), 374.

2

Tenochtitlán and Mexico City under Aztec and Spanish Rule

When Hernán Cortés reluctantly decided to destroy the Aztec capital of Tenochtitlán—in an effort to sever ties with an imperial past—he doomed a city that not only was unique in the pre-Hispanic world but also was one of the greatest cities of its time. Of its European counterparts, only Paris had an equally large population, and certainly not the cities of Iberia. It is virtually certain that no other pre-Columbian center possessed such a large population or covered such an extensive area, and, with the possible exception of Teotihuacán at its apogee (circa A.D. 300–600), none acquired such definitely urban characteristics and functions as the Aztec capital.

Yet even more significant than Cortés's decision to raze the Mexican capital was his determination to rebuild it on the same spot. The following selections, by French anthropologist Jacques Soustelle (1912–1990) and North American historian Charles Gibson (1920–1985), are designed to suggest to the reader certain patterns of continuity and change that developed when a predominantly Spanish city was substituted for a Native American one. Two important subthemes may be identified: 1) how the layout and ecology of the city came to play a significant role in the lives of its inhabitants; and 2) how the city was often an arena for social accommodation and conflict, in which a variety of institutions—political, social, and economic—were employed to control, exploit, incorporate, or marginalize individuals or groups within society.

Soustelle, who spent most of his career as an ethnologist and ethnohistorian in Mexico, draws primarily upon the literature of the conquest and native pictographic records to artistically recreate both the physical and human landscape of Tenochtitlán on the brink of its fall. Three major access causeways converge at the center of the city, funneling antlike columns of citizens toward the midpoint, where an imposing civil-religious-mercantile complex controls the urban pulse beat. As Soustelle's "tour" continues, it becomes clear that religion is the powerful cement of this highly stratified and differentiated society—the great market of Tlatelolco abuts onto the temple precinct. Merchants returning from a successful business trip mount the steps of a temple and show thanks by offering sacrifices. Youths enrolled in calpulli *(clan) schools receive their religious training while simultaneously learning the martial arts. And soaring above it all is the ubiquitous white form of the pyramid, the leitmotif of the Aztec city.*

Soustelle's synthetic study of Aztec urban society was built upon the work of an earlier generation of scholars, most notably the treatment by archaeologist George Vaillant. Subsequent research, including the massive program of salvage archaeology undertaken in connection with the construction of Mexico City's metro system, while yielding a harvest of new findings, has neither diminished the narrative value of Soustelle's account nor challenged its major interpretations.

Charles Gibson, the leading ethnohistorian of his generation, examines the human consequences attending the city's design after the conquest. In his classic work, The Aztecs under Spanish Rule, *he retraces Cortés's early blueprint for a* ciudad de españoles *surrounded by the remnants of the four original Indian barrios, an arrangement that inevitably brought an expanding Spanish society into intimate and multifaceted contact with a declining indigenous population.*

Both Soustelle and Gibson concern themselves with how the city is articulated in a larger sense. Each attempts to show how urban authority and control are exercised and to identify the institutions to which the ordinary people must accommodate themselves, or in some manner resist. Soustelle suggests that daily existence in Tenochtitlán meant participation in a common life. Individualism and deviance were discouraged and frequently severely punished. This was understandable in a society that lived on "intimate if uncomfortable terms with the supernatural powers."* *Propitiation of the gods was an endless task in which every individual was asked to take part; indeed, each knew his social obligations to the letter. Gibson, on the other hand, examines a postconquest society in which the Indian was often at a loss as to what his responsibilities were. He was used by the Spanish as a source of labor and, ultimately, of tribute, and at the same time was expected to fulfill his obligations to his former Indian lord. While some creatively fashioned alternatives to complying on all fronts, others adapted by adopting some of the ways of the conquerors. Gibson's discussion of the urban Indian economy and its craft guilds illustrates this second approach.*

Seen from the perspective of the dominant group, Mexico City was a Spanish city, surrounded by an Indian population that existed only to serve it. A variety of edicts and measures was designed to keep the Indians out and the Spaniards in. A repartimiento (forced labor draft) was instituted to secure a work force and depended in large part on social controls applied by Indian lords whom the Spanish had co-opted into their system. Although initial attempts were made by the missionary friars to educate

---

*George C. Vaillant, *The Aztecs of Mexico* (Garden City, NY: Doubleday, 1941), 233.

and provide services to the Indian community, the philanthropic impulse
subsided quickly as the indigenous population declined in the face of
European diseases.

However, as Gibson demonstrates, the colonial urban experience assumed a rather different character from what the Spanish had anticipated.
The official segregation policy proved a total failure as progressive miscegenation and demographic decline readjusted the racial balance and
altered the human geography of the city. Meanwhile, the de facto Spanish
policy of neglect and exploitation served mainly to perpetuate a vicious
cycle of misery, revolt, and repression.

JACQUES SOUSTELLE ◆ Daily Life of the Aztecs on the Eve of the Spanish Conquest

General Appearance—Roads and Traffic

As Bernal Díaz [del Castillo] says, the conquistadores "saw things
unseen, nor ever dreamed": all the eyewitnesses concur in the astonishing spendor of the city. Even [Hernán] Cortés, the most coldly calculating of them all, is free in his praise. The proud hidalgo, writing to
Charles V, goes so far as to say that the Indians "live almost as we do in
Spain, and with quite as much orderliness." He adds, "It is wonderful to
see how much sense they bring to the doing of everything."

On the 12th of November, 1519, four days after their entry into
Mexico, Cortés and his chief captains went to see the market and the
great temple of Tlatelolco with the emperor Motecuhzoma II. They went
up the 114 steps of the *teocalli* and stood on the platform at the top of the
pyramid, in front of the sanctuary. Motecuhzoma took Cortés by the hand

and told him to look at the great city and all the other towns nearby on
the lake and the many villages built on the dry land. . . . This great
accursed temple was so high that from the top of it everything could be
seen perfectly. And from up there we saw the three causeways that lead
into Mexico. . . . We saw the aqueduct that comes from Chapultepec to
supply the town with sweet water, and at intervals along the three causeways the bridges which let the water flow from one part of the lake to
another. We saw a multitude of boats upon the great lake, some coming
with provisions, some going off loaded with merchandise . . . and in
these towns we saw temples and oratories shaped like towers and bas-

From *Daily Life of the Aztecs on the Eve of the Spanish Conquest*, trans.
Patrick O'Brian (London: Weidenfeld and Nicolson, 1961), 9–15, 4, 18–20, 22–
30, 32–35 (originally published as *La vie quotidienne des aztèques à la vielle de
la conquête espagnole* [Paris: Hachette, 1955]).

tions, all shining white, a wonderful thing to behold. And we saw the
terraced houses, and along the causeways other towers and chapels that
looked like fortresses. So, having gazed at all this and reflected upon it,
we turned our eyes to the great marketplace and the host of people down
there who were buying and selling: the hum and the murmur of their
voices could have been heard for more than a league. And among us
were soldiers who had been in many parts of the world, at
Constantinople, all over Italy and at Rome; and they said they had never
seen a market so well ordered, so large and so crowded with people.

The witnesses all record the same impression: lofty towers rising
everywhere above the white, flat-roofed houses; a methodical, crowded
business, as of an ant-heap; and a perpetual coming and going of boats
upon the lake and the canals. Most of the houses were single storeyed,
low, rectangular, and flat roofed. Indeed, only great men's houses were
allowed to have two floors; and in any case it is obvious that buildings
raised upon piles in a yielding soil were in danger of collapsing as soon
as they passed a given weight, except in the comparatively rare case of
their being built on a more solid island or islet.

The majority of the houses, with their windowless facades hiding a
private life led in the interior courtyards, must have been like those of an
Arab town, except that they were built along straight roads and canals. In
the suburbs there were probably still to be found the primitive huts of the
early days, with their walls made of reeds and mud, and their roofs of
grass or straw: but on the other hand, the nearer one came to the great
teocalli and the imperial palaces, the grander and the more luxurious the
houses became; there were the palaces of the high officials and those that
the provincial dignitaries had to keep up in the capital, and then the official buildings such as the House of the Eagles, a sort of military club; the
calmecac, or higher colleges; and the *tlacochcalli*, or arsenals.

There was no monotony in all this. Here and there, from among the
close-packed roofs, the pyramid of a local temple would rise up: in some
streets the houses served as stalls for jewelers, or for goldsmiths, or for
workers in feathers: in others there would be the warehouses of the merchants. And although there was little free space apart from the great
squares, Mexico was not a town without verdure: each house had its own
inner court, and the Aztecs have always had a passion for flowers. There
were still the mixed flower and vegetable gardens of the country round
the suburban huts, sometimes made on the floating *chinampas*; and the
flat roofs of the great men's palaces were crowned with green.

"The principal streets," writes Cortés, "are very wide and very straight.
Some of these, and all the smaller streets, are made as to the one half of
earth, while the other is a canal by which the Indians travel in boats. And
all these streets, from one end of the town to the other, are opened in such

a way that the water can completely cross them. All these openings—and some are very wide—are spanned by bridges made of very solid and well-worked beams, so that across many of them ten horsemen can ride abreast."

Throughout its whole extent, even to its center (for one could row into the palace of Motecuhzoma), Mexico was a city of lake dwellers, and it was joined to the shore by the three raised causeways that Cortés and Díaz speak of. The northern causeway, starting from Tlatelolco, reached the land at Tepeyacac, at the foot of the hills where the sanctuary of Tonantzin, the mother-goddess, "our revered mother," used to be, and where there is now the basilica of Our Lady of Guadalupe. The western causeway linked Tonochtitlán with the satellite town of Tlacopan. The third, to the south, made a fork, of which the southwest arm finished at Coyoacán, and the eastern at Iztapalapan. At the junction of the arms stood a two-towered redoubt, surrounded by a high wall with two gates in it, and entirely commanding the approaches. It seems that it was only the southern causeway that had been fortified in this way: for it was from this side that the forces of Uexotzinco, an unconquered city on the other side of the volcanoes, might one day launch an attack.

These raised roads were as much dikes as causeways, and the shallowness of the lake had made the building of them comparatively easy: the construction had begun with two parallel lines of piles, and then the space between them had been filled with stones and beaten earth. Here and there the dike was broken to let the water flow under wooden bridges, for the lake had quite violent currents at times, and it would have been dangerous to bottle them up. The roads that were thus formed by the top of the dikes were amply wide enough, as Cortés says, for eight horsemen abreast: the one that ran from Iztapalapan to Mexico was about five miles long, and, according to Bernal Díaz, it "ran so straight that it bent neither little nor much."

The causeways showed the main lines along which the city had developed from its original center: one axis ran from north to south along the line from Tepeyacac to Tlatelolco to the great temple of Tenochtitlán and so to Coyoacán; and another from west to east, from Tlacopan to the middle of Tenochtitlán. Eastward the town had been stopped by the open lake, and one had to go by water to Texcoco, the starting place for the inland journey toward the mysterious Hot Lands, which had always fascinated the Indians of the high central plain.

Public Buildings, Squares, and Marketplaces

The central square of Tenochtitlán seems to have coincided almost exactly with the present Zócalo of Mexico City. It was therefore a rectangle of some 175 by 200 yards, with its shorter sides on the north and south. The northern side was limited by a part of the precinct of the great temple, which at this point was dominated by the pyramid of a temple of the sun; the south was bordered by a canal running from east to west; the east by the houses of high dignitaries, most probably of two storeys; and the west by the front of the imperial palace of Motecuhzoma II, which stood where the palace of the president of the republic now stands.

This great central square is splendid enough today, with its cathedral and the presidential palace; but what a prodigious effect it must have had upon the beholder in the Tenochtitlán of Motecuhzoma. State and religion combined their highest manifestations in this one place, and they gave a deep impression of their majesty: the white front of the palaces, their hanging gardens, the variegated crowds perpetually coming and going in the great gateways, the crenellated wall of the *teocalli*, and, standing away one beyond another in the distance like a people of unmoving giants, the pyramids of the gods, crowned by their many-colored sanctuaries, where the clouds of incense rose between banners of precious feathers. The upward sweep of the temples and the long tranquility of the palaces joined there, as if to unite both the hopes of men and the divine providence in the maintenance of the established order.

The Mexican city is above all the temple: the glyph that means "the fall of a town" is a symbolic temple half overturned and burning. The very being of the city, the people, and the state is summed up in this "house of god," which is the literal meaning of the Aztec *teocalli*. One of the prime duties of the sovereign since the beginning of the city had been "the defense of the temple of Uitzilopochtli." The temple was in fact a double temple. The pyramid rested upon a rectangular base whose north-south axis was 110 yards long and its east-west axis 88: the pyramid was made up of four or perhaps five elements, each stage being smaller than the one below it. Only the western face of the pyramid had steps, a very wide double stairway edged by balustrades which finished almost vertically before reaching the platform at the top. The stairs had a balustrade at the edge which began with great serpent's heads: one of these heads was recently exposed in an excavation near the cathedral. The stairway had 114 steps, and it was one of the highest known in Mexico—the temple of Texcoco had one of 117 and that of Cholula 120, according to Bernal Díaz. The height of the pyramid was probably about 100 feet.

The two sanctuaries were raised side by side upon the flat top of this enormous plinth: the one to the north, painted white and blue, was sacred to Tlaloc, the very ancient god of rain and green growth; the one to the south, ornamented with carved skulls painted white on a red background, to Uitzilopochtli. Each opened toward the west by a wide door that had the sacrificial stone in front of it.

The twin roofs, pyramidal in shape, were made of a wooden frame covered with cement and lime, and they were prolonged skywards by a kind of wall or crest very like those that are found upon Mayan buildings and which are designed to increase their apparent height. The roof of the sanctuary of Tlaloc was encircled by a wavy wreath of shells to symbolize water, while that of Uitzilopochtli was decorated with butterflies—fire and sun. Where the balustrades ran up to the platform there were statues of men with their hands arranged to hold the poles of the banners that were hoisted on certain great holidays—banners made of the splendid feathers of tropical birds. These flag holders were a particular characteristic of Toltec architecture and sculpture, which the Aztecs had adopted. Serpents' heads, side by side, formed a "hedge of snakes," *coatepantli*, all round the pyramid: this was also typically Toltec.

Such was the monument that rose in the center of the city and the empire, colossal yet harmonious in its dimensions, surrounded with veneration and with terror. It was said that uncountable golden jewels and gems had been hidden in the foundations, mixed with the stones and the cement by the order of the emperors. Bernal Díaz avers that this tradition was true and that when the Spaniards destroyed the *teocalli* they found the buried treasure.

At the time of which we are speaking, the double temple of Tlaloc and Uitzilopochtli was not alone. By its size and its height it was the dominant member of a veritable religious city studded with pyramids and enclosed by a serpent-headed wall (*coatepantli*) which must have measured some 440 yards in length from east to west, and 330 in width. This wall ran along the side of the central square and then by the palace of Motecuhzoma.

A great many subsidiary buildings were attached to the temples—places for prayer, penance, or sacrifice. One of these was the *quauhxicalco*, "the place where there is the *quauhxicalli*" or bowl for the sacrificed heart of the victims; and here the emperor and the priests fasted and did penance by thrusting agave thorns into their legs and offering the blood to the gods. Others were the *tzompantli*, where the skulls of the sacrificed men were shown. And there was the *temalacatl*, a huge round of stone laid flatways upon a low pyramid, where courageous prisoners, tied to it by a loose rope, fought their last fight against the Aztec warriors. The *calmecac* were at the same time monasteries and schools. The priests lived in them, austere men, worn out by fasting, severe in their black robes and long hair; and it was here too that the young men of the ruling class learned the rites, the writing, and the history of their country. Each temple had its own *calmecac*, where the priests and their pupils lived together.

But the religious quarter also contained some more secular buildings. To begin with, there was the *tlachtli*, the court for the ball game that was an amusement of the upper classes. The ball game was esteemed by all the civilized nations of ancient Mexico: the people of Tenochtitlán had taken it from their neighbors in the valley, who, in turn, had had it from the Toltecs, who were passionately addicted to the game. There were several buildings called *tlacochcalli* or *tlacochcalco*, "house of the javelins," which served as arsenals, not only for the possible defense of the temple, but for general military operations. They were guarded by soldiers, and a high military official, the *tlacochcalcatl*, was responsible for them. Two houses were used as inns "for the lords of the Anahuac, for those who came from distant cities. And Motecuhzoma honoured them highly, giving them presents, splendid cloaks, precious necklaces or magnificent bracelets." And finally, there was the *Mecatlan*, a building specially for the school of the *tlapizque*, the musicians who played the flute or other wind instruments on ceremonial occasions.

This, in all its living complexity, was the shape of the vast collection of houses, high and low, of towers, walls, and roofs, embroidered with bas-reliefs, brilliant with whiteness and color. Here was the birthplace of the city, when it came into being around a reed-woven hut; and it was here that the city was to perish, under the thunder of guns and the roar of the blazing temples.

But as the city and the state had grown, so too their rulers, like their gods, had exchanged poverty for wealth, the reed hut for the palace. It seems that each emperor was determined to build his own house. The palace of Auitzotl, to the north of the great *teocalli*, was still standing when the Spaniards came to Mexico; so was the palace of Axayacatl, where they stayed. This one, as we have seen, was opposite to the western side of the wall of serpents. As for Motecuhzoma II, he lived in the huge palace called "the new houses" (*casas nuevas*), whose size and luxury plunged the adventurers into astonished admiration. This palace, which was to the east of the square, occupied a rectangle each of whose sides measured some 220 yards. This, too, was a town in itself, with many gateways through which one could go into it, either on foot or by boat.

The sovereign's apartments were on the upper floor, according to the *Codex Mendoza*, which also shows us the rooms kept on the same floor for the kings of the associated cities, Texcoco and Tlacopan. The ground floor housed what one might now term the prime movers in public authority and government—the supreme civil and criminal courts and the special tribunal that judged dignitaries accused of crimes or of serious misdemeanors, such as adultery; then the council of war, which was attended by the chief military commanders; the *achcauhcalli*, the place for the officials of the second rank, who carried out the judicial orders; the *petlacalco* or public treasury, where there were large stocks of maize, beans, grain, and other victuals, as well as clothes and all kinds of merchandise; and the "hall of the *calpixque*," the officials responsible for the exchequer. Other parts were used as prisons, either for prisoners of war or for ordinary criminals.

But besides these there were a great many halls and courts which were attuned to that luxurious and sophisticated way of life that the Mexican emperors had grown used to—a way of life that the higher dignitaries imitated, no doubt, as far as their means would allow them. The young men would come from the local schools in the evening to sing and dance, while skillful singers and musicians were ready in another room, in case the emperor might have some desire to be gratified: they were ready with drums and flutes, bells and rattles, everything their master could ask for. Here, also, were the craftsmen whose delicate fingers chiseled the jade or melted gold or built up the feather mosaics piece by piece; farther on there was the *totocalli*, "the house of birds," which resounded with the song of all the winged jewels of the tropics; elsewhere jaguars and pumas roared from the wooden cages. The rarest flowers from all the regions had been planted in the gardens, and medicinal herbs; and there were great sheets of water with ducks, swans, and egrets.

The central square of Tenochtitlán, like those of the other districts, had also to serve as a marketplace. "This town has many squares," says Cortés, "on which there are always markets, and in which they buy and sell." "But," he adds, "there is another, twice the size of the town of Salamanca, completely surrounded by arcades, where every day there are more than sixty thousand souls who buy and sell, and where there are all kinds of merchandise from all the provinces, whether it is provisions, victuals, or jewels of gold or silver."

This obviously means the marketplace of Tlatelolco. The people of Tlatelolco had always been known for their devotion to trade, and after the town had been annexed it became the chief business center of Mexico. All accounts speak of the extraordinary variety of the enormous market in the same way, and all agree as to its orderliness. Each kind of merchandise had its own customary and defined place, in streetlike rows, "in just the same way as it happens in my own country, at Medina del Campo," writes Bernal Díaz, "when they have the fair." In one place there would be jewels of gold and silver for sale, and precious stones and the many-colored feathers brought from the Hot Lands; in the next row there would be slaves, resigned and waiting for their purchasers, some untied, some wearing heavy wooden collars; farther on, men and women bargaining over cloaks, loincloths, and skirts, made of cotton or the cloth obtained from the fiber of aloes.

Shoes, ropes, the skins of jaguars, pumas, foxes, and deer, raw or tanned, were piled up in the places kept for them: and there was a quarter reserved for the feathers of eagles, sparrow hawks, and falcons. Maize, beans, oil-bearing seeds, cocoa, peppers, onions, a thousand kinds of green stuff; turkeys, rabbits, hares, venison, ducks, and the little mute hairless dogs that the Aztecs so loved to eat; fruit, sweet potatoes, honey, syrup from maize stalks, or the juice of the agave; salt; colors for dyeing and writing, cochineal, indigo; earthenware of every shape and size, calabashes, vases and dishes of painted wood; flint and obsidian knives, copper axes; builder's wood, planks, beams, firewood, charcoal, resinous torches; paper made of bark or aloes; cylindrical bamboo pipes, charged and ready for smoking; all the produce of the lakes, from fish, frogs, and crustaceans to a kind of caviar of insect eggs, gathered from the surface of the water; matting, chairs, stoves.

"What more can I say?" cries Bernal Díaz. "There were even several boats for sale, which, saving your reverence, were filled with human excrement; they were moored in the marshes not far from the market, and they were used for tanning skins. I say this, although I know very well that it will make a certain kind of person laugh." On every hand there was this great accumulation of provisions, an unheard-of plenty of all manner of goods; and up and down between the stalls the dense crowd, unhurrying, grave; not a noisy crowd, but one that hummed or murmured, as Indian crowds do to this day. In this marketplace, says Cortés, "there are places like apothecaries' shops, where they sell medicines ready to be taken, ointments and poultices. There are barbers' shops, where one can be washed and trimmed; there are houses where, upon payment, one may eat and drink." And there were women who cooked on their stoves in the open air, and offered the customers their stews or spiced maize porridge, or sweetmeats made of honey with those excellent maize cakes called *tlaxcalli*, the Mexican tortilla; or savory tamales, whose steamed maize crust was stuffed with beans, meat, and pimentoes.

One could wander all day long in this festival of trade, taking one's meals there and meeting one's friends and relations; and many did, strolling up and down the alleys lined with tottering mounds of fruit or many-colored clothes all spread out. One could talk at length to an Indian woman squatting behind her vegetables or amuse oneself with the savage aspect of an Otomí come down from the hills to sell a few hides; or one could gaze enviously upon a *pochtecatl*, a merchant, just back from the fabled regions of the southeast, with his parrot feathers, his jewels of translucent jade, and his air of wealth.

The impassive guardians of the market, the *tianquizpan tlayacaque*, paced up and down the vast square, silently overseeing the crowd and the tradesmen. If any dispute arose, a buyer protesting that he was cheated, for example, or someone seeing his stolen goods exposed for sale, then instantly everybody concerned was taken off to the court that sat without interruption at one end of the market, where three judges continually took turns and gave their verdict on the spot. If a wrongdoer were fined he would send for his family, and they might be seen coming, gasping under the load of *quachtli*, the lengths of cloth that were used for money. And the crowd, satisfied, would return to its round, moving like a nation of ants between the covered galleries that lined the square, at the foot of the tall pyramid of the temple of Tlatelolco.

The Problems of a Great City

So huge a town and so numerous a population must have set its rulers problems undreamed of by its founders, two centuries earlier. The question of feeding it presented no difficulty, judging by the plenty in the marketplaces; and in fact innumerable boats perpetually converged upon it, loaded with provisions. It may be observed, in passing, that water transport was by far the most effective kind, in a country that did not possess a single packhorse, cart horse, cart, or any other land vehicle, nor any creature that could take the horse's place.

But the grave problem of water was exceedingly difficult to resolve. Nature has so made the Valley of Mexico that it suffers from two opposing disadvantages: it suffered then, as it does today, from either too much water or not enough—flood or drought. In the rainy season, unbelievably violent storms fill the bottom of this huge basin in a few minutes with a mass of water that can only escape very slowly. In the dry season there is great difficulty in supplying the city with drinking water and water for the gardens. Evaporation was gradually lowering the water level, and already the part of the lake round Mexico was quite shallow: though indeed at that time the climate of the valley must have been better than it is today, upon the whole, and less subject to violent extremes. The drying-up of the city's own immediate lagoon, as part of the struggle against the danger of flooding, has done nothing to improve the climate, either.

In the beginning, the Mexicans can have had no difficulty at all with drinking water: the springs on the central island were amply sufficient. As we have seen, they still answered part of the city's needs in the sixteenth century. The water of the lake itself, however, was useless, being too brackish; and when the unfortunate defenders of the city were reduced to trying it, it only made their sufferings worse.

As the population increased, the springs were no longer enough. The only solution was to bring in water from the springs that flowed on the mainland. Perhaps for some time the Mexicans were satisfied with carrying over pots of this water by boat, but very soon this must have appeared quite inadequate and the idea of the aqueduct must have arisen. The aqueduct was built under Motecuhzoma I, and it ran from the spring [of Chapultepec] to the very middle of the city, in the enclosure of the great *teocalli*, a distance of rather more than three miles. It was made of stone and mortar, and, as all the accounts agree, it had two channels, each the width of a man's body. Only one was used at a time, so that when, after a given period, it had to be cleaned, the water could be turned into the other.

As the number of people still increased, so, in its turn, the aqueduct of Chapultepec became inadequate. The construction of the second, which was begun and finished under Auitzotl, shows both the amount of the town's expansion and the intelligent activity of its rulers. This aqueduct, which brought the water for Coyoacán, ran alongside the Iztapalapan causeway. It may therefore be said that the Mexicans solved the first of their two great problems, that of drinking water; but that the solution to the second, the danger of flooding, was precarious and incomplete: indeed, even now it is still not entirely done away with, in spite of modern machinery.

There is another question that should be looked at for a moment—the question of urban sanitation. Tenochtitlán no more had main drainage than the Rome of the Caesars or the Paris of Louis XIV, so the foul waters flowed into the canals and the lake; fortunately the lake had enough in the way of currents to ensure a certain degree of outflow. In certain places, "on every road" says Bernal Díaz, there were public latrines with reed walls against the public gaze: no doubt the boats mentioned by the same conquistador in his account of the market came from here. In passing, it may be observed that the Aztecs understood the manuring of the ground with night soil.

Garbage was dumped at the edge of town, in the marshy wastelands, or buried in the inner courtyards. The upkeep of the streets was the responsibility of the local authorities in each quarter, under the general supervision of the *Uey Calpixqui*, an imperial official who issued directions, in the manner of a prefect. Every day a thousand men were employed in the cleaning of the public thoroughfares, which they swept and washed with such care that according to one witness you could walk about without fearing for your feet any more than you would for your hands. It is quite certain that at the beginning of the sixteenth century the city appears to have been healthy, because of the abundance of water, the cleanly habits of the people, and the mountain air. There is no mention of a single epidemic in the *Codex Telleriano-Remensis*, which nevertheless carefully sets down all remarkable happenings and calamities, very heavy rains, earthquakes, comets, and eclipses of the sun: the same applies to the *Codex of 1576* and the *Codex Azcatitlan*. The first great epidemic ever known in Mexico was when a Negro from Cuba, who came with the Spaniards, brought the smallpox: it devastated the country, and carried off the emperor Cuitlahuac.

Tenochtitlán as a Young Capital

Modern observers differ widely in their interpretation of the scene that has just been described. What in fact was Tenochtitlán? A very big Indian village, a swollen pueblo? Or an Alexandria of the Western world? "Although socially and governmentally Tenochtitlán was distinctly an American Indian tribal town, outwardly it appeared the capital city of an empire," says [George] Vaillant. Oswald Spengler, on the other hand, classes Tenochtitlán among the "world cities," the symbols and the materialization of a culture whose greatness and whose decadence is summed up in them.

I must admit that I do not know what is meant by "an American Indian tribal town." If it means that Mexico was not really the capital of an empire, and that behind the brilliant setting there was nothing more than what might be found in any Arizona village, then it appears to me that it is refuted by the most unquestionable facts. There is as much difference between Mexico and Taos or Zuñi as there is between the Rome of Julius Caesar and the Rome of the Tarquins—the adult must not be confused with the embryo.

But neither can it be claimed that Tenochtitlán was one of those rich, sophisticated, and ossified cities which are the elegant tombs in which their own civilization stiffens as it dies. It was the young capital of a society in full development, of a civilization in full progression, and of an empire that was still in the making. The Aztecs had not reached their zenith; their rising star had scarcely passed the first degrees of its course. It must never be forgotten that the town was destroyed by the Spaniards before it had reached its two hundredth year, and that its true rise only began with Itzcoatl, less than a century before the invasion.

It is true that in so short a time the evolution of men and institutions had been extraordinarily rapid; and this evolution had certainly been hastened by the vitality of a young nation with a rich cultural inheritance in its hands. But their vitality, far from diminishing, continued to increase and to give continual signs of its presence; the time of weariness and decline had not yet come. Nothing had even begun to weaken their upward impetus before the irruption of the Europeans stopped it dead.

It is for this reason that the Mexico of 1519 has nothing of the look of a city that is finished, a dead soul in a dead stone shell. It is a living organism that has been animated these two hundred years by a raging lust for power. The empire is still growing towards the southeast; the social structure is in a flux of change. There is no hint of old age in this picture. The Aztec world is only just reaching its maturity; and the capital, neither primitive nor decadent, is the true image of a people which is looking from the height of its domination forward to new horizons.

Let us look at this town again, and listen to it. There is nothing feverish in its unceasing, orderly activity; the crowd, with its brown faces and white clothes, flows continually along the silent facades of the houses, and from time to time one catches the scent of a garden through an open doorway; there is not much talking, and that little is in murmurs which scarcely rise above the quiet brushing sound of bare feet and sandals. If one looks up, there are the sharp lines of the pyramids against the brilliant sky, and farther on the two great volcanoes rear up their dark forests and their eternal snow. Men pass by, trotting with their foreheads bowed against the band that supports their burden: there are women with baskets of poultry or vegetables. Beside them the canoes glide past without a sound upon the canal. Suddenly the cry of "The Emperor!" runs from mouth to mouth, and the imperial retinue comes into view; the crowd opens, and with lowered eyes the people throw flowers and their cloaks under the feet of the emperor as he comes, attended by dignitaries, in a glory of green feathers and golden jewels.

Even at noon it is cool in the shadows of the walls, and at night it is positively cold. The streets are not lit at night: and the night, as everyone knows, is the time for the fierce, uncanny beings that loom at the crossroads, for Tezcatlipoca, who challenges the fighting men, and for the baleful *Ciuateteo*, the she-monsters that haunt the shadows. But unlike our European towns of the same period the city does not suspend all life until the morning, for in Mexico the night is the most important time for visiting, and the red light of torches is to be seen in the doorways and reddening the darkness over the inner courtyards. It is at night that there are parties to celebrate the return of caravans, and at night the priests get up at regular intervals to celebrate their services. The darkness, already torn by the flames from the huge tripods loaded with resinous wood on the steps of the *teocalli*, reverberates with the sounds of flutes and voices from noble or commercial banquets, and the beating of the temple gongs.

It is a vivid, complex life, the reflection of a many-faceted, much-stratified society with powerful currents running through it.

CHARLES GIBSON ◆ The Aztecs under Spanish Rule

In the Valley of Mexico the conquistadores established one *ciudad de españoles*, Mexico, or as it was known for a time, Mexico-Tenochtitlán. The decision to found the city on the site of the ruined Aztec capital was Cortés's own, and it prevailed against a contrary majority opinion of his followers. The decision meant that the city would always be dangerously exposed to flood, that its environs would be swamplands, that it would face unusual problems of water supply and commodity provision, and that relations with Indians on the island site would be of exceptional intimacy. For Indians, the site of the colonial capital required unique adjustments in labor and tribute. City life promoted miscegenation and the nonagricultural trades. City influences merged at all points with the myriad other forces that affected native peoples.

The Physical and Administrative Setting

Inside the city, the first Spaniards began by marking off the central portion, an area of some thirteen blocks in each direction, as the zone of white occupation. The region immediately surrounding this *traza* then comprised the colonial Indian community of San Juan Tenochtitlán, which consisted of the outer portions of the original four Indian barrios: Santa María Cuepopan (Tlaquechiuhcan) to the northwest; San Sebastián Atzacualco (Atzacualpa) to the northeast; San Pablo Zoquipan (Teopan, Xochimilco) to the southeast; and San Juan Moyotlan to the southwest. Each of the four was L-shaped at one of the four corners of the interior *traza*, and each necessarily gave up a portion of its territory to the Spanish center. The *traza* was symmetrically laid out with streets flanking rectangular blocks. Though some modifications in its size and internal form were made, its orderly plan always contrasted with the irregular disposition of streets in the Indian wards, and its monumental public and private buildings stood in equally sharp contrast to the Indians' adobe houses. The four barrios continued to be subdivided into lesser units—also called barrios—and many of these lesser units retained their locations and

From *The Aztecs under Spanish Rule: A History of the Indians of the Valley of Mexico, 1519–1810* (Stanford: Stanford University Press, 1964), 368, 370–73, 376–77, 380–85, 387–90, 395, 397–402.

native names through the colonial period. At the northern end of the island bordering Santa María and San Sebastián was the distinct Indian
cabecera of Santiago Tlatelolco, likewise divided into barrios, and separated from Tenochtitlán by the canal called Tezontlalli.

San Juan Tenochtitlán and Santiago Tlatelolco, generally called *partes*
or *parcialidades* of the total city, had separate Indian *gobernadores* and
separate Indian cabildos throughout colonial times. By the middle years
of the sixteenth century, Indian alcaldes were alternating among the
Tenochtitlán barrios in the system of rotational representation based upon
the surviving four-part division. Beneath the main four parts the lesser
barrios were governed by *tepixque*, *merinos*, *mandones*, and similar officers* precisely as in other Indian communities. In both *parcialidades*,
and again as in other towns, the barrio subdivisions had functional mean-
ings for community organization. When the Indians of Tenochtitlán
complained to Spanish authorities about excessive demands by the
sixteenth-century Indian governments, the particulars of the complaint
were specified barrio by barrio. When the Indian governments undertook
to organize labor for community tasks or for the construction of buildings
for Spaniards, the work was subdivided among the lesser barrios. And
when the Indian governments exacted tribute from the Indians of
Tenochtitlán and Tlatelolco, the allotments and procedures of collection
were similarly organized in accordance with the barrio subdivisions.

Both San Juan Tenochtitlán and Santiago Tlatelolco, as *cabeceras*,[†]
also had jurisdiction over a number of estancias[‡] located outside the urban area. But each also had a large number of other estancias that were
located closer to the city. Some were subdivided and shared between
Tenochtitlán and Tlatelolco, and within Tenochtitlán some were affili-
ated with one or another of the four barrios. The estancias, like the barrios, performed functional roles in the Indian governments, and like the
estancias of other *cabeceras* they were liable to the tribute and labor demands of their *cabeceras* in Indian service.

The Beginnings of Accommodation

Spanish civil government paid little attention to this complex Indian organization. But the ecclesiastical government immediately recognized the

---

*Subordinate officials at the town and *calpulli* levels.
†The capital or head town of a local Indian ruler—as such, the seat of Indian
government, nobility, tribute collection, and recruitment of labor.
‡An Indian community subordinate to the *cabecera*; synonymous with *sujeto*;
usually one *calpulli*.

Indian subdivisions and organized the missionary church in accordance with them. Under the direction of Cortés and Fray Pedro de Gante, in the first postconquest years, each of the four Indian parts of Tenochtitlán became a distinct ecclesiastical unit.

In both Indian government and ecclesiastical organization, however, the relationship progressively broke down. By late colonial times a number of the *sujetos* of Tenochtitlán and Tlatelolco had become pueblos with their own *gobernadores*. The various *parcialidad* controls over the distant estancias were gradually abandoned. In the early nineteenth century Tenochtitlán still retained a tribute-collection authority over Xalpa, Chalmita, San Lucas Tepetlacalco, and Popotla, but the communities themselves fell under the political jurisdiction of the intendant of Tacuba. Save for these four, the tribute jurisdiction of Tenochtitlán and Tlatelolco was reduced to a small area, and even within this area some semi-independent communities with *gobernadores* existed. Beginning in the late sixteenth century ecclesiastical dependence upon the original Indian form similarly broke down. By the early seventeenth century the city was divided into three *parroquias* for Spaniards and seven for Indians, with their areas in some instances overlapping.

It would be possible to trace the history of the ecclesiastical jurisdictions in Tenochtitlán and Tlatelolco in much greater detail. But the essential fact is that the various changes of the late sixteenth and early seventeenth centuries represented departures from the original Indian organization and corresponded directly to subsequent changes in the city's population. Progressive miscegenation, the spread of non-Indian populations outside the *traza*, and the penetration of the *traza* itself by native peoples were represented in other changes. At first it had been ruled that no Spaniard could live north of the *traza* in Santa María, San Sebastián, or Tlatelolco, and in 1528 all grants there were revoked. Thirty years later, however, the Spanish cabildo successfully defended its authority to assign properties outside the *traza*, and Indian and Spanish dwellings became steadily more interspersed.

In the late seventeenth century, following disorders in the city, efforts were again made to separate Indian from non-Indian inhabitants. Urban regulations of the 1690s redefined the limits of the Spanish center, forbade Indians to establish residences there, and required native immigrants to return to their original communities. Subsequently some of these same rules were repeated. But the failure of all such efforts was expressed by the new subdivisions, ecclesiastical and secular, of the late eighteenth century. In the 1770s, with the secularization of San José, three new parishes were created. Their boundaries on the edge of the city were fixed essentially by the boundaries of the surviving Indian barrios, but all the parishes included Spaniards, Indians, and others, without ethnic separation. The equivalent secular divisions were revised several times in the late eighteenth century, most notably in the creation of eight major and thirty-two minor wards in 1782. The wards, like the parishes, followed the boundary lines of some of the original Indian barrios, but other barrios were subdivided and regrouped and in general the effort was made to organize the city in a rational eighteenth-century form. The regulations spoke, as had preceding regulations, of a separation of Indian peoples in the city for ecclesiastical and tribute purposes. But the new system, once established, did nothing further to separate Indians from other inhabitants.

Demographic Decline and Spanish Neglect

The urban white population appears to have changed in inverse ratio to the attempts made at Indian Hispanization. In the sixteenth century, when Spaniards were few and Indians many, serious efforts at Indian education were made. Later, when [the] Indian population declined, these attempts were abandoned.

The decline of educational institutions in the city during the late sixteenth century and after may be taken as symptomatic of the subsequent Spanish neglect of formal Indian teaching. The Colegio de Santa Cruz (for example) never fulfilled the original hope that it would serve as a seminary for an Indian clergy. When the ecclesiastical council of 1555 forbade the creation of an Indian priesthood, the *colegio* lost one of the principal reasons for its existence. Latin, logic, philosophy, and theology were dropped from its curriculum. Viceroys after Luis de Velasco failed to support it, and efforts were made to divert its income to other recipients.

Other institutions in the city dedicated to the welfare of Indians were always limited both in number and in influence. The Jesuit Colegio de San Gregorio had only seventeen Indian students in the 1590s, shortly after its foundation, and some of these were diverted to the labor gangs of the repartimiento system. In 1728 it had only fourteen pupils, and after the Jesuit expulsion in the 1760s it ceased to function. The Hospital Real de Indios, the most enduring of the institutions for nonwhites, had eight wards, two doctors, and two surgeons in the eighteenth century, and an average of about three hundred patients. Its continued existence, while other institutions for Indians failed, may be explained by the fact that it was maintained by the Medio Real in Indian tribute.

Apart from the decay of the formal instructional institutions, Spanish neglect of the Indian population of the city is documented in numerous ways. Frequent commentaries refer to the untaught, unsettled, and criminal character of the city's mixed population, its *pueblo bajo* of Indians, Negroes, mestizos, and mulattoes. Murder was reported to be a daily occurrence during the late sixteenth century. Pitched battles between the Indians of Tlatelolco and those of the adjacent Tenochtitlán barrio of Santa María were traditional annual events. In the eighteenth century the number of homicides was reported to have increased, and the Spanish government specified severe punishment for Indians who carried arms. Spaniards spoke repeatedly in late colonial times of the vile, vicious, fetid, homeless, and unclothed population of the city, living in filth and disease and drunkenness. Alexander von Humboldt estimated in the first years of the nineteenth century that ten or fifteen thousand of the city's inhabitants were sleeping in the open. The extreme urban squalor aroused repeated comment, in conjunction with observations on the depressed state of Indians and mestizos. It is clear from the accounts that urban poverty in the seventeenth and eighteenth centuries had a special character, distinct from that of the towns and countryside, and that large portions of the late colonial city were slums.

On two occasions the urban masses rose in revolt against the Spanish government. The first uprising, in 1624, occurred at a time of high maize prices and of sharp disputes between the viceroy and the archbishop. A crowd of Indians and mestizos stormed the viceregal palace, denounced the viceroy as a heretic, and in other ways demonstrated partisanship for the archbishop. The second uprising, in 1692, also came at a time of high prices and was even more violent. It resulted in damage to the Spanish *casas de cabildo*, the viceregal palace, the jail, and other buildings. Indians were reported to have planned the revolt over a period of three months and to have selected a native king to lead them, their intention being to burn the city and slaughter the Spaniards as they fled from the houses. The Indian leaders were executed, and in both instances the disturbances were quickly suppressed.

Institutions of Exploitation: Repartimiento and Tribute

Efforts by Spaniards to organize the city's native population were directed primarily toward securing labor and tribute. Until 1564 the Indian population paid no tribute in money or in material goods to Spanish authorities, their tribute obligation being regarded as commuted to labor service for the city's need. In the earliest period a substantial part of this service was devoted to the individual governors of the Spanish state. All the first heads of state—Cortés, Alonso de Estrada, Nuño de Guzmán, Ramírez de Fuenleal, Antonio de Mendoza—received the direct service of the

Indians of Tenochtitlán and Tlatelolco. Through the sixteenth century, in an extension of this early service, Indians of the city were required to supply firewood, fodder, and water for the personal use of the viceroy and other royal officials.

A more productive form of Indian organization was devoted to the construction of buildings. Apart from private residences, many of which were built with early encomienda labor, the major building operations of the sixteenth century were the monasteries of Santo Domingo and San Agustín, the Franciscan chapel of San José, the Cathedral, the Hospital Real, the *casa de fundación*, and the *casa real*. Relatively little major new building was begun in the late sixteenth century, but many existing structures required repair, and the constant sinking of the heavy buildings meant that new floors had to be laid and pillars and doorways elevated.

Other undertakings related to causeways, street pavements, canals, bridges, and the supply of water. The original Aztec causeways, connecting the city with Guadalupe to the north, Tacuba to the west, and Mexicalzingo and Coyoacán to the south, remained the principal causeways of the colonial period, but they were continually modified, strengthened, and repaired.

At all stages of these various enterprises—buildings, causeways, streets, canals, and water supply—Indian labor was recruited by repartimiento. The officials in charge were variously the viceroy and his subordinates, the *obrero mayor* of the city's public works, special urban *jueces repartidores*, the Indian *gobernadores* of Tenochtitlán and Tlatelolco, and the Indian *mandones* and other barrio officials. Tenochtitlán and Tlatelolco were separate subdivisions in the early labor drafts, each with its *juez repartidor*. In the early period Tenochtitlán and Tlatelolco alternated in the service for Viceroy Mendoza. In the second half of the sixteenth century, with the establishment of the *jueces* and of percentage quotas, both *parcialidades* became liable to the organized repartimiento and, as in other towns, repartimiento labor for Spaniards functioned side by side with the native *coatequitl* for Indian officials and the communities. Laborers were conducted by *merinos*, *alguaciles*, and others from the local barrios to the *jueces repartidores* and by them assigned to employers. Unlike the agricultural repartimiento, the urban drafts always classified workers in the two categories of skilled and unskilled workers, the former called *oficiales*, and the latter at first called *maceguales* and later generally called *jornaleros* or *peones*. *Oficiales* were principally carpenters and masons and were in great demand by Spanish employers. In the 1570s, Tenochtitlán and Tlatelolco were each expected to give 300 Indians in monthly rotation, of whom 240 were to be *peones* and 60 to be *oficiales*. From this labor pool the viceroy, the members of the *audiencia*, and the other royal officers were entitled to draw as many workers as they wished for personal services; the Chapultepec aqueduct was to receive fifty; the Monjas de la Concepción thirty; the Dominicans eighty for the building of their monastery and twelve for regular services; and other recipients numbers in accordance with preassigned quotas. Because the original liability of the city's Indians to labor in the maintenance of causeways, aqueducts, and streets was in lieu of tribute liability, no wages were paid in these tasks until the 1550s.

Abuses, Revolt, and Repression

As in agricultural repartimiento, pressures in urban repartimiento induced irregularities, coercion, and illegal manipulations of the conditions of employment. The Indian *gobernadores* of Tenochtitlán and Tlatelolco connived with Spanish employers to sentence Indian debtors to *obrajes* and other enterprises, outside of repartimiento. Within repartimiento, *repartidores* yielded to extreme viceregal and *audiencia* demands for Indian masons, carpenters, tailors, smiths, candlemakers, and servants, and to the requests of other royal officials for skilled and unskilled workers. Laborers were taken from the Chapultepec aqueduct and privately turned over to individual employers. Indians worked and were not paid. The monasteries, churches, and private persons with licenses for woodcutting (notably in the *montes* of Chalco province) sold the licenses to contractors, who exploited and defrauded the Indian woodcutters. *Repartidores* made preferential assignments, favoring some employers with *oficiales* and full quotas, ignoring other employers, and holding workers for special purposes. Private employers sequestered workers and hired them out for profit, to the point [that] the viceroy in the early seventeenth century allowed the public works authorities of the city to offer advanced wages in an official and competing system of peonage.

Labor obligation was held to be the justification for the early tribute exemption of the Indians of the city. But one must remember that the native governments of Tenochtitlán and Tlatelolco, like those of other communities, had traditionally been supported in the pre-Spanish period by contributions from Indians and that this intra-Indian taxation was at no time included in the exemption. The early colonial records of intra-Indian tribute indicate continued contributions of fish, frogs, salt, fowl, *petates*, and other goods for the *gobernador* and community. The tribute was increased to two *reales* by Spanish order in 1549, and applied both to the Indian government and to the support of ecclesiastics, and although this was the equivalent of similar tributes in other towns it aroused immediate Indian opposition in the city. Several Indians were hanged in the middle sixteenth century for their refusal to pay it. In the 1550s and early 1560s the tax was collected in the form of one-half *real*, or one-half *real* and ten *cacaos*, every eighty days (as in the original Aztec system) to make a total of between two and two and one-half *reales* per tributary per year. The exemption thus applied only to the additional tribute for the Spanish government, and it continued to be justified in terms of the urban Indians' labor on the public works.

The city's exemption from normal tribute received criticism in the royal interest as early as the 1530s, and in the 1540s an ineffective assessment was proposed, at four thousand pesos per year. An inquiry made by the *oidor* [*audiencia* judge] Alonso de Zorita disclosed that the Indian government in Tlatelolco was already collecting more tribute than would have been paid to the royal treasury, and that it had taken over fifty thousand pesos in advance. A royal order requiring full tribute payment in the city was then issued in 1551. But the definitive regulation was made only in 1564 under the stimulus of the royal investigator Jerónimo de Valderrama. Tributaries of Tenochtitlán and Tlatelolco were required for the first time to pay one peso and one-half *fanega* [about a bushel and a half] of maize apiece per year, with half payment by half tributaries, widows, widowers, bachelors, and spinsters. Because the city was not a producer of maize, commutation of the maize payment at three *reales* per half *fanega* was permitted. Renewed Indian resistance took the form of open rebellion in both Tenochtitlán and Tlatelolco, with an attempt on the life of the *gobernador*. Some fifty Indians were captured and the *gobernador*, alcaldes, and *regidores* of Tenochtitlán were jailed for their failure to collect the tax and maintain order. Indians stoned the community house of Tenochtitlán, and in Tlatelolco the collectors were stoned and further imprisonments followed.

Other Institutions of Accommodation and Conflict

By the late sixteenth century the Indian government had lost nearly all its original authority over commerce and other areas of economic life within the city. Regulation of markets and supplies had fallen wholly to Spaniards, and the Spanish state had assumed control over both the white and the Indian economies, as well as over the intermediate exchanges that affected both. A major change in urban Indian commerce during the sixteenth century was the decline of the Tlatelolco market and the concentration of the main exchanges in Tenochtitlán. The Tlatelolco plaza was still attracting native buyers and sellers to a number estimated at twenty thousand in the middle 1550s. But by the early seventeenth century an observer could say of the Tlatelolco market that "it means less for what it is than for the memory of what it was." The San Juan market near the southwest corner of the *traza* was equally large and continued to be used extensively, while the Tlatelolco market declined.

The orderliness of the Indian markets, which had so impressed the first Spaniards, had broken down in San Hipólito by the 1560s, and the Indian markets suffered disarrangement after the Spanish manner. The efforts of the sixteenth century to confine sellers of chickens, fruit, *atole*, and other foods to the plazas were unsuccessful, and in the seventeenth century Indians were permitted to sell foods freely in or out of the plazas. In late colonial times Spaniards, Indians, and mestizos were helter-skelter in the markets. Stalls, no longer limited to the marketplaces, were scattered throughout the city. Indians trafficked in goods from house to house and hawkers roamed everywhere.

An important difference between the economy of the city and the economy of the towns relates to those Indians who became artisans in the crafts of Spanish urban society. The sixteenth-century record refers to a huge number of such crafts and in effect confirms the statement of a Spaniard of 1569 that there was then no trade in the city that Indians had not learned. The full list includes swordmakers, glovemakers, glassworkers, saddlers, bellmakers, blacksmiths, and tailors. By the end of the first colonial generation Indians were manufacturing doublets, waistcoats, breeches, and all Spanish garments. Though imitative, these first-generation Indian craftsmen appear to have been remarkably positive and eager, and it may be suggested that the disciplines of preconquest craftsmanship were such as to encourage ingenuity in novel circumstances.

It should be added that a strong economic motive likewise encouraged craftsmanship among the Indians of the city. By the midcentury skilled Indian embroiderers and silver workers were making as much as a peso per day, or more than the best-paid *gobernadores* outside the city. Carpenters were making four *reales* per day in the early 1560s and masons three, while *peones* were making only one *real*.

In the original Indian craftsmanship of Tenochtitlán and Tlatelolco, as in that of some other large communities of the valley, each person and family worked at a particular skill, and specializations were handed down through families from generation to generation. Groups of artisans had lived together in the barrios of the preconquest city. The noteworthy fact for the colonial period is that even in the congested and disorganized conditions described above this family tradition and local specialization persisted. This does not mean that all individuals in a barrio pursued an identical occupation, but that one or several activities predominated to a greater extent than free choice or normal distribution would have allowed.

For a time in the sixteenth century it appeared that Indian organizations approximating guilds might be created to oppose the Spanish guilds. Indeed, the original Indian craft barrios in some ways resembled, and thus offered precedents for, urban Indian guilds. The native lacemakers in the city in 1551 were sufficiently organized to make a common appeal to the viceroy in protest against Spanish lacemakers who entered their houses, seized their goods, and molested them in other ways. Among the candlemakers in Tlatelolco, procedures of examination and supervision by an Indian inspector were in operation in 1551, precisely as in the guilds of Spaniards. Systems of apprenticeship and examination leading to viceregal licenses for itinerant trade or for establishing shops were in effect for other Indian crafts. The Indian shoemakers of the city in 1560 were organized as a formal body of craftsmen with designated shops, and one of their number served as examiner, with judicial powers. Their economic problems closely paralleled those of the Spanish shoemakers, for Indians who were not official craftsmen intruded on their market with inferior shoes and sold them outside of the designated shops.

The exclusion of such Indian craft groups from the Spanish guilds was a policy expressed in several viceregal and guild statements, to the effect that none of the specified regulations for manufacture were to apply to Indian craftsmen. The point was made regarding the silkmakers' guild in 1556, the painters' and gilders' guild in 1589, and the hatmakers' guild in 1592, and it was surely implied in a number of other guild regulations, for it followed a general order of the Crown. The purpose here was to maintain the Indian economy free from Spanish interference, and the result was to create an atmosphere favorable to the development of distinct native craft organizations. The final result, however, was not two competing guild systems but the incorporation of native labor within the Spanish guilds. Already in the 1540s certain guilds, including the saddlers and the embroiderers, had undertaken to bring native *oficiales* within the processes of guild examination.

In some cases the guilds of the seventeenth and eighteenth centuries reacted against urban miscegenation, taking refuge in an insistence on ethnic purity and on the quality of professional white craftsmanship. The regulations of the painters' guild specified in 1686 that all apprentices were to be Spaniards. The ordinances of the makers of gold and silver wire in 1665 required that only Spaniards could submit to examination, "for it would not be right for any other to be examined in so noble an art." The dyers boasted in 1685 that their guild consisted entirely of Spaniards and that no examinations were permitted for Indians, mulattoes, or mestizos. The smiths and veterinarians, seeking to retain some of the dignity that Hispanic tradition associated with horsemanship, asserted in the early eighteenth century that all apprentices were to be "Spaniards, pure and without stain, as demonstrated through presentation of their baptismal records, for ours is a noble profession."

But in the complexities of the city's late colonial economy such ethnic distinctions could not be consistently upheld. Some guilds explicitly admitted qualified Indians, Negroes, mulattoes, and mestizos to all offices, including that of inspector, while others formally prohibited them only from the rank of master. A common eighteenth-century phrase referred to the *"maestros y indios"* of a given craft. But Indian maestros were recognized in many crafts, and a guild policy of exclusion had become self-defeating and unenforceable in late colonial society. Far more characteristic of that society than the cautious rules of the Spanish craft guilds was the mixed labor force of the royal tobacco factory, founded in 1789, which numbered between six and nine thousand and consisted of men and women, Indians, and all mixed classes.

3

Viceregal Lima in the Seventeenth Century[*]

Bernabé Cobo

Translated by Sharon Kellum

Sixteenth-century chroniclers of the Peruvian conquest era focused on three major themes: the loss of the Inca state (for example, Garcilazo de la Vega); the soldier's eye view of the conquest (for example, Francisco de Jerez and Pedro Pizarro); and the turbulent civil wars that pitted conqueror factions against one another. Internecine Spanish strife combined with the ever-present threat of Indian rebellion to delay the Crown's consolidation of the Peruvian territories. It was not until the reign of Viceroy Francisco de Toledo (1569–1581), three decades after the conquest, that domestic peace was assured. This forceful viceroy reorganized colonial administration, established the forced labor draft, or mita, *and crushed the last heir of the Inca line. Thus, the frenzied looting of the conquest years gave way to a more methodical exploitation of the colony's resources. Ships laden with Peruvian silver left Lima's port of Callao to rendezvous with the Indies fleet and returned with luxury goods and immigrants for the booming seacoast cities.*

Consonant with the new timbre of life in the colony, a second generation of chroniclers arose to record the transition from a society of conquest to a true colonial society. Completed in 1639, Bernabé Cobo's Historia de la fundación de Lima *was one of the first works of this new genre, for it neither looked to the Inca past nor emphasized the epic deeds of individuals but rather detailed the organization of creole urban society and the mercantile system that sustained it. Although Cobo acknowledged his debt to earlier chroniclers, he cautioned against complete acceptance of their writings. He suggested that the desire for fame and*

From Historia de la fundación de Lima, in Colección de historiadores del Perú (Lima: Imprenta Liberal, 1882), 49–80 passim.

[*]The editors express their gratitude to Ann Twinam for her assistance in editing this chapter and preparing the introductory note.

reward sometimes swayed these writers to exaggerate or romanticize the events they portrayed.

Cobo's personal experience accounted in part for his determination to convey an accurate picture. Lured by tales of El Dorado, fourteen-year-old Bernabé Cobo had left his native province of Jaen and sailed to the Indies in 1595. A stopover in Santo Domingo and a fruitless quest for treasure along the Venezuelan and Colombian coasts gave him a more realistic picture of the New World. Cobo sailed for Peru, arriving in Callao in 1559. Two years later he entered the Jesuits' San José Seminary in Lima. He divided the next thirty years of his life between Lima and its provinces, and between his vocation as a Jesuit and the writing of history. In 1630, Cobo was transferred to Mexico, but he returned to Peru twenty years later and died there in 1657.

Cobo's account of Lima is more descriptive than analytical, yet his narrative conveys a dynamic vision of Lima's growth and the city's interaction with its immediate hinterland and the European metropolis. Cobo proudly proclaims that the City of Kings is both "court and emporium . . . a kind of perpetual fair for the entire realm." The Lima of Bernabé Cobo is chameleon-like in its changing urban form, expansive in its remittance of specialized goods and services to the interior, yet ultimately dependent on imports of grain for its very life and of luxuries for its frivolous moments.

Cobo wrote and revised the Historia *over a period of twenty-eight years (1611–1639). His comparisons of the Lima of his youth with the city of his mature years provide a range and depth not often found in chronicle writing. Indeed, a variety of prominent twentieth-century Andeanists regards Cobo to have been the most "scientific" and comprehensive of the early colonial* cronistas.[*]

A comparison with the chronicler who was Cobo's closest contemporary, Fray Buenaventura de Salinas y Córdova, is instructive. Cobo's stylistic superiority and greater breadth of vision are widely acknowledged,[†] yet on certain issues Fray Buenaventura's Memorial de las historias del Nuevo Mundo Pirú *provides a refreshing counterpoint to Cobo's* Historia. *Salinas y Córdova was equally proud of Lima's achievements and growth, but the Franciscan's perspective on the city's development as a native-born Limeño differed from that of his Jesuit counterpart. It is not unusual that Salinas should rail against the "unjust privileges" that* peninsulares *(Spanish-born subjects, such as Cobo) enjoyed at the expense of* criollos

---

[*]See, for example, John Rowe, "Inca Culture at the Time of the Spanish Conquest," in J. H. Steward, ed., *Handbook of South American Indians* (New York: Cooper Square Publishers, 1963), 2:194; and John Murra, "The Economic Organization of the Inca State" (Ph.D. diss., University of Chicago, 1956).

[†]See, for example, Luis E. Valcarcel, introduction to *Memorial de las historias del Nuevo Mundo Pirú* by Fray Buena Ventura Salinas y Córdova (Lima: Universidad Nacional de San Marcos, 1957), xi.

like himself. What is noteworthy is that he couched his diatribe in terms of Peru's increasing dependence on Spain and Europe. In an especially revealing "dialogue" with "the fabulous [silver] mine of Potosí," Fray Buenaventura laments that of the mine's legendary riches Peruvians take "only the heat of the ore's brilliance . . . giving everything else over to the King . . . [and to] all the other foreigners who come to exhaust your rich veins." *

Unlike Salinas's Memorial, which was printed in Lima in 1630, the Historia de la fundación de Lima *was not published during Cobo's lifetime. The forgotten manuscript disappeared, possibly during the expulsion of the Jesuits in the eighteenth century. In 1870, Peruvian scholar M. González de la Rosa discovered a copy of the* Historia *in Seville's Biblioteca Colombiana and published the work in 1882 as the first volume in his series* Historiadores del Perú.*†*

The Form and Greatness of the City Today

The houses built at the beginning to shelter the settlers were of simple construction that lent itself to the materials available at that time. All the houses fit into the first two blocks surrounding the plaza, the number of residents being so few. The remaining site plan was being established by the regiment for those who came to settle nearby, and there was enough space to allot in this manner for many years. The blocks that were laid out were surrounded by adobe walls and turned into orchards and farmworkers' huts for Indians and blacks, or what we used to call *corrales de negros*, some of which have lasted until our time. In the thirty years since I came to this city, I have seen many houses built, so many that no single block is left in the layout of the city where Spaniards' buildings are not found. Because of the upheavals and civil wars that ensued in this realm three or four years after the founding of Lima, and lasted for more than fifteen years, the city experienced very little growth in all that time. But once the noise of arms ceased, the climate improved and the Spaniards began to enjoy peace and quiet. Lima caught its breath and launched into such great growth up to 1629 (the year in which this is being written) that it has achieved a very prosperous course of uninterrupted growth. Nor can one foresee the end or limit to Lima's growth in the future.

*Salinas y Córdova, *Memorial*, 86, 268.
†Biographical data on Cobo come from M. González de la Rosa's introduction to Cobo's *Historia*, 7–21. Cobo originally planned to write a three-part *Historia natural de Indias*, part one to include a description of New World flora and fauna and parts two and three to contain histories of Lima and Mexico. Colonial sources indicate that Cobo completed the three volumes, but only excerpts from Vol. I and the complete version of *Historia de la fundación de Lima* (Vol. II) have survived.

It seemed to the settlers that they were greatly extending the city's dimensions and design when they were laying it out, believing that however much the population grew it would take a lot to manage to fill the site they were planning and dividing up. Yet their estimate fell far short of the magnitude that the city has achieved in view of the fact that Lima today occupies twice the space that the settlers allotted in planning it. Four thousand houses have been built here, along with those of the neighborhood and parish of the district, with Indian houses numbering about two hundred. The remainder are for Spaniards, and of these, six hundred stand along the other side of the river in the neighborhood called San Lázaro, after the parish church located there. All these dwellings together house five to six thousand Spanish inhabitants, who when combined with those coming and going, add up to twenty-five thousand souls. There are thirty thousand black slaves of all ages and sexes, about half of them living most of the time on the small farms and country estates of this valley, and as many as five thousand Indians of every age. All these groups together total sixty thousand persons of every kind living in Lima. Things of this world are so unstable and so subject to change and variation that the industry and foresight of men are not enough to prevent or defend against such changes. We have a good example of this unpredictability in the subject we are discussing. The settlers expended great care and diligence in establishing this city with the order and arrangement noted and in anticipating the accidents that can alter a city without changing its shape and design. Despite all this, in the few years that have passed here, the city of Lima—without having suffered the calamities of fires, sackings, and sieges that have befallen cities in Europe—now has a shape and state so different from the one the settlers provided on founding the city that it is amazing.

The Plazas and Public Buildings

The public buildings of Lima have the advantage over the private residences in grandness and splendor. Most of them are found on the main plaza, the most spacious and best laid out that I have seen, even in Spain. The plaza takes up an entire block, including the width of the four streets that surround it on all sides, and thus on the four sides one can survey more than two thousand feet. The plaza is very level, with a large fountain in the middle, two rows of buildings with porticos featuring stone columns, a brick arcade, and many large balconies and windows. Along one of these two sides are the offices of the cabildo [the secular town hall], more imposing and magnificent than the rest of the buildings on that side, with very showy covered corridors in front of the chamber of the *ayuntamiento* [city council], a large and beautiful structure. Beneath these porticos stands the city jail, with a chapel so large, well decorated, and well attended that it could be called a church, along with the offices of the clerks, particularly those of the town hall, where the district magistrates meet and decide legal cases.

The other row of buildings with porticos consists of shops of different kinds, most of them occupied by hatters, silk merchants, and retailers. The block on this side is split in half by a street so narrow that we call it "the Alley." It leads to the street of the silversmiths and is lined on both sides with nothing but shops. On the third side of the plaza are the main church and the archbishop's quarters. The magnificence of these buildings makes this side of the plaza the most ornate and showiest of all. The church fronts onto the plaza via the three main doors (of its seven), with two towers on the sides, one on each corner. The rest of this row of buildings is occupied by the archbishop's offices, which are magnificent and have splendid windows, particularly in the living quarters and the hall of the ecclesiastical council, which were built during the lifetime of the third archbishop. On the fourth and last side of the plaza, which slopes down toward the river along the north bank, are the royal offices, palace, and home of the viceroys. It is the largest and most luxurious structure in this kingdom because of its grand site and the great effort expended by all the viceroys to make it resplendent with new and expensive buildings. Scarcely a single viceroy has not enlarged it with some room or distinguished addition, and hence the structure has acquired the majesty that it represents today. The building is low, only one story tall, with spacious tile and flat roofs. In addition to the rooms and apartments where the viceroy lives with his family are the courtrooms and halls of the *audiencia* [royal tribunal], which deals with civil and criminal matters, all these chambers being expensively appointed.

After the founding of Lima, this plaza stood with few decorations, surrounded by the humble buildings erected at the beginning, with the gallows in the middle, right where the Marqués [Francisco] Pizarro put them, until the administration of Viceroy Count of Niebla undertook to improve the plaza. The first thing he did was to take the gallows out of the plaza and move them to the side toward the river. He also began construction of the porticos and ordered that running water be installed in the city and that fountains be built, beginning with the one in the plaza. All of this was started at that time but was completed only gradually and with the support of Viceroy Don Francisco de Toledo.

The commerce and bustle of those who continually people this plaza is very great. More than a quarter of the plaza, in front of the main church, is taken up by the market, where all kinds of fruits and other foods are sold by so many blacks and Indians that it looks like an anthill. And so that this multitude of common people will not lack for mass on fiesta days, a low mass is said for them from a balcony or corridor of the main church, which dominates the entire plaza. The items found in this market are anything that a well-supplied republic could desire for its sustenance and comfort. Many little stalls are set up by street vendors, Indians selling a thousand trifles. All along the row of buildings of the palace, a string of booths or wooden stalls belonging to vendors with a few things to sell are set up leaning against the walls, as well as many other little portable stalls along the two rows of buildings. In the marketplace, on the side of the town hall offices, public auctions are always being held where old clothes are sold at low prices along with everything needed to furnish a house.

The eight streets that lead into the plaza are the main ones and the most heavily traveled in the city. The street that goes to the Convento de la Merced is the one we call Merchants' Row because it is lined with expensive shops run by wealthy merchants. It is very beautiful and fresh because the southerly wind fans its length, and covered by awnings in the summer, it offers much coolness and shade. On Merchants' Row are found all the hustle and bustle of merchandise not only from this city but from all over the realm because every part of the country does business with the merchants along this street. The second-busiest street runs nearby at a right angle to Merchants' Row and is called the Street of the Blankets; it runs westward to Holy Spirit Hospital. This street got its name from the fact that in the early days, most of its shops sold native clothing, Indian garments, blankets, and undershirts. Now the street has expensive shops with Spanish clothing like those on Merchants' Row, although not as many. The rest of the street is occupied by workers plying various trades.

The third-busiest place in Lima is the intersection of the two streets on the corner of the main church: one heads right toward the south and runs into the Convento de la Encarnación, and the other runs east to the Convento de la Concepción, both of which are for nuns. The first road is known as the Street of the Second-hand Clothes Sellers, after the shops along it that sell ready-to-wear clothing, old and new. The second street has only one row of shops because it faces the main church.

The four other main streets also bear much traffic and trade, and although they have no stores, they are lined with the shops of many workers. In addition to these streets that head straight out to the edges of the city are others with lots of businesses, like the ones running into the back of the plaza on all four sides, especially the street of the silversmiths, the one that goes from the Jesuits' headquarters to the parish of San Sebastián, running more than a quarter of a league in length.

The Abundance of Provisions

A sufficient argument for how well Lima is supplied with everything needed for human life is that provisions today have the same price and are found in the same abundance as they were thirty or forty years ago, when the city had less than a third of its current population and not nearly as many Indians living in the region. The reason is that all the tilling and trade in matters pertaining to the sustenance of the republic have also been increasing while the republic has been growing. Regarding the most necessary and common food, which is bread, I can say that the republic always has plenty. In the thirty years that I have lived here, I have seen no more than two or three rather lean and expensive years when the price of wheat rose to twelve or fourteen pesos at most per *fanega* [about a bushel and a half], a price equaling thirty *reales* in Andalucía. The ordinary price of wheat usually ranges from two to four pesos, lower in years of plentiful harvests because great quantities of wheat are imported in addition to the eighty thousand *fanegas* harvested in this valley. The port of Barranca alone sends to Lima each year fifty to sixty thousand *fanegas*, which are harvested in the valleys of Pativilca, Barranca, and Zupi, twenty-six leagues from here. And this figure does not count the wheat brought to Lima from the valleys of Santa, Guarmey, Guáura, and Chancay, all to the north of this city (Santa, the most distant, is sixty leagues away). No less comes to the city from the valleys in the southern area—Mala, Cañete, Chincha, and Pisco. Thus a hundred and fifty thousand *fanegas* of wheat and almost as much corn come into the city each year by sea. It is noteworthy that when a shortage of wheat does occur, the poor and less prosperous people substitute for bread many other plentiful foods made at times in this country, such as cassavas, sweet potatoes, potatoes, *achiras*, and other kinds of roots that the Indians eat instead of bread. To remedy the need that used to arise during lean times, the city has a public granary, where quantities of wheat are gathered and shared at the discounted rate of five pesos per *fanega*.

No less abundant than bread is meat, although in the beginning both were in short supply until the seeds and herds brought from Europe started to multiply. They began to slaughter the cattle from Spain in 1548 because the herds had already grown so rapidly. In that year, on December 17, the town council designated a site for butchering on the edge of the river and ordered that on two days a week, Tuesdays and Saturdays, a meat market be set up where all kinds of meat would be sold, Castilian as well as native. In addition to this slaughterhouse and meat market, a second one was established recently in 1622; both markets slaughter every market day upwards of six hundred head of sheep and a total of twenty-seven hundred cows per year. A sheep is worth ten *reales*, and twenty-five pounds of beef, five to six *reales*. To appreciate the daily growth of this republic and also the multiplying of the herds, consider this: twenty-five years ago, when Juan Jiménez, an honorable and very wealthy man, started serving as the town supplier, he killed each day no more than three hundred sheep, less than half as many as now, and they sold for the same price that they go for today.

Adding to the above is the great quantity that one always finds of produce and greens, not only the kinds native to this country but those brought from Europe. In one respect, Lima has the advantage over cities in Spain: here it is not necessary to wait for the right time of year to enjoy these things, as people must in Spain, because here the entire year is the appropriate season. Nor should one fail to mention the superabundant and excessive consumption of sweets, which are made available in this city by the large quantity of sugar harvested on the outskirts of the diocese. Sugar always sells for such a cheap price that it never exceeds three or four pesos for twenty-five pounds, which would equal six or seven *reales* in Spain. With this surfeit of sugar and the abundance of fruits, it is dazzling to see the infinite varieties of sweet snacks and preserves that are made for treats.

From discussing the food supply, we can come down to the subject of the supply of firewood, which is just as important as obtaining and seasoning food. The lack of firewood has been felt keenly in this city since its settlement, and the shortage has worsened over time to the point that today firewood is the most expensive category of goods to be found. This scarcity is being remedied by planting a grove on the country estates on the outskirts and also by bringing in a lot of firewood and coal by sea from the valleys along the coast.

The Commerce, Fame, and Wealth of This Republic

Lima is the court and emporium as well as a kind of perpetual fair for the entire realm and the other provinces that trade with the city. Here the merchandise brought from Europe, China, and New Spain is unloaded, and here it is distributed to all the areas that do business with Lima. Thus the growing trade and commerce of the city's inhabitants can be readily understood. Most Limeños live by investing their money in trade, buying and selling themselves or via third parties, even if commerce is not their usual occupation. Consequently, the hubbub and volume of business is very great, especially when the armadas are dispatched, the time when installments and payments for purchases and sales are usually due. The royal revenues are collected and sail for Spain along with the silver of private parties, the main product this kingdom sends abroad in return and exchange for the many goods that the fleets bring here. The quantity that leaves each year through the registry office of this city on the fleet sailing to Tierra Firma totals six million ducats or more, in silver ingots, *reales*, and gold bars, not counting another big chunk that trade in New Spain carries off or the amount exiting the port of Buenos Aires. A much greater quantity of silver would leave Buenos Aires were it not for the severe prohibition placed by His Majesty.

In addition to the trade in foreign merchandise, this republic produces other goods of no less consideration or interest, namely, the continual flow that goes to provide the other towns in the kingdom with all the items made by the many workers and craftsmen of all kinds who live here. They are so numerous and varied that I do not know of a trade found in the more populous and well-supplied cities of Europe that is not practiced in Lima, despite its being such a young city. Leaving aside those who know how to cure our bodies, build us houses to live in, and provide us with clothing and footgear (things that cannot be done without), of all the other specialty trades that many other towns must do without, scarcely one is lacking here. Lima has weavers of silk and other rich and costly fabrics, lace- and ribbonmakers, leather embossers, glovers, clog makers, forgers of all kinds of weapons and implements of metal (such as lead, tin, brass, and tinplate), artillery casters, clockmakers, silversmiths, jewelers, sculptors, painters, goldsmiths, glassblowers and makers of all kinds of porcelain (some as well made as the most prized in Spain), crafters of lenses of crystal and glass, printers, and all the other trades invented by human curiosity and self-indulgence that are practiced in Europe. All these trades are carried out in this city by highly skilled artisans who can be sure of making a profit here, which cannot be said for many who live elsewhere in the kingdom. It is an amazing thing to see the large number of shops and workshops operating throughout Lima, mostly along the streets near the main plaza. Just the shops on Merchants' Row number more than a hundred and fifty, not counting the many warehouses found in private residences. And the silversmiths alone line one of the main streets of the city. Hardly a corner lacks a shop or store selling wine and things to eat (we call them *pulperías* here), and there are more than two hundred and seventy of them throughout the city.

The grooming and resplendence of Limeños in the care and adornment of their persons is so great and commonplace that on a feast day one cannot tell by looking who anyone is. Everyone—nobles and those who are not—dress stylishly and richly in silk garments and all kinds of fancy clothing, and with no moderation at all in this part of the world because the *Pragmáticas* on dress that were published in Spain have not arrived here. And to this end, incredible sums are spent on all kinds of silks, fabrics, brocades, delicate linens, and fine textiles. The profit made by the merchants on these kinds of things is also incredible because the goods are all brought by these traders from Europe and other places. Hence in the years when the armada does not arrive or is late, these goods are sold at steep prices and their scarcity is sharply felt. This is what happened recently in 1624, when Rouen cotton reached a price of sixteen *reales* per *vara* [almost a yard] as a result of the fleet not arriving. Similarly, the prices of all goods rise and fall according to their abundance or scarcity. For example, a quire of paper often sells for sixteen *reales*, while at other times, a ream of five hundred sheets is worth no more than that amount.

The growth that I have witnessed in thirty years here in Lima has been in this vanity of dress, finery, and pomp of servants and livery, which is astonishing. Lima has men with an income of three to four hundred thousand ducats from their haciendas and even more; he who has less than a hundred thousand is not normally called rich. Those with fifty thousand ducats or less we count among the moderately endowed, and there are plenty more in the category of twenty, thirty, and forty thousand ducats per year. Those persons of quality and family whose haciendas bring in less than twenty thousand pesos annually are considered poor.

The wealth of most Limeños consists of money and real estate in the form of estates, orchards, vineyards, sugar plantations, woolen mills, cattle ranches, property, and income from inheritances and encomiendas (labor obligations) of Indians. Up to now, fourteen or fifteen inherited estates and entailments have been established in this city, with revenues averaging around eight to ten thousand pesos each, some more and others less but none less than three thousand. Those who enjoy ecclesiastical revenue and receive a salary from His Majesty are numerous, and thus, it can be affirmed that these revenues and payments, whether those of the ministers of justice or those in the military who receive a salary from the king, are the ones that most swell the trade of the republic by distributing among the recipients each year more than a million ducats, all of which end up in Lima.

No less valuable is the wealth of this city in personal property like merchandise and jewels in private homes. The great ornamentation and ostentation of houses in Lima is so extraordinary that I believe one would find that even the poorest and humblest Limeños have some jewel or silver or gold vase in their homes. The quantity of these rich metals and precious stones like pearls, diamonds, and others displayed in table services, household items, and coins is so excessive that knowledgeable persons estimate this wealth at twenty million pesos. Setting aside all the personal goods, wardrobes, tapestries, and all kinds of household furniture and effects and religious objects, let it suffice to say that Limeños' investment in slaves exceeds twelve million pesos.

4

Colonial Buenos Aires[*]

Juan Agustín García

Translated by Sharon Kellum

Juan Agustín García's La ciudad indiana *appeared in 1900 as an amplified version of his earlier* El régimen colonial *(1898) and was praised widely as virtually the first venture into Argentina's colonial history. García began his inquiry into the social formation of Buenos Aires with the city's precarious early years as an armed camp on the periphery of the Spanish Empire. Until late in the seventeenth century the lack of ready wealth in minerals or native labor conspired with the perpetual threats of enemy corsairs by sea and hostile Indians by land to restrict the growth of the settlement and to promote the Argentine cult of courage as a dominant social value. Only those lands nearest to the city were safe for cultivation, and their monopolization by a few large landowners formed a* cintura de hierro *(iron cinch) around the settlement, closing off access to land for the city's less privileged, constricting urban growth, and providing the economic base for a Porteño oligarchy. Thus, the dynamics of land appropriation in the surrounding countryside emerged as a critical determinant of the city's internal evolution.*

García went on to detail the processes by which a powerful few choked off the potential avenues to material prosperity for the mass of the population and undermined the city's moral well-being: the excessive reliance on slave labor, the manipulation of food supplies at the expense of the poor, and the stifling of small business by corrupt and monopolistic authorities. While the many suffered, the few grew rich, accumulating the eighteenth-century fortunes that marked the second stage in the city's evolution. Behind this veneer of wealth, which was the fruit of contraband, slave labor, privileges, and monopolies, García perceived a social organism permeated by lies, fraud, and corruption and perverted by its

From La ciudad indiana: Buenos Aires desde 1600 hasta mediados del siglo XVIII (Buenos Aires: Angel Estrada y Cía, 1900), 50–295 passim.

[*]The editors express their gratitude to Joan L. Bak for her assistance in editing this chapter and preparing the introductory note.

utter scorn for law. Much of the responsibility for this condition lay with the city's unique talents for contraband, condoned and engaged in by all. Yet wealth also brought reforms and recognition to Buenos Aires, culminating in its elevation to the seat of a viceroyalty. In García's analysis of the viceregal years, a new desire for education, a burgeoning pride in the city as patria *(fatherland), and a new faith in a great destiny constituted social forces that held out hope of overcoming the city's moral ills.*

In the colonial transition from impoverished hamlet to corrupt and opulent wealth of a viceregal seat, Juan Agustín García (1862–1923) must have seen continuities with his own time. He was raised in an austere Buenos Aires, still dominated by the unpaved streets and single-storey buildings of colonial days. While he earned his law degree, however, the victory by the national army in 1880 over the secessionist forces of Buenos Aires led to the city's federalization. This event ended seventy years of civil strife and initiated a decade of spectacular urban growth that transformed the city into a wealthy metropolis. García witnessed too the overnight enrichment of the Porteño aristocracy, along with the speculation and corruption that led to the crash of 1890. He never hesitated to censure or ridicule that aristocracy, to which he himself belonged by birth and life-style, and he built a reputation as one of the outstanding social critics of his generation. Nevertheless, as the following selection makes abundantly clear, García was not immune to the racialist notions that his class embraced around the turn of the century.

A professor of law, history, and sociology, García wrote on topics ranging from legal and historical studies to literary portraits of Argentine society and even published several unsuccessful plays. While still in his twenties, he first attracted attention as inspector general de colegios nacionales y escuelas normales, *when he authored an outspoken report criticizing Argentine education for its production of useless* bachilleres *and its complete neglect of technical and commercial training. In 1910 he was one of only four professors to support the appointment of socialist Alfredo Palacios to the Porteño law faculty, and during the 1918 university reform movement he served as intervenor for the Facultad de Filosofía y Letras.*[*]

---

[*]Biographical data come from Alberto Armando Mignanego, *Juan Agustín García, sociólogo e historiador* (Buenos Aires: Est. Gráfico "Tomás Palumbo," 1937), and Narciso Binayán, prologue to García's *Obras completas*, ed. Binayán (Buenos Aires: Editions Zamora, 1955). *La ciudad indiana* has been discussed in the writings of two of Argentina's most prominent thinkers. See José Ingenieros, *Sociología argentina* (Buenos Aires: Editions L. J. Rosso, 1918), 125–40; and Ricardo Levene, *Historia de las ideas sociales argentinas* (Buenos Aires: Espasa-Calpe, 1947), 213–38 ("La realidad histórica y social argentina vista por Juan Agustín García").

The Environs of the City

A fortress atop the hills overlooking the Río de la Plata was the city's original core, the point of support and place of refuge for the new group. In its shadow, and flanked by three convents, grew the hamlet of straw and mud inhabited by the families under the protection of the garrison's soldiers. The settlers tended their small farms, which they could "work and visit with ease every day," and defended themselves against Spanish bandits and aggressive Indians, blacks, and mestizos who chased after their work animals and made brazen attempts on their property and persons, stirring up trouble around the outskirts along the strip of cultivated land that fed the city.

The site was at risk from enemies by land and by sea. The silhouette of some Flemish or English pirate hulk used to appear on the outer edges of the river and leave its sinister imprint on the settlers. It is not surprising that Buenos Aires gave the impression of being an encampment, with its particular kind of severe discipline and the necessity of bearing arms, of always being alert, and of not disappearing without the governor's permission and without leaving behind a replacement well equipped with arms and horses who would protect the community. Periodically, the men and their arms were reviewed. They would file into the main plaza, a large empty space with the fort to the east, the Jesuit-style town hall to the west, and beyond, the pampa that infiltrated the city, invading it as if wanting to merge with it once more and cover the settlement with the "gentle natural greenery of its fields."

Thus, the city's warlike and proud character was formed. It was understood that the life of one's city depended on the strength of one's power and that a moment of forgetfulness or weakness could bring definitive ruin. In such a favorable milieu, the national cult of courage gathered extraordinary momentum, dominating all ideas, aspirations, and sentiments absolutely. Courage was the yardstick of the social values that served to classify men, judge their actions, set the norms of public morality and respect, and create distinct social hierarchies according to the superior qualities that would rule the group in setting themselves up as examples for imitation—all because courage was the most useful and necessary quality.

The City

Don Juan de Garay outlined the plan of Buenos Aires in the form of a grid of twenty-four blocks from south to north, separated down the middle by the main plaza, and eleven blocks from east to west. Spanish law ordained that three areas around new cities must be reserved as common and inalienable property: common land for recreation for the settlers; arable lands bordering on the common land for tending and grazing flocks; and municipal public lands. Planting crops in these open spaces was forbidden. Garay was unable to abide by the legal order, however. The special circumstances defining the new group obliged him to reduce the settled area and bring the population closer to the center and its strength and protection. He therefore divided up the areas that were originally supposed to be public lands and grazing grounds as lands to be farmed, leaving as common land an area measuring twenty-five blocks from north to south by a league [three and one-half miles] from east to west.

The rich lands carved out of the common land, on the right bank of the Gran Paraná and the Riachuelo de las Canoas, were divided into large lots measuring a league in depth by 350 *varas* [965 feet] along the Paraná and by 3,000 *varas* [8,268 feet] in depth along the Riachuelo. Thus twenty-six landholders became owners of all the arable land in the settlement. This arrangement provided land that could be worked and visited daily despite the presence of hostile Indians, according to the original owner's wish. It also offered easy communication with and proximity to the market. Thus was established the iron cinch that would restrict the economic development of Buenos Aires for many years: the basis of a fortune for a few at the price of moral and material poverty for the working majority.

The immigrants who arrived later would find all the sites taken. To establish their farms, they had to either encroach on the public lands, where their situation was illegal and their foothold precarious, or buy or rent from private individuals, who took advantage of their monopoly by imposing relatively high prices on what in reality (and given the larger circumstances) should not have been worth so much. Lacking liberal and scientific careers (which are modern creations) and wealth based on real property (which was then unknown), three paths presented themselves to the hard-working and ambitious individual: working the land, commerce and smuggling, and public office. Land, the basis of the entire colonial economy, had been monopolized by the state, which had divided a limited amount among a small group of privileged persons. The new owners of these large areas of fifty and seventy leagues, which were teeming with animals, could exploit such wealth with only a few workers, most of them slaves. Smuggling was dangerous: it required the complicity of royal officials as well as sizable capital to acquire an entire shipment, charter a ship, and pay the premiums demanded by the captain and crew before they would undertake a dangerous adventure that could end in a lopsided battle with pirates or in being condemned to the gallows.

At the same time, every large-scale enterprise or attempt at daring speculation was impeded by the authorities. The spirit of entrepreneurial adventure was not looked upon favorably because the official perspective envisioned a simple and mediocre life. Fortunes, which were made stealthily by illicit means, were hidden in dread of extraordinary taxes and envy and in fear of possible confiscation. Small business was scorned as a lowly trade: "Let them not mix with those who traffic in and sell merchandise." Government employment, in contrast, brought wealth (if one's conscience had few scruples), high regard, and prestige. This social situation blocked the development of the population of Buenos Aires, despite the abundance of food. A pessimistic outlook, fragmented and anarchic family structure, and the sadness of life were all factors that were at least as important in material poverty as the shortage of wheat and meat.

The Family

In social terms, the traditional family was made up of relatives connected by ties of blood and kinship as well as servants, Indians, slaves, and free laborers, all of them dependents of the colonial landowners. Each of these elements had its role and exerted its influence in shaping the family. First of all, the black slaves—trusted servants, teachers, and companions of the children whom they raised and cared for—imparted to these young charges their vices, flaws, and manner of thinking and feeling, along with the hatred for work, order, and thrift that made up their particular morality and the wastefulness and laziness that characterized their way of life.

Slaves also represented a source of income. Nearly all the families in Buenos Aires lived off slave labor. Slaves monopolized manual jobs and trades, the humble but indispensable functions in urban life. Each house was a workshop or warehouse for workers, who went out every day to sell their labor on behalf of their owner. As a business, slaves were a very profitable way of earning easy money with few risks. For one to two hundred pesos, a slave could be bought who would bring in eight or ten pesos a month and whose maintenance cost very little.

From the time that children opened their eyes, they saw work as the inherent attribute of slaves. Inside and outside the house, slaves were the only workers. And this impression, repeated day after day, wound up tracing a deep imprint on the children's souls, confusing all the good ideas, weakening the resources of their will. Habituated to seeing work performed by vice-ridden and scorned people, the children associated working with the depressing flaw of the black slaves.

Also participating in the family were the Indians who were obligated to provide personal service (*yanaconas*) and the laborers. The former were preferred over slaves for domestic service. Fortunately, the tribes of the pampas turned out to be fierce, and thus race mixing could not take place on a grand scale, keeping the European type pure.

Laborers lived under the protection of the family, like the serfs of the Middle Ages, but in direct contact in sharing tasks and rendering small services. Although laborers were not slaves according to the law and retained their prerogatives as free beings, their social status in reality was analogous to that of black slaves or indentured Indians, and so was their manner of thinking and feeling. Laborers led a wretched existence, living in the poorest huts erected in vacant areas, simple occupants of the empty spaces in the city where they put up their huts. They ate scraps from the slaughterhouse and handouts from the master's house. If one of them turned into a bandit, he would plunder the ranches and farms along with the hostile Indians and fugitive black slaves. Laborers had not the least idea of any possible self-improvement. In their minds, their situation was fixed, like those of their companions in poverty, the Indians and blacks. Work was useless—they could not even find a field to work in! And all the trades within their reach were performed by slaves. The social milieu offered no paths, easy or hard, by which one could journey through life with dignity and pride. Laborers therefore resigned themselves to the status quo, aided by their inherited temperament and trusting their destiny to the kindness of the *patrón*, who protected them enough that they did not perish and with admirable selfishness allowed them to remain sunk in the same poverty.

The economic basis of the family was the uncompensated exploitation of its labor. The system was bad not only because it undermined production with its banal immorality but also because it perverted the most basic notions of good government. Apart from their scorn for hard work, which runs contrary to all progress, the governing classes got used to living and getting rich off the labor of others and to considering rural and urban workers as inferior beings destined by fate to serve them and maintain their comforts and fortunes. This moral corruption—the baseness of ideals, the false sentiments, the vices, the decadence of all these closely related elements—had repercussions on the exploiting family, which represented the crux, the dominant center of the small social group.

The Business of the City

To a certain extent, the colonial economy centered around the city, enclosed within the limits of the village and its outskirts, with little outside trade, its population fixed, renewed only by the natural increase in population, and its needs reduced to what was most indispensable. Buenos

Aires was commercially oriented from its origins, born with an instinct for business, a robust and energetic instinct that was affirmed during the seventeenth century in a curious struggle filled with events, some of them tragic because things were taken to their ultimate extremes. To regularize matters—to avoid the frequent cornering of the market and speculation of the era as well as rapid price fluctuations on items of basic necessity—the governor or the town council intervened constantly, almost paternally. They did so with the laudable intentions of an interested housekeeper who is voluble and frugal but has no inclination to seize every opportunity to make money, which was easy for anyone in a position of power.

One of the main concerns of the town council was the provision of bread, flour, and wheat. In 1652 poor people were dying of hunger while the preachers were clamoring in their pulpits. District officials and other city leaders spread out along the sidewalks exhorting wealthy citizens to bring wheat to the city bakeries, telling them that the governor would pay them a good price. In 1658 the selling of bread in homes was prohibited, a clandestine practice commonly employed to avoid official fees, the vigilance of weights and measures, and taxes. Yet the speculation continued, indifferent to the misery, squeezing the last *real* out of the hungry population.

Whenever it best suited their dealings, a score of prosperous and established persons of influence were able to lay siege to the poor through hunger, by hiding the wheat, restricting sales, and setting up deals with small business owners to make items of basic necessity scarce. State intervention was useless—it could do nothing in that struggle against heartless, implacable individuals who would find loopholes in the laws, lie, and bribe officials of easy and complacent morality. All the circumstances particular to Buenos Aires—its isolation, scarce means of communication and bad roads, and fiscal system that sapped the vitality of the colony—favored iniquitous ways of making money. Because merchants could not fill their pockets through legal import and export trade (except by smuggling), they devoured each other with exemplary alacrity and astuteness. They had not come to the Indies to lead the patriarchal life, nor were they tempted by the idyll of life in the country. Such utter mediocrity of existence was their despair. They longed for a fortune at any cost.

The city council audited the shops and general stores every year, not only to uncover smuggling and confiscate prohibited goods but also because of its tendency to mix into private matters. Nothing was more curious and revealing than its manner of operating. The council investigated the origin of every item of merchandise and the price paid by the merchant, limiting profit to 20 percent.

In reality, and despite the mandates of all the civil and commercial codes, a system of monopolies was established that in the absence of proper legislation, depended totally on the arbitrary whim of officials. Whether for purposes of increasing the revenues of the city council or obeying other motives that could not be admitted, state monopolies were awarded for the exclusive profit of some influential merchant, sometimes to the benefit of the public. At any moment, retailers selling whatever kind of goods could find their operations suspended by order of some high official, and could thus find themselves exposed to ruin and placed in difficult circumstances that were impossible to foresee because the government was creating them according to whim. Thus, an entire sphere of activity that could have channeled the middle class remained closed, filled with obstacles that made day-to-day operation difficult and success impossible. Those sons of average families who did not inherit land found themselves in a sad situation, condemned to perpetual idleness or to working as day laborers, stifling all their ambitions, all the positive impulses that translate into individual wealth and the general well-being of the country.

The Administration of the City

In 1706 the city council was complaining to the king that Governor Antonio Maldonado had filled six vacancies for councillors. The laws gave almost unlimited powers to the governors in their role as presiding authorities of the jurisdiction. In Buenos Aires, these functions were exercised with the greatest latitude. In the session of 5 August 1619, the usher of the city council reported that he had "not called the head sheriff because he has been in jail for many days and has not been found in the city hall; nor has he called on the sentencing magistrate of the court because he too is in jail." In addition to arresting and fining these local officials, the governor (or his lieutenant) lost no chance to make them feel all his scorn as a European and the representative of the king.

The city council could not count on resources other than those authorized by the king and the revenues from public properties. In Buenos Aires, the resources authorized were few and brought in a ridiculous amount: three or four hundred silver pesos per year. Complaints were constantly being made about the city's poverty. In 1779 an official report recounted that due to the meagerness of its revenues, the city found itself in debt by twenty-six thousand silver pesos.

Notwithstanding the modest powers of the city council and its total disregard for the progress of the city, its revenues barely covered the cost of rituals. V. G. Quesada commented, "Among the largest expenditures listed is an entry for the costs of candle wax used in church functions to honor the patron saints of the city, set at the rate of five hundred pesos. Hence, more was spent on candle wax than the municipal revenues were producing." These festivals assumed extraordinary importance: forty-nine days of the year (in addition to Sundays) on which the population was distracted from its tasks. And yet the colonial era was sad, lacking in popular rejoicing, those spontaneous outbursts of traditional merriment seen in other towns. It was a melancholy and taciturn society, as if an aura of dejection or mournfulness had poisoned the atmosphere. Even in those matters that depend on the peculiarities of temperament, Porteños did nothing unless aroused by the official lash. In 1669, despite the ordinance of the city council, people refused to amuse themselves on St. Martin's Day, and it was ordered that "each citizen be fined four pesos and be detained in the public jail."

Thus, since the city's origins, the financial system of Buenos Aires has been characterized by deficit and its administration by lack of planning. The city has been administered in a childish manner, and the necessary has always yielded to the superfluous. Vain and frivolous outlay and wastefulness carried the day in the historical development of this colonial economy. Rather than repairing some road or filling the potholes that made traffic impossible on the main streets, rather than addressing any of the pressing needs left unattended, festival lights, bullfights, and mock war games were funded and the frivolous vanity of the regiment was satisfied so that it could take its place of honor in these productions.

The Capital City

As for the moral values that can be noted in an era lacking literature and art, the new sentiment that appeared in the eighteenth century was the sense of the *patria*. At the beginning of the century, Father Neyra used this term in his travels, without connecting it to the King or to serving him: "So certain is the affectionate bent toward the *patria* that there is no son, however useless he may be, who when inspired will not offer himself either to defend the country, if he hears it being insulted, or to expound on the happiness that the idea of *patria* gives him."

In concept, the *patria* is one's own city. This ancient and classical idea of the city-state fit well into the geographical and political conditions of Argentina. The sense of the greatness of the country served as a basis for pride and self-esteem, which are indispensable for the development of patriotism. Around the end of the eighteenth century, this sentiment was based on the country's short history, encouraged by a few military incidents that were romantic, and embellished enough to impress people's imaginations. The various undertakings of conquest by the Dutch,

French, and English had all been repelled; the adventures with pirates who tried to sack the city—Fontano in 1582, Cavendish in 1587, Pointis in 1698—and the battles with the Portuguese all formed a tradition made popular by guidebooks and almanacs. [Ignacio] Núñez commented [in 1825 that] "knowledge of these actions was common in Buenos Aires among Spaniards and Americans. They had formed among the inhabitants of this city, but more specifically among the sons of the Spaniards, a sense of vanity that was fortified by the progress that the population was making and by the advances being made in their education."

These advances, the main effect of which was to give the city a sense of itself, had been broadcast notwithstanding the radically opposite objectives of the monarchy. The first sign was the intense desire to become informed that ruled those generations: "All the youth, convinced of the inadequacy of their education, try to make up for it by avidly seeking instruction in foreign books. One meets few young people who are not learning, with only the help of dictionaries, to translate French and English, making all kinds of efforts to learn whichever of the two languages they prefer." In 1769, in order to satisfy the fervent wishes of the heads of the families, the city council petitioned the Court, proposing to create centers of learning with the wealth confiscated from the Jesuits. The love of books was widespread throughout America, but especially in Buenos Aires.

The capital was cosmopolitan and replaced the old Spanish animosity toward foreigners and heretics with love and congeniality, captivated by the optimism of the new doctrines of unlimited progress, the generous political and social ideas of the philosophy prevailing in the eighteenth century. And all these moral factors, a mixture of fresh and vigorous sensations and ideas, reacted together to reinforce the sense of the future greatness of the country. That potential for unlimited progress, that brilliant future predicted by the theories of the day was nowhere better realized than in Buenos Aires, a new territory with inexhaustible resources, favorable geography and climate, and wide open spaces where millions could live happily. Their Latin imagination was excited by this dreamed-of prosperity, a wondrous mirage of wealth and culture that stirred their minds and caused them to exclaim in a naive and exaggerated manner:

Calle Esparta su virtud,	Let Sparta speak not of its virtue,
Su grandeza calle Roma.	Let Rome speak not of its grandeur.
Silencio! que al mundo asoma	Silence! For the great Capital of the
La gran Capital del Sud.	South is beginning to appear.

If these notions were not entirely sensible, they *were* effective as a social force. In the course of human development, it is one thing to feel convinced that one's fate is sealed by a miserable destiny, to believe oneself persecuted by misfortune, to be a misanthrope and therefore feeble and sluggish. It is quite another thing to possess the vanity of the presumptuous optimist who throws himself into any undertaking with the deep inner conviction of his own strength, the biased view that the gods are protecting him. Such an outlook can be criticized, especially when it does not succeed, but it generally carries nations, as it does highly gifted individuals, forward to their greatest destinies.

Various obstacles were placed along the city's path toward intellectual progress by the [empire's] refusal to found schools and universities, thus precluding noble callings. It was believed that a port city was not an adequate place to establish centers of learning. They were not wrong, if one bears in mind their political goals. Buenos Aires was not merely a center of exchange for products, a commercial market of the first rank. It was also a place where ideas were circulating faster than goods—an active, impressionable place with a liberal intelligentsia that was sympathetic to everything new. To set up schooling here would have been the same as stirring up ferment, a source of serious upheavals.

The new ideas spread nevertheless. Lacking high schools and universities, Porteños learned on their own, studying without textbooks or professors. The capital's fine private libraries illustrate this, as do the exceptional self-educated men who distinguished themselves.

The Commerce of the Capital

What distinguished the economy of the eighteenth century was the emergence of capital. During the previous century, the conquistadores and their descendants had accumulated substantial fortunes by profiting from the labor of their slaves and workers—labor that was barely repaid with food, that is to say, only enough so that they would not die. At the end of the seventeenth century, a French traveler wrote the following about the wealth of the merchants of Buenos Aires: "The majority of the cattle traders are very rich, but of all the merchants, the most important ones are those who trade in European goods, many of them reputed to have fortunes of three hundred thousand *coronas* or sixty-seven thousand pounds sterling. So that the merchant who has no more than fifteen or twenty thousand *coronas* is considered to be a mere petty retailer. Of the latter, there are some two hundred families in the town." And the estimate was not exaggerated. Its accuracy is substantiated by various data, private donations, and subscriptions provided by the tax records. For example, in 1717, Don Juan de Narbona gave twenty thousand pesos to found the Convento de los Recoletos. This same Narbona, who was a distinguished smuggler, built (this time as the contractor) a convent for Cataline nuns at an estimated cost of fifty-three thousand *pesos metálicos*, which were donated by Dr. Dionisio Torres Briceño. In 1743 the leading citizens got up a subscription of fifteen hundred pesos per head to benefit the Capuchin nuns.

The impression that the chronicles of the seventeenth and eighteenth centuries leave is one of abundance and wealth, an easy life. In the festivals celebrating the coronation of Don Fernando VI, out rode "the troupe of citizens, weighing down their mounts with very expensive saddles and bridles, with beautiful saddle blankets and saddle covers embroidered in Europe with gold and silver as well as some made in this city of braiding and gold and silver fringes, all of them dressed in rich apparel that each had had made for this occasion." Viceroy Nicolás Arredondo said in his report, referring to the construction going on in the city, "It is a marvel to see how houses are being built, every day and in every location; and this lets us know that there are fortunes in Buenos Aires." These fortunes had been amassed in three ways during the seventeenth century and the first half of the eighteenth: by smuggling, by exploiting human labor, and via the monopolies and privileges conceded in order to obtain illicit profits under the pretext of public utility.

A curious economic and social situation fostered and maintained the system of smuggling. Notions of civic morality are readily upset when money is exacted in order to misspend it or to fund an undertaking that is alien or indifferent to the interest of the ones who are paying for it (which is the same thing), leaving the taxpayers surrounded by unmet needs and neglected basic services. It is then easy for individuals to feel themselves victims of an evil and abusive robbing—and with reason. It is also easy for the law to lose its respectability and turn into a means of exploitation. Not only did seventeenth- and eighteenth-century society in Buenos Aires consider these swindles as legitimate acts, but they looked on them sympathetically, a legacy replete with the sentiments of the settlers' adventurous spirit, which had been punished by legislators in defense of odious interests. The Marqués of Loreto commented, "Fraud has more accomplices than the original perpetrators, and they are innumerable. Fraud relies on the remarkable protection that the transgressors are accorded and the protection that they in turn surely provide for those persons whose status and office define them as guardians of the soundest morality."

"Not even the friars in the convents," says [an observer], "were strangers to the temptation of filling their pockets with public funds, and police agents were seen entering the cloister to apprehend offenders among the most honored instructors in theology and members of the governing councils." In the absence of mining, fraud—the basis of all the speculative activities and monopolies already described—allowed one to amass a relative fortune quickly and easily, assuming the interested leniency of the magistrates. Everything came together to favor smuggling: a long and deserted coastline that was almost impossible to patrol and that offered special conveniences for hiding the goods, and the jealousy and discord among high officials, who were not interested in avoiding knowing about the inspection of ships in order to increase their own share of the contraband.

Inadequate legislation, which ran roughshod over the natural tendencies of the country, produced as an inevitable consequence a generalized corruption. The rot began at the highest levels, descending into and invading the entire social organism, eating away at its most vital forces. Those in high places, the wealthy ones, gained the concessions, monopolies, and privileges by bribing officials; others took their chances in committing crimes. From the high official down to the slave, everyone breathed an atmosphere of lies, fraud, and corruption. The society became steeped in scorn for the law, a notion so pervasive and entrenched that before long it became a general sentiment, a part of Porteños that perverted their intelligence and morality.

The Administration of the Capital

The establishment of the Viceroyalty of the Río de la Plata implied the triumph of Buenos Aires, whose importance and value were finally commanding the respect of Spanish statesmen after a century and a half of struggle. The viceroyalty also heralded the beginning of an era of reform, the slow spread of the principles of the new philosophy among the upper classes. There is nothing more useful to forming an idea of this social phenomenon than reading the reports of our viceroys and comparing them with the previous acts of the town councils and the notes of the governors. The report by Viceroy Juan José de Vértiz, a model of its kind, is the most interesting.

Under the title of "general provisions of government," Vértiz enumerated the various measures that he had taken in the branches of justice, police, and finance. He performed as legislator and hygienist, took upon himself municipal functions, and assumed powers that our present-day administration distributes among various offices of importance. In matters of police and health, he ordered cleaning and repair of the streets and sidewalks, guarding of the entrances to the city, and enclosure of the vacant areas, mills, and parks, because at night they were sheltering crimes and delinquents. He also prohibited littering the streets with filthy waste, pillows, and other wrappings used to bury the dead; ordered that reports be made on those who died of consumption, typhus, or any other contagious disease; and forbade mixing of the sexes in the baths and "even the scandalous behavior of taking them during the day in public view."

The *audiencia* [the royal high court of justice], the *junta superior*, and the viceroy held in their hands all the political and financial means of control. Local authorities gradually disappeared from the public arena. The viceroy or the intendant absorbed all the municipal functions. To carry out the tasks, a *junta municipal* [municipal council] was established, made up of the mayor, two councillors, and the *procurador* [town administrator], which was responsible for managing all the funds "without allowing the body of the *ayuntamientos* [town councils] to be able to meddle in this matter or to impede by any pretext whatever the dispositions of its *juntas municipales*."

Thus, while Buenos Aires was developing in wealth and population, its cabildo [town council] declined in practice and legal theory in direct proportion to the importance of the official who was representing the king. Before, as long as the city was poor and insignificant and administered by a third- or fourth-rank magistrate, the town council retained a certain active role and influence, albeit always relative and derivative in that at bottom, the council depended on the whim and goodwill of the governor. But once the viceroyalty and the intendencies were established, the cabildo turned into a modest subordinate office and ultimately disappeared without out anyone noticing its death throes, the last pitiful shudders of its extinction. The cabildo had vegetated during the prolonged colonial siesta. It lacked the moral and material force that animates and sustains legal institutions, allowing them to develop freely and exercise all the influence of which they are capable. The cabildo had not known how to inspire respect and support. The public awareness that invigorates institutions and gives them verve and energy results from the arduous labor of continual vigilance and self-sacrifice for the common good.

5

Bahia in the Late Colonial Period[*]

Luis dos Santos Vilhena

Translated by Gerald G. Curtis

The port city of São Salvador da Bahia de Todos os Santos, commonly referred to as "Salvador" or simply "Bahia," served as the capital of colonial Brazil from 1549 to 1763. An administrative, commercial, and ecclesiastical center, located in an important sugar-producing area, Bahia ranked as Brazil's largest city until the early nineteenth century, and since then has functioned as one of two regional metropolises in the Brazilian Northeast.

Headed by a governor-general and later by a viceroy, the government at Bahia theoretically ruled all of Brazil in the name of the Portuguese Crown. Because of tenuous communications, however, the viceroy's practical influence extended only to the adjacent captaincies of Sergipe del Rei to the north and Espírito Santo to the south, as well as to the interior of the large captaincy of Bahia, which included the districts of Ilhéus, Pôrto Seguro, Jacobina, and the Recôncavo, a fertile sugar-plantation zone surrounding the capital. Brazilian cities outside this region—Belém, São Luís, Recife, Rio de Janeiro, São Paulo—enjoyed direct maritime communications with Lisbon, bypassing Bahia entirely. After 1763 the governor at Salvador continued to administer the affairs of Bahia and its subordinate captaincies, Sergipe and Espírito Santo.

The best surviving description of colonial Bahia comes to us from the late eighteenth century, after the viceregal government had moved to Rio de Janeiro as a result of the gold rush in Minas Gerais and Spanish military threats in the extreme South. Luis dos Santos Vilhena, a native of Portugal who taught Greek at Salvador between 1787 and 1799, recorded his impressions of the city's physical appearance, society, and economy in a series of long letters to a correspondent at Lisbon. These letters, first

From *A Bahia no século XVIII*, vol. 1 (Bahia: Editôra Itapuã, 1969), 40–139 passim.

[*]The editors express their gratitude to Bainbridge Cowell, Jr., and Darrell Levi for their assistance in editing this chapter and preparing the introductory note.

published in 1922 in two volumes entitled Recopilação de noticias soteropolitanas e brasilicas, *contain trenchant observations on urban problems of the time, along with detailed descriptions of government buildings, fortifications, social and racial groups, population, occupational structure, commerce, food supply, diseases, and educational establishments. These topics, which fill the first eight letters, comprise the most interesting part of Santos Vilhena's account; he devoted most of the remaining fifteen letters to exhaustive listings of religious orders, magistrates, governors-general and viceroys, bishops and archbishops, plus second-hand descriptions of the other captaincies in the colony.*

Commenting on Bahia's social scene, Santos Vilhena vented his elitist and racist attitudes. To him, the mulattoes and blacks displayed pretensions to higher status totally unbecoming their humble position in society. Poor whites, in similar fashion, refused to practice mechanical trades, relegating such lowbrow tasks to people of color. Many whites, according to Santos Vilhena, aspired to nobility or at least to minor-gentry status, and some, especially Portuguese immigrants who had started out as clerks, backed up their claims by assembling sizable fortunes in commerce. Others procured bureaucratic employment, "which could not possibly be appropriate for black people." Miscegenation, it seems, provided opportunities for mulattoes to acquire wealth; a sugar planter's illegitimate child, for example, might inherit his father's landed estate. All told, Santos Vilhena's account indicates considerable social mobility, more than he—or we—would have expected in a colonial plantation society.

Not surprisingly, Santos Vilhena noted the number of beggars who infested the streets of Salvador. These included former slaves, too old or too crippled to work, whose owners had freed them to avoid the expense of providing food and shelter. The description leaves no doubt that colonial Brazilian cities contained a large population of marginal, underemployed persons—a problem that persists two centuries later.

Salvador's commerce, on the other hand, made it the busiest port in Brazil. Sugar and tobacco constituted the main exports, in exchange for which the city imported European goods—manufactures such as hardware and textiles, foods such as salt, codfish, and wine—and African slaves. The overseas trade of Bahia reached many parts of the world—to western Europe via Lisbon and Oporto, to the Guinea coast and Angola in West Africa, and (illegally) to the Portuguese outposts of Goa in India and Macao in China.

Bahia also drove a brisk trade with other parts of Brazil. The city received foodstuffs, such as jerked beef and manioc flour, from Ceará, Rio Grande do Sul, and other captaincies along the coast, sending in exchange goods imported from Europe. Ranchers sent herds of beef cattle to Salvador from as far away as the São Francisco Valley in the west and Maranhão in the north, sometimes covering distances of more than a thousand kilometers.

Not all who styled themselves merchants deserved the title, according to Santos Vilhena, since many of them had insufficient capital or merely served as comissários *(agents) for Portuguese houses. Santos Vilhena disapproved of the activities of such lesser businessmen, claiming that they upset the dealings of more established merchants. It appears, in other words, that the wealthiest firms no longer enjoyed the cozy oligopoly they once had and that the commercial economy of late colonial Brazil allowed at least some change for the rise of new capitalists. Santos Vilhena's biased opinion in this matter reflects the traditional social distinction between big merchants on the one hand, and petty traders and shopkeepers on the other. As it does today, the city in Santos Vilhena's time had large numbers of street vendors and market stalls retailing a wide variety of wares, especially food.*

Under the rubric "administrative disorganization," Santos Vilhena deplored the expenditure of municipal funds to benefit private citizens who happened to have friends or relatives on the senado (city council), an inevitable abuse in a personalistic society. He also criticized the city council's subservience to the governor-general and to the high court (relaçao), a situation frequently found in Latin American capitals, colonial and modern. In a revealing passage, Santos Vilhena complained about the acrid debates in the council, implying that the members no longer came exclusively from the ranks of the sugar planter elite. Elsewhere, Santos Vilhena dealt with what he called "urban vicissitudes," which continue to plague Brazilian cities in the twentieth century: landslides wreaking death and destruction, streets too narrow for traffic, meat shortages and high prices engineered by speculators, epidemics caused by unsanitary conditions, and, in general, inadequate physical planning.

Throughout his letters, Santos Vilhena looked at Bahia and at Brazil with the eyes of an administrator. Given better organization, he felt, the colony could produce far more wealth and its people could enjoy a higher living standard. The system of slave labor, to him, symbolized all that was wrong with Brazil—peasant farmers, not slaves, were what the country needed. This theme of Enlightenment liberalism was to echo throughout Latin America for the next hundred years, generating schemes for rural colonization by European immigrants. On the whole, however, Santos Vilhena believed in a hierarchical society. As Carlos Guilherme Mota has pointed out, Santos Vilhena wanted to reform the colonial order, not destroy it.*

The Bay of All Saints is situated at 13 degrees south latitude and 345 degrees, 36 minutes longitude along the meridian of the Ilha do Ferro [Iron Island]; its bar is extensive and admirable, measuring some two-

*Carlos Guilherme Mota, "Mentalidade ilustrada na colonização portuguêsa: Luis dos Santos Vilhena," *Revista de Historia* 35, no. 72 (October–December 1967): 405–16, esp. 413.

and-a-half to three leagues at the mouth in such a form that a joined armada may enter through it. Its port has some notable advantages since the inlet is formed from Santo Antônio da Barra to the Itapagipe beach, the result being one of the finest of gulfs and one free of islands.

A little less than a half-league inside the bar, and along the base of the mountain that accompanies the seashore, lies the city of Salvador, beginning at the beach located at Preguiça and extending as far as Jiquitaia, with a crooked but continual street and properties with three- and four-storey houses and other large buildings. Along the entire length of this settlement, which they call Praia [Beach] or the Lower City, extend streets which end at the seashore. By means of seven pathways that go up the hill as if seeking the plains toward the East, a link is established between the Lower and the Upper City which runs in the same direction as the mountain along a similar street, with no small twists in it. At its greatest width the city may measure between four hundred to five hundred *braças* [an old linear measurement equal to about 22 meters]. Salvador's large buildings, churches, and houses for the highborn are, because of taste or by chance, old-fashioned, with the exception of a few which are more modern.

There are in the city noble edifices, large convents, and rich, well-kept churches. There are also three public squares or plazas including the New Compassion Plaza where the regiments from the city garrison normally hold drills. Seven streets empty into this square and it may become more uniform in the future when some buildings are erected to adorn its appearance.

Palace Plaza is square and is embellished on the south side by the palace of the residence of the governors; on the opposite side is the mint and two private properties. To the east lies the large Council House and jails, and opposite that are the palaces of the High Court, the main Guard Corps, and two insignificant buildings. Six streets branch off from the square and communicate with the whole city.

The Terreiro de Jesus is the third plaza, in the form of a rectangle. Its west flank is decorated by the famous church and part of the school which belonged to the Jesuits but is now destined to be the Military Hospital after having fallen into abject ruin. Facing this is the Church of the Tertiaries of São Domingo with its noble, modern consistory. To the north lies the church which belongs to the Brotherhood of the Clergy of St. Peter, still unfinished.

It is not just in the body of the city that her grandeur consists but in the six districts that surround her. Among them are the district of São Bento, the largest of all and the most pleasant; the whole of it lies to the south on a plain, with spacious streets, tidy churches, and a number of houses belonging to nobility. The Beach district is opulent because of the merchants from the plaza who frequent it, but it possesses no churches, fortresses, or better buildings.

One begins to sense why the former inhabitants selected the site for this city on the slope of a hill, above a steep bluff, full of many breaks and inclines, without access by land, except for three roads.

~ To anyone not deprived of the use of his eyes and reason, the neglect of the former inhabitants is clear in regard to permitting the construction of buildings wherever anyone wished, without any thought for the future. First and most obvious was their allowing the Benedictine religious to take over a plain next to the city and to found thereon their large monastery, depriving the city of the most appropriate and only site for a citadel in which the garrison could take refuge in case of need. This is the only hill from where the city can be bombarded, as was shown during the first invasion by the Dutch in 1624, who from that same site attacked and took the city. This perhaps would not have occurred had that advantageous post been occupied by a fort rather than a convent.

The consequences of another similar oversight have not been nor will they be less grievous; I am referring to the construction of enormously heavy buildings on the top of the mountain which on the east side overlooks the sea which slaps at its base. The latter is cast up with a wall which Nature most appropriately created for defense and suitable for the offense of anyone wishing to attempt its invasion. The main buildings which gravitate toward the hill are the Diocese Cathedral; the palaces of their excellencies, the governors and archbishops; the palaces of the High Court; the House of Mercy with the Hospital and Asylum; the school and large church which belonged to the Jesuits; the Church of the Brotherhood of the Clergy, transferred today; the parish of the Sacrament of the Rua do Passo; a church and consistory and other possessions belonging to Our Lady of the Conception of the Mulattoes. These are followed by an infinite number of private dwellings, built not only on the top of the hill but all along the slope, and most of these on points from which by some miracle of Providence they do not fall, inasmuch as they are all made of bricks, built on slender pillars of the same material, constructed on steep cliffs and without any earth to secure the supports. The sight of this strikes terror in the boldest and most fearless, and as if this lack of order were not enough, they allowed the whole mountain to be stripped, pulling all the earth into the sea from the foothill, upon which may be seen rising very tall dwellings of three, four or more stories. On top of it, finally, another city is founded, the one which, as I said, they call Praia, somewhat inferior to the Upper City in regard to width, and of the same extension, while equal in purpose and greater in riches, for the heart of commerce is there.

The base of this mountain is a sandy, black stone. Most of this rock is so concentrated that many or most of the buildings do not have their foundations upon it but rather upon earth, which is a red, almost sandy clay. These are the causes for the fact that in 1795 no less than twenty properties along the high mountain near the Fort of São Francisco slid down, crashing into the fort and ruining many other properties located in Praia.

More lamentable was the misfortune which occurred on 1 July 1797, because of the collapse of the remains of a wall which the Brotherhood of the Clergy had had improperly constructed on top of the mountain to secure the church, which was cracking. The wall collapsed, because of the extended and continued winter, upon another mountain below, making it run down in such a way that fifteen dwellings that were erected at the bottom were all leveled, burying many people, some who lived there as well as some who were passing along the two streets between which the dwellings were located. Some of the bodies were disinterred, but the majority were left underneath the debris on purpose long enough for them to decompose, and this in order to avoid any epidemic or plague caused by the infection of the air or any rotten particles which could evaporate.

Two effects came about as a result of chance, or because Providence allowed it, which meant much less destruction than might have been otherwise: the first was the collapse of the houses as soon as the stability of their foundation failed, because if they had toppled frontwards they would have knocked down more than twenty very high houses facing them and the destruction would have stopped only at the edge of the sea; and second, the fact that part of the collapsed wall fell behind the thick new wall built upon a rock, which through His Majesty's funds, is being constructed at great expense, and which holding back a great flow of earth, obstructed the ruin of some high dwellings which, had they fallen, would have tripled the destruction because of the steepness of the terrain where they are located, and which would also have ended in the sea, burying an infinite number of people and property.

~ There are in this city, and in all of Brazil, I believe, branches of many illustrious families if the surnames are not illegitimate. This is an uncertainty to which we are led by our ordinances and some of our laws where we see the quality of the people who began to populate this vast region, without our being persuaded, nevertheless, that all the families proceed from similar trunks; for noble families have come to Brazil for many and varied motives. The truth is that the passage of time has caused considerable confusion between nobles and base plebians: there are some who take pride in tracing their ancestry from *caboclos* [half-breeds] or from Indians, while others glory in descending from some of the illustrious governors who formerly governed not only this captaincy but all of Brazil, or from some of the various personages who at different times arrived at this port.

It is certain that there is no lack of individuals who will not hesitate to weave a more extensive genealogy than do the Hebrews and to debate nobility with the great ones of the entire world, when theirs may very well derive from a lack of restraiht on the part of their fathers or grandfathers, a nobility discovered on a coat of arms which for twenty-some *mil-réis* they have sent from the Court; given the nature of those who broadcast stains on others' reputations, it would have been better had they not been discovered. There are others whose parents came to Brazil not many years ago to be clerks, if they had the talent for such, and since fortune was good to them and they collected great wealth, their children feel that the emperor of China is unworthy to be their servant. There are others, however, who were obsessed with the idea of being nobles before they had the means to display that illusory nobility, and if they come to possess something of their own, they are so taken with the surnames of many of the illustrious families from the Court, and are so puffed up with their imagination, that in their opinion a duke amounts to nothing. There are others who are imbued with false enthusiasm and who think they are something in this world, living in their houses and surrounded by sordid misery, so when they go out they bedeck themselves in such a manner that it is difficult for them to revere even God. However, there are others, who being truly noble and rich, live and conduct themselves according to the dictates of modesty, reason, and civility, following completely an entirely Christian ethic.

Those who are in the military branch, however, become unbearable because of their lack of understanding of what it is to be honorable men. Any of them, from an ensign to a *coronel*, thinks of himself as the non plus ultra of nobility, without their actions ever agreeing with the duties of the forum in which they find themselves or the post or rank which they occupy: there are some such who, being no more than a domestic servant or an add-on in an aristocratic family who have come as governors, want to be the great Tamerlane.

The soldiers, however, aside from the scanty instruction in regard to their duties, may pass as examples of insubordination and insolence, for their conduct is quite unworthy of emulation. In general, the people are all lazy, most of the craftsmen not working as long as they have something to eat, although they are extremely skillful when the situation requires it of them. Ordinarily they are sociable and fun loving, and in general they are good men.

Almost all the rich mulattoes aspire to noble status; they are very vain and disdainful, not very friendly with the whites or the Negroes, for different reasons. The poor fellows esteem themselves no less than the whites, being quite audacious; the native-born Negroes imitate them and are all gifted with the ability for the employments they wish to pursue. There are many emancipated Negroes among those who have come from the coasts of Africa, who are always humble, more inclined to the whites than to the mulattoes and native-born Negroes. This does not fail to contribute to a useful and appreciable equilibrium; all whites who have no public employment, emancipated mulattoes, and liberated Negroes are soldiers in the different military corps, the line troops as well as the urban militias, those of the latter being obliged to buy their own uniforms as soon as they enlist.

~ There are some who estimate the population of the city of Bahia at eighty thousand souls; I, however, believe that those who set the figure at less than sixty thousand are more correct; and anyone estimating fifty thousand for the *recôncavo* [district] I believe is not far from the truth; and if the rest of the captaincy reaches one hundred thousand that is many. You know, however, that this calculation must be considered an approximation because an infallible figure is almost impossible to ascertain. A third of all these inhabitants may be whites and Indians, and the other two-thirds, Negroes and mulattoes.

I do not consider it agreeable to political and economic dictates to allow the city to fill up with the three kinds of beggars: whites, mulattoes, and Negroes. The whites, if they are men, are usually sailors who are ill in the hospital where they find precious little charity. As soon as they can lift their heads they are turned out in the street to convalesce and since they lack the means to care for themselves, they go petition the faithful. Because this trade is less arduous and just as profitable as that of a sailor, they embrace it in such a way that rarely do they put it aside again; instead, they normally frequent the taverns where most of them die, consumed by firewater and rum, because they rarely drink wine due to its higher price. The white women come from among those who can no longer seek their life, according to the common phrase, and this because of the violence and diligence with which they sought it while they were able, the State paying for their disorders.

The mulattoes and blacks are usually blind, crippled, old, and disabled, most of them coming from the misunderstood charity of some and the scandalous inhumanity of others. I call misunderstood charity that practiced by those gentlemen and ladies who leave emancipated slaves and female slaves without a trade, to die, without any legacy or support. If they are old they are able to do little or nothing and they want to work in order to obtain sustenance, for which cause they soon become beggars and therefore a burden to the State. If they are young they desire nothing more than to show those who are captive the difference between freedom and captivity, which they make them see by giving in to the vices that idleness suggests to them. Since there is no one to correct them and warn them they end up dying as drunkards or in the dungeons, and if they are fortunate, many of them spend the rest of their lives in forced labor. If they are women, and young, they generally prostitute themselves with such lassitude that within a short time they are helpless, paralyzed, and consumed by misery, some of them begging at the doors in order to feed themselves. This would not take place were they to remain subject to someone who would not allow them to surrender to the torrent of vices in which they engulf themselves, someone to sustain them, to cure their illnesses, to free them from crime, etc. It is doubtless a great work of mercy, that of freeing our captive brothers, but it seems more in conformity with reason and justice that those who are freed maintain this nature and quality, ever responsible to a guardian or director who will forcibly dissuade them from evil and direct them to good, not leaving them to their own brutal volition.

There is certainly no injustice in calling someone inhumane who, because he can no longer afford a slave, casts him out of his house, a slave who, during his time of service, has gone blind or become disabled in such a way that he can no longer serve. The oxen of the Israelites were more fortunate than the slaves of such masters, and if these deserve the name inhumane, I am unaware of the one which should be given to those who keep blind and crippled slaves in captivity without giving them any type of sustenance and send them out to beg from the faithful so that at the end of every week they may pay them four hundred-some *réis*, a sentence of harsh punishment.

Moreover, it does not appear to be a very discreet policy to tolerate crowds of Negroes of both sexes in the streets and public squares of the city, performing their barbaric *batuques* [Afro-Brazilian songs and dances] and playing their many and appalling *atabaques* [a kind of drum]. They dance indecently, singing Gentile songs, speaking several tongues, and this with such a horrendous and dissonant hubbub that they cause fear and wonder even among the most dauntless, considering the consequences which could result therefrom, given the number of slaves in Bahia. They are a fearful company, and worthy of close attention but for the interference of the rivalry that exists between native-born blacks and those who are not, as well as among the diverse nations that make up the slave trade coming from the coasts of Africa.

It would be greatly desirable that these slaves be placed in such a state of subordination that when it comes to showing respect, they would consider any white man to be their master, and not display the arrogance generally seen among the slaves who are the property of those who, because of their qualities, employment, and possessions, stand out. These blacks do not hesitate to treat all other whites with the unpleasantness and lack of regard which they observe in the treatment received from their own masters. Very limited must be the knowledge of anyone not recognizing the paramount importance of such a policy of slave subordination in a city populated by slaves, boorish and as untamed as wild animals.

Another principle to consider is that the Negroes in the State of Brazil are detrimental, and since it is they who handle all servile work and mechanical arts, there are few mulattoes and rarely any whites who wish to do that type of work, without excepting those indigents who in Portugal were never more than servants, waiters, and hoe diggers. It can be observed that he who comes here serving some minister is a good servant only so long as he does not reflect upon the fact that in his master's house he is employed performing those services which in other houses are duties belonging only to Negroes and mulattoes. For this reason the servant shortly begins to pester his master to fit him into some public employment not assigned to Negroes, and some masters employ these servants in such a way that the masters themselves feel persecuted and badly served and they end up putting the servants out in the street. If, however, the master delays in making this decision, the servants anticipate it and think it a better fate to be a vagrant, to go about starving, become a soldier, and sometimes a thief, rather than serve an honorable master who pays them well, and sustains and esteems them. All this to avoid doing the work that the Negroes do in other houses.

The same fate befalls the maids who accompany the ladies who come from Portugal, because for the same concern they either put themselves or they are put out in the street, preferring to subject themselves to the sad consequences of misery rather than live harbored in a house that will honor and sustain them. The daughters of the country are of such a stamp that the daughter of the poorest, most abject man, the most helpless, emancipated little mulatto, would rather go to the gallows than serve even a duchess, if there were any in the land; and this is the reason why there are so many lost and miserable women in this city.

White men who are natives of the country become soldiers, shopkeepers, scribes, clerks, officials or judges in some court, officers of the treasury, or some other public occupation removed from the domain of the Negroes, such as surgeons, pharmacists, port pilots, teachers, boat captains, clerks in waterfront warehouses, etc. A few others, although rarely so, find employment as sculptors, goldsmiths, painters, etc.

Not a few attended classes in the Royal Schools that His Majesty has set up in this city from which have come excellent students for the priesthood and other areas of letters. As soon as their parents see, however, that the schools are the targets toward which the officers and soldiers in charge of recruits first direct their shots, and that these recruiters yank their children out of the schools, the children having no immunity, privilege, or exemption of any value, and persuaded that the State needs no more ecclesiastics nor any other employment related to letters, these parents resolve that they do not wish to sacrifice their sons by exposing them to the rancor of overbearing and imprudent military men.

~ The income of this City Council is a large amount and transactions incumbent upon it are very frequent. A lack of effective economic governance is due to the lack of personal respect of many of those who annually enter into that governance, since they are more interested in their own welfare and that of relatives and friends than they are zealous of the public welfare. Hence, they conspire so that the City Council may have many and very costly works carried out, which prove to be useful only to some private individual, the engineer or construction foreman who directs them, and the contractor who accepts them. Of such a nature are some of the pavings of streets and razings of hills which amount to twelve, fifteen, and 20 thousand *cruzados,* and are useful only to powerful individuals at whose doors the works terminate, and this to increase the value of their country houses. They use the pretext that a road can be built in that direction toward some unimportant fountain or little pond used for daily needs, when the blacks who are going to carry the water would be greatly obliged to them if they didn't do the paving because of the harm it does to their bare feet.

There are and have been others who, because their chaise does not roll smoothly on the street or the pavement next to their property, believe strongly that the City Council, in the name of public welfare, should have those areas raised or lowered or paved at once. By these and similar ways a large part of the City Council's income is dissipated, funds which should have been applied to other highly urgent needs, indispensable to the public.

There are three causes which explain why many feel that the City Council will never be able to achieve a state of what we might call order. The first is that the Council president, who is always the district judge for civil matters, or, in his absence, the criminal judge or the one assigned to orphans, can never deliberate without much opposition from the city councilmen and procurator. Since the latter must be drawn from the most unassailable and independent members of the nobility, they are in a position to prepare many trivial matters and have them introduced improperly in the agenda. To effect this, they make use of the pledges of individuals who quickly lend their support in the selection of the agenda matters; and when they prepare to name aldermen, it is with a previously determined intention to obtain from their companions a thousand things which are unfair, tending to their own benefit and that of relatives, friends, and patrons, in spite of opposition by the president, which they immediately suffocate with a plurality of votes.

Another source of disorder in the City Council is the ascendancy over the Council which the Supreme Tribunal of the High Court has claimed. Typically, when the City Council desires to have some infractions of municipal laws expunged, including directives from their excellencies the governors, the aggrieved party registers an appeal before the High Court and is already sure of a favorable decision when the appeal is made. Thus, ordinances and repeated directives become invalid before the City Council, or rather the deluded president, as perverse individuals raise their hands to strike when the president obstructs their aspirations. Now this hardship which the City Council suffers from in its deliberations in economic governance is worthy of much reflection, especially in a chamber which represents a citizenry so worthy of consideration as that of Bahia. Because of these and similar disorders it turns out that there is no people as poorly governed in regard to the economy and the police. I do not recall having been in a land such as this where there is not one span of unused land on the city's outskirts for a public square or park for the people, to the extent that there is not even a place to get rid of garbage, and the excuse will not wash that everything is taken and walled in.

The third cause then are the frequent directives from their excellencies the governors who, suspicious perhaps of the sinister intentions of some of the diverse members who make up the City Council each year, have arrogated to themselves the majority of its prerogatives, placing the Council in such a state that it is unable to deliberate anything worthy of consideration without being supplied with a directive.

~ Everyone engaged in commerce knows that the public square in Bahia is one of the most active in the Portuguese colonies and that its commerce, quite in spite of the involvement of foreign nations, causes privation only to the vassals of the Portuguese Crown, for the latter are not allowed to maintain trade or export goods except to Portugal and some of her colonies or domains, such as the whole coast and interior of Brazil, the Azores Islands, the Cape Verde Islands, the Kingdom of Angola, Benguela, Mozambique, the Islands of São Tomé and Príncipe, as well as the gulf ports and the coast of Guinea. The corps of merchants existing in Bahia is made up of 164 men (there may be a few more than I have stated) and some of these are merchants in name only, with an abundance of personages about whom we are ashamed to acknowledge that they engage in business. However, each one avails himself of whatever he has; would that these were the least of their faults. Not all those who make up that number are registered but they are called agents. However, since all of them transact business, pay duties, and transport valuables, let us grant them the consolation of calling them merchants, whatever their nature may be. There is no doubt that these illegitimate souls must have had their apprenticeship in business because of the torture to which they often subject the legitimate merchants, causing such disorder in the purchase of valuable products that they ought not to be purchased if it is just to make up the necessary shipments. Otherwise unavoidable damage occurs, and who does not recognize that, all told, this is prejudicial? Perhaps this is the reason that of the three public squares in Rio de Janeiro, Pernambuco, and Bahia, the latter has the reputation of being the least policed while thus far being the most opulent.

The export trade from this public square consists of the production from 400 sugar mills and plantations, that is, 260 in the *recôncavo* of Bahia and 140 in the district of Sergipe del Rei, as well as other products from exports and imports handled in this market and directed to the two markets in Lisbon and Oporto. Trade from ports on this continent consists of jerked meat and corned beef from Rio Grande de S. Pedro do Sul, ample wheat flour, many green hides, and some cheeses, much tallow in loaves and candles, besides a great quantity of corn. For all this they receive much salt purchased here through the contract administrator. Many provisions come from Europe, including some sugar and confectioneries, as well as poorly behaved slaves whom their masters have sold off there; most of the aforementioned products, however, are purchased on a cash basis.

Commerce today between this public square and Minas Gerais has diminished considerably, ever since the average Mineiro began to travel regularly to Rio de Janeiro, a distance of eighty leagues from their capital, while Bahia lay some three hundred leagues distant. Trade from Bahia consists of plentiful slaves which Rio cannot supply with requisite abundance; white cloth and some which is colored, weapons and hardware, powder, and lead; some liquid food products; hats, and a few other baubles and knickknacks. Most of the Bahia trade, however, is with Minas

Novas and Jacobina. From this last district large cattle drives come to Bahia, but by the time they get to the city, for the most part they are already in the hands of the detestable middlemen. A great deal of cotton also comes in and a little gold; very little of this metal comes in from Minas Gerais, however, and most of it surreptitiously, as well as a few mules which are ordered. Most of the gold from Minas Gerais comes in the same way as well as stones, whether topazes, drops-of-water [hyalites], aquamarines, amethysts, etc.

Trade with the Azores Islands and Madeira consists of the importation of wines, rum, English china made from stone powder, some cloth made from cured linen and some from uncured, sewing thread, and a little pork. In regard to exports, I am of the opinion that it does not go beyond a little sugar and sugar cane rum. I am persuaded that this trade, because it is quite infrequent, is very weak. The export trade from Bahia to Angola consists of bundles of sugar, kegs of rum, some tobacco in rolls and powder, much hardware of all kinds, coarse cloth fit for blacks, and much *simbro*, which is a small conch which collects in this area along the seashore, as well as some other articles which I do not recall. Imports consist of slaves which are transported from Angola and Benguela to work in the sugar mills, in the fields, and in other workshops in Brazil as well as a great deal of wax, half-cured and unfinished.

From here they export to the different ports of the Guinea coast, Príncipe Islands, and São Tomé much of the tobacco which is discarded after shipments to Lisbon and India under His Majesty's auspices, although it is reduced to much smaller rolls. They also send out much rum, and conch, which serves as coin among the Negroes; and in exchange for these goods come boats loaded with slaves as well as a few pounds of gold dust. There is less contraband today than what used to arrive abundantly on our vessels; and this from the trading posts that the English, French, Dutch, and Danes used to maintain in the above-mentioned ports. Many of our people were obliged by force to take these goods; most of these same individuals, however, bought them willingly and introduced them into this city with immoderate profits for those who ran the risk of stealing His Majesty's import duties. Much cotton cloth, commonly called *panos-da-costa* [cloth from the coast], also comes in, and because it is a product manufactured by the Negroes, it enters duty-free.

⁓ In this city there is not just one market square but also a few places called *quitandas* [free markets], where the Negro women gather to sell everything they bring, whether it be fish, half-baked meat which they call *moqueada*, pork fat, whale meat during the fishing season, vegetables, etc. There are three of these *quitandas* throughout the whole city, the first one being in the Beach. The second was in unseemly fashion located in the plaza or Terreiro de Jesus, but is located today on a street called Nova, where there are few houses and where the City Council built some small houses to rent to the women who run the *quitandas*. These, unfortunately, are so small that no one wanted to rent them. The third *quitanda* is at Portas de S. Bento, where the City Council had some other huts built which, because they are more roomy, are hardly ever available for rent. After the fortress at Portas de S. Bento was judged worthless, because it is set so far into the city, His Majesty granted a benefice to the City Council in order that a market square might be established in that plaza; the truth, however, is that up to the present the city still does not have the market.

Since the public square at Portas de S. Bento has not been employed for any particular purpose, there could have been set up at that location a fish square, which Bahia still lacks, although because of the heat, fish could not be kept there very long. The most appropriate place for a fish market would be on the beach itself, where fishermen might be obliged to display their fish for sale to the public for one or two hours after they come ashore, the heat not allowing any greater delay. By the same token, anyone found selling fish in any other place should be punished. This should certainly apply to the Negro fishwives, called *ganhadeiras* [street peddlers], if they buy fish in some other place without showing the necessary customs clearance. If the proper practice were followed, there would be no illegal fish eaten in this city after being weighed and purchased because the sea in this area is abundant in fish. However, the fish inevitably goes through four or five hands before it gets to those who finally buy it to eat it. Everyone knows of this disorder but no one changes it because it is a somewhat exclusive business belonging to the *ganhadeiras*, who ordinarily are or were slaves in wealthy or so-called noble houses, where no one wishes to meddle. If one did, it would most certainly go badly for him because of the interest which these ladies normally have in that trade. The *ganhadeiras* sell the fish to other black women to be sold again, and this transaction they call *carambola* [swindle]. Fish remains expensive because en route, before it arrives in port, it is snatched away from the fishermen by several minor officials who, using the pretext that it is for their superiors, take it for the price they want and hand it over to the above-mentioned *ganhadeiras* or other black women with whom they have a business arrangement.

Of equal or greater dimension has been the disorder caused by these same individuals, brazen and protected as they are, with respect to meat. Not content with a meat tax of six hundred *réis* per *arrôba* [equal to about fifteen kilograms], a price which was in force until the year 1793 or 1794, the monopolists worked until a tax of eight hundred *réis* per *arrôba* was put into effect. Since they were still not satisfied with this price, however, they decked out an anonymous orator, one who naturally had his own interests at heart, who presented a formal and eloquent petition. With that oration, longer than the annals of Aragon, they take to the field, attract supporters, and obtain four hundred or so signatures of men of good reputation, thereby remaining free from any restriction on the price of meat. In the weeks preceding the price rise, only sixty, fifty, or thirty head of cattle would come in and in some of those herds not one steer.

However, in the following week the suppliers went to Jacobina, which is 100 leagues from Bahia, and to Piauí, which is 250 leagues away, besides other interior areas, and that same week they came into the city with some 400 head. In short order they earned, if it can be called earning, substantial capital on the cattle they brought in surreptitiously, to the detriment of the City Council's income, the thirds belonging to His Majesty, and the Literary Subsidy; today, however, they earn less, and sometimes they even lose money. This is because, in the first place, as soon as the news about the freeing up of the price of meat arrives in the interior, very few, if any, cattle breeders come down with their cattle because they put any price on them they wish at the gates of their ranches. In the second place, the poor who do not have the means to buy expensive meat do without, or they buy it in the afternoon when it *breaks*, which is what they call it when the price comes down. This happens when the meat is half rotten and good for nothing except to give to the dogs or throw into the sea.

These and similar disorders come as a result of the profiteering monopolists, and since the soldiers, too, are sure to enter into this brotherhood, I will report to you some of the functions of their group, reminding you that in order to become familiar with the giant you have only to see his finger, and similarly, by a claw you may judge the size of a lion. Much to be noted and even more to fear is the ascendancy which the soldiers have arrogated to themselves over the people, committing abuses well worthy of being suppressed. One of the most egregious of these is seizing control of the public meat markets on the occasions when there is a shortage of meat, by violently entering the butcher shops, removing the quarters of beef by force, wrenching it out of the hands of slaves, and especially from the ministers, using the pretext that the ministers are no more privileged than the soldiers. Often the president of the City Council has had to go personally to the scene of the disorders which the soldiers create, and has been treated by some of them with less than decorum and respect. There have been times when they have broken down the doors of the butcher shops which he has ordered closed to avoid those very disorders. Their audacity and insubordination have gone so far, that in order for their own general to have meat on Holy Saturday in 1797, it was necessary to have a steer butchered within the patio of the palace itself. These procedures would be less scandalous if the soldiers took only the meat they needed but they take additional portions and hand them over to the black women with whom they have their dealings. These women, known as *cacheteiras*, prepare the meat on a *moquém* [a type of grill], and sell it bit by bit, robbing the miserable poor who have no other way to obtain it.

Groups of black women go out with small boxes full of cloth, most of it either contraband, pilfered, or purchased from foreign vessels which dock here. Such vessels leave loaded with money; others come from trading posts along the coasts of Guinea and Mina, thus avoiding the customs duties which go to His Majesty and eluding the appropriate laws which forbid such behavior, aided by the venality of the guards, not only civilians but also soldiers, some of whom consider themselves blessed when one of these assignments falls to them. Of course, there are, nevertheless, many guards who are extremely honest. The same black women bring other types of cloth which receive customs clearance; and no one disturbs them nor demands an accounting from them out of respect for the powerful houses to which they belong, the latter a safe-conduct which frees them from all danger; and sad the fate of anyone who meddles with them. However, black women who do not belong to first-rate houses draw a license from the City Council in order to sell, free from the snares of the vigilant tax collector.

Given the way this tax collector carries out the duties of his employment, one may also judge the political and economic regime of this city. When he makes an entry in his books, he has already computed the number of small stores and taverns there are thoughout the city and the outskirts. Then he calculates the adjustment to be made for each one so that from those adjustments the collected revenue will be assured and his own earnings not small. With this calculation done beforehand, he projects, concludes, and draws up the terms with the usual clauses and with reputable guarantors. When this is done he goes out and concludes the aforementioned adjustments with the small grocers and tavern keepers, agreeing not to heckle them the rest of that year if they give him so much, usually 12,000 *réis* or more. When this adjustment takes place then this huckster is able to steal in safety, a term of the adjustment being that he will be warned right away whenever there is to be a general *correição* [on-the-spot investigation by an official].

WHO CANNOT SEE that inactivity on the part of the whites is the cause of the blacks' laziness? Why can't those in Portugal who lived only from their hoes learn how to dig in Brazil? Why should those who only knew how to obey want only to command? How much would these blessed lands produce if they were cultivated by other hands, and not those of savage Negroes who for the most part only scratch the surface? What utility would be garnered if they were cultivated by perceptive men, men of talent!

If only such views on economic policy were to occasion a change in the system which might be embraced and followed! No land would be more prized for its opulence and abundance than Bahia if there had been a productive and politic government here; and if slaves had never come into the land, these being the cause of its backwardness and poverty.

6

Bogotá in the Nineteenth Century

Miguel Samper

Translated by Sharon Kellum

Miguel Samper's Miseria en Bogotá *(1867) is at once descriptive and prescriptive. Against the backdrop of Colombia's colonial and contemporary strife-torn past, the author paints an urban canvas of Dantesque proportions. The streets are no longer safe or clean: "Swindlers, idlers, lepers, drunks, pickpockets, and madmen infest the plazas." The city has become a vast arena in which the cunning and prodigal gratify their inflated appetites. In the face of acute political unrest, confidence has disappeared and credit all but dried up, to the detriment of capitalist and worker alike. This panoply of internal parasitism—the city's inability to employ and provide for its own population—is linked to the larger problem of external parasitism and economic dependency.*

Arguing persuasively that Bogotá's condition and destiny are inseparable from that of Colombia as a whole, Samper makes the social condition of Bogotá his departure point for a more comprehensive view of Colombia's post-(or neo-)colonial predicament. By inserting the city into the larger framework of national politics and economy, the capital's octopus-like hold on the nation is exposed and analyzed. Samper traces Bogotano domination back into the viceregal past when, in the pursuit of metropolitan ends, imperial policymakers established the city as an artificial power base of monopoly and bureaucratic privilege. Independence, according to the author, merely transferred the locus of sovereignty to Bogotá; if anything, the magnetic "force of attraction" which the capital exerted on the rest of the country became "more intense."

Samper's eschatological vision of the city—his image of the future Bogotá—stands in bold contrast to his pessimistic description of present reality. He did not consider it farfetched to conjure up the image of a harmonious, productive society centered around a capital which, once a parasite, might serve as a powerful engine for national development. Like

From *"La Miseria en Bogotá" y otros escritos* (Bogotá: Universidad Nacional de Colombia, 1969), 7–102, 135–93 passim.

Capelo, Santos Vilhena, and García—fellow children of the Enlighten-
ment—Samper was not above moralizing, and, like these writers, he pro-
vides a prescription for his city's future development. Moreover, in
Samper's case, the prescription is painstakingly detailed and explicit—a
proper blueprint dictated by the author's lifelong commitment to Euro-
pean, predominately British, liberal utilitarian principles.

An avid reader of Thomas Macaulay and the other leading propo-
nents of classical liberalism, Samper early acquired the free-trade men-
tality that was to characterize his political and economic writings.
Educated as a lawyer, Samper was encouraged to develop his liberal
philosophy by his teacher, Ezequiel Rojas, a renowned utilitarian. Signi-
ficantly, Samper's subsequent career as a merchant, publicist, and states-
man was the very model of the bourgeois ideal, testifying to the consistency
of his beliefs and even winning him the respect of his political opponents.
Indeed, one distinguished Conservative contemporary dubbed him a Co-
lombian William Gladstone. Shortly before Samper's death in 1898, the
Liberal Party, which had long frowned upon his political moderation,
belatedly expressed its admiration by nominating him as its presidential
candidate.

There is much in Samper's analysis of Bogotá that suggests the
nineteenth-century British liberal tradition. For example, to illustrate the
Bogotá of the future, the author invokes images of Birmingham and
Glasgow at comparable stages of development, complete with clanging
anvils and "a thousand factory furnaces burning night and day." Simi-
larly, Samper's insistence on comercio libre, *thrift, tolerance, and the*
guiding role of an industrial bourgeoisie—all of which find expression in
his formula for alleviating parasitism—accords with the main tenets of
the Victorian industrial age. Indeed, Samper's "modernizing" discourse
remains current in our own era of economic integration and "free trade."

Samper's radiografía (X ray) *of Bogotá, however, is rooted in a deeper*
cultural tradition. The attentive reader will encounter a peculiarly Latin
approach to the city, a Hispano-Catholic orientation that the author's
liberal ideology cannot successfully mask. Samper had a holistic vision
of Bogotá, an integral perception of society in its historical, physical,
sociological, political, economic, and moral dimensions. Accompanying
this total view was an organic ideal for urban and national society. It was
not enough merely to seek the "political kingdom" by putting an end to
the debilitating civil wars that were ravaging Bogotá and creating condi-
tions upon which parasites preyed. It was not enough to dismantle tariff
barriers and abolish commercial monopolies. Nor was it enough to in-
culcate habits of savings and hard work while discouraging gambling,
begging, and drunkenness. Saving Bogotá would take all these reforms
and something more. For Samper, it was a question of morality in the
larger sense, or what he called a matter of "regeneración." *In the Bogotá*
(and by extension, the Colombia) of the future, capitalist and artisan would
work together as productive members of a larger enterprise or whole.

Samper believed that once the broader moral question had been solved, Bogotá's natural advantages—climatic, demographic, and mineral—would assert themselves and propel the city and the other more backward regions of the nation forward.

Rarely does a prophet get the chance to comment on and revise his original vision. In 1896, almost three decades after the appearance of Miseria en Bogotá, *Samper published a brief "Retrospecto" in which he brought his study up to date. The* "cuadro de miseria" *had been alleviated to a great extent: the streets were cleaner and lepers were now being cared for by the Society of St. Vincent de Paul. Material improvements could be seen everywhere—telegraph, railroad, and postal services had been extended, public lighting improved, and modern aqueducts and plumbing introduced. Nascent industry (such as iron, beer, and glass) had made great strides, and some artisan trades had been revived.*

Although the patient had improved over the thirty-year period, Bogotá had not recovered. Far ahead of his time, Samper sounded a warning of impending ecological disaster as necessary timber resources in the city's hinterland were being rapidly depleted. More important, the parasites had not disappeared; they were, in fact, as cunning and dissolute in their habits as ever. And whereas Samper had been able to report in 1896 that civil discord had subsided under the rule of dictator Rafael Núñez (1880–1894), less than three years later Bogotá and Colombia fell headlong into the most disastrous civil war since Independence. In bloodletting that foreshadowed the twentieth-century "Violencia," more than one hundred thousand Colombians lost their lives, commerce was ruined, and production rendered almost negligible. Miseria *continued to reign in Bogotá.* [*]

Diagnosis of the Patient

My purpose here is to present some of the facts characterizing the state of backwardness and decadence of this society so that once the causes are known, the complaints can be heard and the efforts of all can be directed against them. If one examines the condition of the various social classes that make up Bogotá, the portrait that results from this description can only crush the spirit of all who take an interest in their own fate and in the fates of their families, their friends, and their fellow citizens. Of all the capital cities in South America, Bogotá has remained the

[*]Biographical material on Samper may be found in the introductory articles to Miguel Samper, *Escritos políticos-económicos de Miguel Samper,* 4 vols. (Bogotá: Editorial de Cromos, 1925), and in the essay on the Liberal statesman by his Conservative rival, Carlos Martínez Silva, "El gran ciudadano," in *Escritos varios* (Bogotá: Editorial Temis, 1954), 246–55. Jaime Jaramillo Uribe devotes a chapter to Samper's political and economic thought in his *El pensamiento colombiano en el siglo XIX* (Bogotá: Editorial Temis, 1964).

most backward, unable to sustain comparison with Caracas, Lima, Santiago, or Buenos Aires. Let us see how this city presents itself to us.

Beggars fill the streets and plazas, exhibiting not only their abandonment but also an insolence that ought to provide much food for thought, given that they demand alms, and anyone who refuses them is left exposed to insults that no one thinks of trying to stop. Begging in a fertile country with a benign climate, where industry is only beginning to exploit the resources offered by nature, is an alarming fact in more than one respect. But not all the beggars show themselves on the streets. The majority of the city's poor, whom we know by the name of *los vergonzantes* (the shamefaced), hide their poverty, burying themselves with their children in dilapidated dwellings, where they suffer the horrors of hunger and nakedness. If it were possible to take a census of all the persons in Bogotá to whom the name of *vergonzante* is applicable, the total would be terrifying and the danger would be perceived as more imminent.

Parasitism is so developed here that deciding whether to answer a greeting is today a matter to ponder carefully. And paying one of those Castilian compliments, such as "I am at your service," or "Command me," constitutes a real threat to one's pocketbook. Little by little, those smiling and open countenances characteristic of our climate, our race, and our traditional and daily habits are disappearing because each smile is a stimulus and each stimulus brings a bloodletting. The streets and plazas of the city are infested with pickpockets, drunks, lepers, loafers, and even crazy people. Nightfall places everything sacred at the exclusive disposition of crime or vice. Incredible scenes take place only a few steps from the door of the cathedral. The means employed to satisfy brutish appetites is no longer seduction but assault. The family home offers no protection—neither for its walls, glass doors, and windows nor for the family's rest and sleep.

The material decay goes hand in hand with the moral decay. The state of the streets, with their piles of filth, is suitable only for guaranteeing unsanitary conditions. The water service or supply is such that the houses that should get water will quickly depreciate after being burdened with a tax favoring the bricklayers and plumbers. Street lighting, except on a few commercial streets, comes to us from the moon. In sum, the municipal administration of Bogotá is little short of worthless, owing in large part to the fact that the city too has been robbed of its substantial assets. And although some of them have been ordered returned, we do not know if the municipality has begun to receive the revenue. What more can be added after finding out that the evening sessions of the state legislative assembly run the risk of being held in the dark?

If from these facts that make us ashamed and require courage to make public we go on to consider the condition of the working classes, the picture will be no less somber. The laborer does not find steady work, nor does the shop manager receive payment for his efforts. The landlord collects neither leases nor rents; the shopkeeper neither sells nor buys nor pays nor is paid. The importer sees his goods slumbering in the warehouse and his wallet full of promissory notes. The capitalist receives no interest, the employee no salary. The carts and mules wander around empty; the buildings remain unfinished; the farmers sell their potatoes, wheat, honey, and other products at awful prices; cattle and horses are hard to find yet cheap. There is no currency, or at least the legitimate kind is scarce. Credit has disappeared because there is no trust, and the small amounts of capital that manage to circulate are hoarded. Public creditors are viewed as speculators and are not paid. There is no confidence in the administration of justice, and at the mere threat of a lawsuit, the owner is ready to pay the ransom. Finally, the sense of insecurity has reached such a point that it is considered a hostile act to call someone rich. The disease is moral, social, and political. The ability of the doctor would have to equal the magnitude of the ailments that overwhelm this debilitated society.

In drawing together my reflections on Bogotá, I cannot fail to note how, from the beginning, Bogotá assumed the character of a consumer city on a grand scale and a producer city on a limited scale. Leaving aside the habits developed in the residents by the domination of one race over another, it is enough for my purpose to observe that since its founding the city has been the seat of a rigorously centralized government. A large part of the civil and ecclesiastical contributions collected throughout the country were being consumed in Bogotá. These funds were intended either to sustain the governing retinue of both kinds of authorities or to construct public works that were very useful from many perspectives but were not productive for the country in general.

Bogotá was the capital of a Spanish viceroyalty. This single circumstance provides some basic data for my purpose. We appreciate the benefits deriving from the Christian civilization imported by the Spanish conquistadores, but the religious war, the oppressive spirit (which was exacerbated among the Spaniards by the secular battle against the Moors), and the Spanish monarchs' and monks' hatred of the heretical Reformation and all reform combined to set the tone of the national character. And this combination of vices and violent ideas, mixed together with some virtues more heroic than practical, was the legacy that the Spaniards brought to America.

Thus were established the principles underlying the colonization of what is now Colombia: in the areas of industry and commerce, monopoly, privilege, and exclusive profit for the mother country; in politics, absolute centralization and the predominance of the conquering race; in science and arts, ignorance; in philosophy, abasement of the spirit; and in religion, intolerance and fanaticism. Development of physical facilities was attended to with the excessive amount of work imposed on the indigenous peoples and the unfortunate Africans. Development of moral faculties was addressed by dividing the human flock into herds, the seed of all vices for the masters and the slaves as well as the main cause of the perversion of ideas and feelings that now afflicts us. Development of intellectual faculties was dealt with by repressing or prohibiting all teaching that might tend to dissipate ignorance and prejudices or spread accurate ideas about the arts and sciences. Finally, the development of industrial faculties was addressed by total isolation from the civilized world, commercial privileges favoring certain ports of the metropolis, monopoly in certain industries and the prohibition of others, tribute and taxation in their most oppressive forms, and the maximum exploitation of the soil and the people of America for the exclusive advantage of Spain. Having such elements defining its formative years, Bogotá came to be a city that was essentially parasitic due to its origin as the seat of those classes that were dominant, exploitative, or nonproductively consuming. The policies of the viceroy, the royal tribunal, and the whole apparatus governing a vast colony extended throughout the territory and encompassed all interests and all relations, making the capital a center of power and the residence of a swarming retinue of civil and military employees, applicants, dismissed public employees, pensioners, lawyers, clients, and adventurers of every kind.

If political centralization was itself a focus of attraction, the commercial centralization resulting from it did not take a back seat. Given the regime's absorbing nature, Bogotá, as the center of consumption of goods, was bound to attract and monopolize trade. The merchants of Seville (the only ones who could send expeditions to these areas during certain periods and in quantities taxed in advance) used to send to Cartagena and afterward to Santafé [de Bogotá] the cargoes that the colonial metropolis distributed throughout the territory. The fate of our agriculture remained subject to the interest of the metropolis in promoting it from points best situated for transporting weighty products, which at the same time gave the government the advantage of dispensing with the opening of roads in South America. Taxes and monopoly undertook to kill those products whose appearance worked against isolation.

The religious ideas of those times, reinforced by the not very tranquil consciences of those who lived off the spoils and oppression of indigenous peoples and blacks, ended up invigorating these causes of industrial backwardness by giving birth to an infinity of foundations established for the purpose of getting to heaven, which tied up real estate and contributed to paralyzing the development of industry. Convents, ecclesiastical foundations, and trusts of all kinds multiplied rapidly and brought more nonproductive inhabitants to Bogotá. The convents were also inexhaustible sources of subsistence for many poor people; and just as nothing attracts flies like honey, handouts distributed without judgment nurse mendacity. It is gratifying to see the spirit of charity that reigns among us, but we cannot condone as conducive to good habits the giving of alms to all those who disguise themselves as unable to work.

The elements that worked together to form the city of Bogotá as the capital of the viceroyalty (which it remained until the era of Independence) arose from having implanted in the city an artificial center of power and political, religious, commercial, and industrial influence within whose organization parasitism, more or less disguised, played a considerable role.

Independence transferred the seat of sovereign power to Bogotá; and the presence of high officials inevitably exercised a force of even more intense attraction. The form given to the republic from 1821 until 1850, when decentralization began to prevail over centralism, as well as the increasing complexity of the governmental apparatus created by this decentralizing trend, worked to expand the number of jobs in Bogotá.* The city also grew because of the army's great expansion during the war, with numerous personnel on active duty adding to military pensioners. In addition, the contracting or acknowledgement of domestic and foreign debts, payment of taxes, contracts that gave rise to public service, and other such activities made the general treasury a powerful magnet and endowed Bogotá with a new class of public creditors.

Note how insubstantial and unproductive were the results of the political change brought to Bogotá by Independence. An excess of

---

*Samper is referring indirectly to the ascendance of the Liberal Party during the first half-century of independence. Taking their cues from Francisco de Paula Santander, the Liberals tended to favor a decentralized state. The Conservatives, in contrast, regarded themselves as the spiritual heirs of liberator Simón Bolívar and favored a strong state. The Conservative trend became increasingly popular during the final decades of the nineteenth century, under the leadership of Rafael Núñez.

employees, pensioners, soldiers, clerics, and lawyers combined with exchange of the city's capital for certificates of public debt were the two factors that made Bogotá a city that produces only salaries, pensions, revenues, fiscal profits, and fees. What remains is to describe the influence exercised by the passions and political parties on the varied and contradictory facts I have been presenting in order to arrive at proof that the great common result of these political parties is insecurity, the source of all the evils that appear today concentrated in poverty.

Today the political parties have become disoriented and are beginning to break down. Insecurity has become our political atmosphere. It envelops us and penetrates us and has become one of the elements of the climate, the molder of our habits, customs, and institutions. And insecurity will lead us into a social situation more monstrous than that of the Berber states, where barbarism does not even coexist with the traditions of Christian civilization. Insecurity is worse for wealth than swamps are for health, and it is more severe in its consequences than sterility of the soil. Industry, aided by security, has tamed the wrath of the sea. Today, industry is converting the desert sands in Algeria into arable fields and has exhumed in Suez the remains of a civilization buried by insecurity for many centuries.

Capitalists and workers prosper and suffer together, and it would be pushing them toward suicide to revive rivalry and envy among them. So too parasites should respect the property owners and the workers not merely out of moral obligation but also out of self-interest. The parasitic classes, compelled by the vote, would have to give up their places in society to the working classes, who would begin the rebirth of the political parties by electing to public office candidates who are above all honorable. When public opinion solidifies and functions, its force is irresistible, and thus it rarely has to resort to violence. Peace must be created to reestablish security. Under its aegis, poverty will disappear with the thrust of the united and harmonious forces of intelligence, capital, and labor.

If the reader will allow it, I will conclude in the style of a proclamation:

Workers: Defend yourselves from the parasites; punish fraud and bad political habits; do not support filthy journalism with your subscriptions; regenerate the political parties with your direct action and make them purify their doctrines; go to the ballot boxes; clean up all the assemblies, judgeships, and public offices of every kind; unite around the law and defend it.

Parasites: Respect the workers, not only out of moral obligation but also out of self-interest; remember the hen who laid the golden eggs.

Colombians: Anarchy is invading us, letting loose in the towns unleashed passions that are more destructive than the lava from our volcanoes; save us.

Citizens, citizens, defend your cause.

Liberalism's Prescription

The law is not called on to intervene in production or to make changes but for the sole purpose of assuring producers of the fruits of their labor and verifying the transfer of wealth from one set of hands to another by means of contracts and legal transactions.

In a new country that marches steadily from backwardness toward progress, the work that is most stimulating and enriches most quickly is manual labor, provided that it is accompanied by frugality, thrift, savings, and all the habits that favor the creation of capital and homes where legitimate ties unite the spouses and children. The habits that never lead to these results are unreliability in work, insubordination, quarreling, frequenting gambling dens and taverns, sensual passions, and disputes over politics. A workplace flourishes when the boss has not caused a lack of trust or antipathy in the customers by disturbing behavior; when he dedicates himself to the work with zeal; when he uses his savings to improve his equipment and to select and acquire new materials of good quality; when his conduct inspires confidence and facilitates his credit for stocking raw materials at good prices or providing the means to pay the workers while the job is being completed; and when, in the end, everyone —bosses and workers alike—lives convinced that peace is the first requirement for both the poor and the rich and that harmony should reign among them, a peace that only parasites can disturb.

When the rich feel threatened by the hatred and envy of the poor, they limit their consumption and hide or export their capital. Both results are fatal to industry and hurt the poor especially. Consumption by the wealthy is what nourishes employment of the poor because the wealthy are the ones who use more stockings, clothing, and saddles. Thus, if fear should inspire in them the desire to emigrate, the shops would close at the same time as the factories. Yet capital cannot create anything unless labor makes it productive. Without capital, goods like calfskins and pigskins, fine cloth, suspenders, and all the rest could not come to Bogotá, nor could capital create any business without the workers, who convert these items into salable goods.

Products made in Europe are manufactured by large factories that use all kinds of machinery, buy large quantities of raw materials, and realize endless savings due to the size of the business establishments and the variety of their stock. The result is the greatest economy possible in all operations and expenditures. In Bogotá, work is carried out in small shops with materials that are mostly foreign. These materials are inferior in quality, and thus the end product cannot turn out to be durable. They are bought in small quantities and at high prices because no shop can import them on its own account. Machines are not employed, notwithstanding the relatively low cost of machines for sewing cloth and leather. Moreover, the work in general is executed neither very promptly nor very well.

Many of these inconveniences would be smoothed out by peace and, above all, by reestablishing trust between workers and capitalists because despite everything, some large factories—if endowed with enough capital to obtain raw materials and to be equipped with machines and good tools—would prosper. Wages must be lower in Bogotá than in any European city because here workers do not have the needs and expenses imposed by the change of seasons. They can count on twelve hours of free daylight year round, with the climate permitting the same capacity for work every day, and the distances between homes and workplaces are insignificant.

If one adds to these considerations others of a broader and more lasting nature, it will be easily understood that the future of Bogotá basically must be in manufacturing and that perhaps the nineteenth century will not end without active productivity replacing the current apathy. A great population center that does not know how to employ its workers and an accumulation of considerable capital lacking fixed investment are two elements that naturally invite manufacturing industry. These elements, assisted by the natural talent apparent among us and the climatic advantages just mentioned, could achieve a formidable productivity. Moreover, the raw materials are at hand as a result of the diversity of climates created by the latitude and the height of the mountains combined with the mineral wealth of the soil, especially iron and coal, which are to industry what meat and bread are to nourishment.

Often, I let my imagination travel forward in time through these regions in the twentieth century, when they all may be dedicated by the hand and genius of mankind to fostering industry, that magic wand given to the viceroy of creation instead of a scepter. But what advantage could my readers reap from daydreams? Let us return, then, to the current year of our Lord, 1867.

If one wanted to proceed methodically in industry here, the first thing should be to produce cheap and good-quality iron and to turn over to teaching and travel, as their major goal, the acquiring of technical and practical knowledge in the natural sciences, mechanics, arts, and the agricultural and manufacturing industries. Young Colombians who can educate themselves abroad would do much more for themselves, their families, and their country by looking to the United States as the best school for acquiring professions of certain advantage. There they could stay at U.S. farms and factories until they acquired the technical knowledge, methods, and procedures for cultivation and manufacturing. They could also learn those American habits and that genius for business that foster self-confidence at all times and places and inspire the "go-ahead" with which mountains are overcome, chasms are skirted, and the progress is made that astonishes and intimidates the Old World.

With cheap iron and some men who have the means of setting up shops and factories as well as the necessary know-how to direct workers and even teach them as needed, Bogotá would become within a few years the theater of powerful manufacturing activity. Cables, nails, hoes, axes, machetes, plows, hinges, screws, locks, bits, shovels, scythes, spurs, fetters, and many other items produced in Bogotá would be 300 percent cheaper than those brought in from Europe. Next would come rudimentary machines, like those for threshing and winnowing, which would be used to harness the soil's productive forces and the mine's riches, then tools and more refined objects, and finally, steam engines. Copper, lead, and their alloys when combined with other metals would give rise to new industries. And who knows whether the proximity of textile materials, aided by the opening and improvement of roads, might not allow us to arrive at the road to freedom that protection would otherwise prevent us from reaching.

Imagine the magnitude that iron production can achieve by focusing on just two items: pipelines and rails. The municipality of Bogotá does not allow cart traffic along the city streets for fear of breaking the baked clay water pipes in the conduits. Consequently, Bogotá is perhaps the only city in the world with a population of sixty thousand where one never sees or hears the wheel, that throne of industry. Modern cities possess huge networks of pipes underground to carry water and gas to all public places and private dwellings. They are like a forest that displays above the surface the branches and leaves of the trees whose trunks are sustained by millions of underground veins in which water and electricity circulate, like sap. Rails and telegraph wires snatch the wings of time and fix them in the ground in order to advance life via the rapidity of motion, and when they begin to spread out over our plains and to penetrate the folds of the mountain ranges, a thousand ovens glowing day and night will testify, as they do on the outskirts of Birmingham, Liège, and Glasgow, that the iron industry can never rest.

I will conclude by reminding the artisans of an old Spanish proverb: "Padre pulpero, hijo caballero y nieto pordiosero" (Storekeeper father, gentleman son, beggar grandson). What I mean to say is that the class called the bourgeoisie in France, which among us translates into "the middle class," the one that enjoys the comforts of life without the boredom of idleness, has no barriers protecting it from being invaded by poverty other than foresight, thrift, saving, and frugality, which when combined with work yield capital. I say, look at that privileged class in which you believe the rich live and you will find that the gentleman, the scholar, and the capitalist were all born of the humble shopkeeper or the honest laborer who saved for his children. Now look among the beggars at those children who sell little boxes of matches on the streets, and you will find many offspring of the families who at one time were called noble and great, families led into ruin by gambling and idleness. Believe me, public tranquility, harmony among the working classes, and good morals and work habits are the only correctives for poverty and the true sources of progress and freedom.

Retrospective (1896)

Let us consider the debit side of life in Bogotá. We continue to find greed, luxury, dissipation, drinking, and gambling running up mounting debts in our city. Private wealth is displayed in almost all the buildings. Facades like palaces on private dwellings and cramped interiors are the main features of our new style of building. In the new little hovels in the neighborhoods away from the center of town, the stone facades, encrusted with ornamentation, showcase bad taste. And the extraordinary rise in the prices of lots and building materials is causing a reduction in the space allotted for each dwelling. In the main part of the city, the old houses are being rehabilitated, but by dividing them into two or three parts. In many instances, the stairs are slender tubes too narrow for pianos, buffets, or tenants who are too stout, and thus everything has to be hoisted or lowered by pulleys or scaffolds in order to go in or out via the balconies. Such houses really ought to be equipped with their own capstans.

Turning from the buildings to the ornamentation of the drawing rooms, we find that they have become caricatures of museums. The strangest objects are exhibited in them: testacea shells at the foot of console tables, miniature painter's easels, little gilded canes holding up little chairs, with the choicest trifles consisting of wedding gifts and even folding screens. To all these are added venerable old tables, chairs, and other odd furnishings from the colonial era, properly touched up and bought at a good price, thanks to the fashion of the times.

Deserving of special mention in this review of luxury is the ostentation with which weddings are celebrated today. Apart from the increased and even extravagant expenditures that the bride's parents make to receive their guests for a day, the number of invitations multiply the costs extravagantly, turning a simple family party into a happening of great moment in the city. The guests compete among themselves over the value and uselessness of their gifts. Hence the necessity of storehouses stuffed with such objects and the consequent dedication of sizable amounts of capital to their importation and renovation.

Bogotá is also well endowed with new specialty stores. Large jewelry shops, clock shops, and stores for wedding gifts and expensive trinkets adorn the busiest streets. For the children, there are fabrics and dresses, hats and high-priced toys, all of which prepare the new generation for the frugal life that will make them strong adults. And now that we have stumbled onto the subject of frugality, it is necessary to mention here the splendid sites dedicated to gastronomy and the shops and stores that sell the most exquisite products from the famous Morton factory, along with wines and liqueurs of the finest kinds. In such establishments and in the cafés and restaurants, gentlemen of leisure dedicate themselves to treating one another to lunches and dinners. Members of the fair sex, however, are deprived of partaking of those delicacies, which rarely reach the forsaken home.

The use of distilled liquors is taking hold despite the heavy taxes passed on them. Cigarettes are the inevitable companion of that habit. Although the police prevent public displays of drunkenness, it cannot be denied that drinking is the scourge of our society today; the point is proved by the growing number of establishments set up especially to satisfy that vicious habit. Drinking is also the source of many illnesses, which are dealt with by new pharmacies, and thus whenever a new bar opens, it is not long before the concomitant drugstore appears nearby.

Nor has gambling been left behind. Greed stimulates it, and the public lottery (established by a recent law) spreads and promotes gambling with a solicitude worthy of banks and other savings institutions that the legislators do not encourage—perhaps to avoid creating competition with the lottery. Flocks of children run through the streets pestering everyone with tickets for the next drawing, and it becomes clear that the youngsters will serve their first apprenticeship in their careers as gamblers by investing their own savings in what they are selling. In the railway stations, the lottery ticket is the first thing offered to any traveler arriving or departing from Bogotá.

Without having given up its dark dens of vice, gambling now occupies splendid premises as well. In some of the houses of what is today called high society, it is considered chic to follow dinner or tea with a roll of the dice or a round of baccarat. If the unlucky guest delays somewhat in paying the debts contracted, the amiable host turns into the stern master of a gambling house to make good on them.

It should not be surprising that criminality has grown, despite a more efficient police force. The vices and appetites not satisfied, as well as those that unfortunately are, lead to crime and to the madhouse. Suicide was almost unknown among us earlier; today, it too is one of the solutions for ending the struggle for survival.

THE COURSE OF three centuries has not taken from the capital its parasitic character. Many of the taxes and revenues collected by the national and departmental governments from those living in other parts of the country continue to be invested in the capital. Indeed, it can be said that the main industry of Bogotá consists of attending to the spending of the budgets. If the city has made progress, it is because the tribute that comes from other places to be consumed in the city has also increased.

This parasitic progress is being threatened by a decentralizing tendency that seems unstoppable. This fact can be confirmed by observing what has happened to the administration of the various departments in civil and ecclesiastical matters as well as the establishment of new bishoprics separate from the Bogotá see. Industries, commerce, and manufacturing in the capital are not keeping pace with the progress that has been achieved in the new centers of Medellín, Bucaramanga, Cúcuta, Cali, and Pasto.*

Bogotá ought to aspire to a more honorable and fruitful destiny than that of taking advantage of much of the national budget. The relative isolation of the high mesas of Cundinamarca and Boyacá created by mountainous terrain, the rich deposits of salt, rubber, iron, coal, limestone, sulfur, and other raw materials of great value to industry as well as the

*Recent urban research confirms Samper's observation on the rapid development of Colombia's secondary centers and Bogotá's concomitant decline as a "primate city" during the second half of the nineteenth century. According to Richard Morse, Medellín, Cali, and other regional centers generally outgrew Bogotá during this period. See Morse, *Las ciudades latinoamericanas*, vol. 2, *Desarrollo histórico* (Mexico City: Sep Setentas, 1973), 33–35.

concentration of capital and labor in the city all invite Bogotá to become a powerful center of manufacturing. For now, the main industry is the one engendered by politics, which in turn benefits the political parties to the detriment of the solutions urgently required by difficult problems in the economy. The outcome of the current situation is the rising rate of interest, an obvious signal that capital lacks what labor craves. When salaries are sufficient for the well-being of the classes that receive them, the two necessary agents of production demonstrate that there is progress, and capital does not delay entry into the fortunate region that wants it. If on the contrary salaries oblige workers to curtail their food intake or the quality of their diet and to let their clothes fall into tatters, then interest and salaries become social plagues that reveal a basic flaw in the political regime. Insecurity is the name of this defect; poverty was its fruit in 1867, and it remains so on the date on which I finish this retrospective.

7

Lima in the Nineteenth Century*

Joaquín Capelo

Translated by Sharon Kellum

As Peruvians surveyed the national scene in 1895, they could find little cause for optimism. Lima, the City of Kings, had just recovered from the ignominy of being occupied by a victorious Chilean army. Defeat in the War of the Pacific (1879–1883) had not only wounded national pride but also foreclosed Peruvian exploitation of the southern nitrate fields. The guano boom had collapsed, leaving unfinished railroads and an insupportable foreign debt in its wake. Within the continent, Peru seemed to be standing still while other South American countries were capitalizing on newly developed export products. Peruvians watched with envy as Argentine beef and wheat, Brazilian and Colombian coffee, and Chilean nitrates brought prosperity to their respective capital and regional cities. It was amid this climate of national defeat and economic stagnation that Joaquín Capelo wrote his Sociología de Lima, *a blistering denunciation of Limeño social and economic organization.*

As a civil engineer, politician, and writer, Capelo was intimately involved in Peruvian life at the turn of the century. The War of the Pacific found him supervising the construction of fortifications for Lima and Callao in 1880–81. In the war's aftermath, Capelo headed the government's public works section and in 1885 was elected to the constitutional assembly. During the 1890s he engineered the construction of Peru's via central *(main thoroughfare), wrote a book about this experience, and then served as Minister of Development. The new century saw him hold that office a second time, head the Corps of Road Engineers, and serve in the Senate, where he was noted for defending workers and Indians and denouncing militarism.†*

From Sociología de Lima, vols. 1–3 (Lima: Imprenta Masias, 1895–96), vol. 4 (Lima: Imprenta La Industria, 1902); vol. 2, 82–147 passim, and vol. 3, 127–260 passim.

*The editors express their gratitude to Ann Twinam for her assistance in editing this chapter and preparing the introductory note.

†Bibliographical data comes from Neptalí Benvenutto, *Parlamentarios del Perú contemporáneo* (Lima: Imprenta Malatesta, 1921), 52–55; Juan Pedro Paz

Drawing on nineteenth-century European thought, Capelo organized his Sociología *along "organic" lines. He viewed Lima much like a living body with a physical structure requiring nourishment, coordination, and education. This perspective led him to divide the work into four books dealing with the "physical" (physical plant, services), "nutritional" (occupations, income distribution, production), "relational" (public opinion, industry, institutions), and "intellectual" (schooling, publishing, university life) dimensions of the city. Thus, in undertaking his analysis, Capelo assumed the role of physician in pointing out the diseases affecting the urban body.*

The excerpts included here, when taken together, represent Capelo's diagnosis of Lima: the patient was suffering from chronic malnutrition. Capelo assumed that the sustenance of any city derived from the wealth produced by its inhabitants. Unfortunately for Lima, large sectors of the population—servicios menores (minor services), contratistas (contractors), and parásitos (parasites)—consumed the city's resources but did not replenish them. Furthermore, those classes most capable of multiplying Lima's existing wealth—the traditional elites and would-be entrepreneurs—failed to do so. Small shopkeepers and tradesmen were forced to borrow from the entrenched commercial elite at high rates of interest. Many led a precarious existence or went bankrupt, stifling commercial variety and innovation. Moreover, the traditional duties and obligations imposed by the extended-family system further burdened the marginal entrepreneur striving to better his or her lot.

Capelo's talents as diagnostician far exceeded his ability to prescribe for Lima's maladies. In retrospect, his proposals for change were at once confusing and contradictory. He readily acknowledged the industry and creativity of foreigners, for example, but rejected the fashionable conclusion that immigration would solve the problems he had identified. Capelo's work has lasting value, however, in being far more than a detailed portrait of turn-of-the-century life in the Peruvian capital. His dissection of Limeño society revealed the very skeleton—the underlying patterns of society, economy, and culture—common to many if not all cities of the Latin American species. For that reason, the Sociología de Lima *remains a classic in urban literature as well as a Latin American archetype.*[*]

Soldán, *Diccionario biográfico de peruanos contemporáneos* (Lima: Librería Gil, 1921), 82.

[*]Richard M. Morse, "The Lima of Joaquín Capelo: A Latin-American Archetype," *Journal of Contemporary History* 4, no. 3 (July 1969): 95–110. The Spanish edition appears as "Estudio crítico: La Lima de Joaquín Capelo: Un arquetipo latinoamericano," in *Lima en 1900* (Lima: Instituto de Estudios Peruanos, 1973).

The Minor Services

B y the heading of *servicios menores*, we mean all those services, generally manual labor, in which human beings produce wealth merely
by cooperating to preserve already existing wealth rather than by making
a particular object (as the industrial worker or craftsman does), or by
adding to persons or things useful qualities that give them a new value
(as the scholar or artist does), or by bringing together elements capable of
producing benefits by the fact of their union (as the banker, statesman, or
politician does). The minor services, however humble the status of the
job may be, nevertheless have a positive value: one earns a living; the
bum and the criminal steal it. The most humble servant is infinitely superior to the idler, the thief, and the murderer.

The ranks of the minor services are always filled with numerous personnel. The statistics reveal no less than 5 percent of the population in
domestic service alone. In Lima, if one looks at just the servants' guild
and those registered with the agencies, the number would not exceed five
thousand, divided almost equally between men and women. But if one
considers all those who perform minor services as a whole—whether in
their own homes, or by living with families (almost as members), or as
butlers, gatekeepers, and doormen—I believe we come much closer to
the truth in estimating the number of persons who earn their living by
providing services in Lima at thirty thousand.

Within the category of minor services, one can distinguish service
provided by children from that provided by adults. The latter form a permanent population that aspires to no other mode of life, while the children serve temporarily, as long as their parents are able to send them to
school, and afterward they go on to learn a trade or spend their lives as
simple laborers. The sense of independence is very pronounced in Lima
among all the social classes, and inferior status is accepted only out of
dire necessity.

Minor services should also be differentiated according to the nature
of the tasks that each branch entails. At the bottom of the ladder we find
the *muchacho*, the young helper in every small household, even among
the humblest and poorest families. The *muchacho* is the errand boy who
does the shopping in the neighborhood stores, tidies up the house, serves
at the table, and works hard for himself and the family of which he is a
part. He generally does not earn a salary, but the family takes care of all
his needs.

The *muchacho* usually wears hand-me-downs from the household,
eats everything the family eats, and is scarcely made to feel the inferiority of his position. The young boys who grow up in this manner usually

maintain respectful affection for everyone in the household. And when later they leave in search of a job, they never stop coming back to see the family in which they received their first instructions in learning how to live.

On the second rung from the bottom come the servants per se, whose number I have calculated at three thousand men and two thousand women. This population is made up entirely of mixed races, men of color, Orientals, and some Indians from the most backward places. Those found in this class accept inferior status as a permanent status and remain in it, whether by reason of being accustomed to that life, or having a low level of intelligence or a narrow horizon of aspiration, or perhaps at bottom, out of a certain moral laziness about changing a status whose inferiority has not been perceived and whose abandonment would demand efforts that these individuals are not capable of producing.

Poor people do not have servants as such, nor are they abundant in the middle class. The households of the rich always have servants, but their number is not large, generally one or two except in special cases. The hotels, schools, convents, and boardinghouses are the establishments where the greatest numbers of servants are found.

After servants per se come the butlers, doorkeepers, and trusted assistants found in all large houses and even in some middle-class homes, where one person generally fills all three posts. The butler is the middleman between the servant and the housekeeper, and thus the responsibility falls to him to distribute conveniently each day the work that they must do and to watch over its execution, completing it himself as necessary and performing those services that presume a certain appropriate education to carry them out properly. The doorkeeper is valued less for the services he performs than for his honesty and personal formality, his job being mainly to watch over and look after the house.

The *hombre de confianza* (as we call him for lack of a better name) is the one closest to the head of the family. Generally, he is attached to the family by feelings of deep gratitude or receives the broad protection of the house. This trusted assistant does not live in the family home nor does he associate his style of living with the servant class. Usually, he has various and diverse tasks, but the main one is disposing of the confidence of influential persons.

The women who lend their services to the families in their homes fulfill different functions, among which can be distinguished housekeepers, wet nurses, and seamstresses who do the mending. Between the seamstresses and the wet nurses is an intermediate class of trusted nannies who are never lacking in comfortable homes, their main purpose being to accompany and serve the little girls they have raised and for whom they have as much feeling as if they were members of the family. This class is generally is made up of *muchachas de color* who are used to dealing with respectable people.

The class that we are studying is perhaps the one that, after the wealthy class, has the best life, certainly not because of the little it possesses but because in being unaware of how much it lacks, this class makes the most advantageous use of the little it has. In this class of the minor services, marriage is not a burden but just the opposite: a husband and wife earn enough to live so that if they unite to form a family, their expenses diminish, thus preserving their earnings as a whole. Living in the family's home saves money on room and board at least, and their children encumber them for only the first five years, thereafter entering into earning their own living when their personal labor is incorporated into some household or into the same one where their parents live.

On another score, public diversions—bullfights, theater, circus—are cheap for the humble folk. For forty cents, they can enjoy any function, and they need no special clothes to attend it. If they get sick, the hospital takes charge of caring for them without any expense on their part. In case of a death in their household, they will not lack for friends of their same class who will quickly get up a collection to take care of the burial expenses. Thus, all seems favorable to this social group that we have located at the bottom of the ladder.

I am nonetheless very far from lending support to a related opinion on this subject. I do not agree with [Count Leo] Tolstoy, the incomparable philanthropist of modern Russia, that human happiness can be found among this deprived class, in which one can scarcely distinguish a human being from a domestic animal. The class that we have examined is in general very unfortunate. And it falls to the superior classes worthy of the name to make every effort on behalf of the servants to awaken to the moral life (which is to say to the emotional and intellectual life) this group of beings who merely vegetate.

Contractors and Auctioneers

The contractor and the auctioneer are clever types of men, enterprising and business-oriented. For them, everything is money, everything has a price, and everything is possible. The contractor studies the small mishaps of things as to how much advantage they may provide, and he makes a thorough analysis of each official and public employee, which allows him to be up-to-date on whatever has to do with the official as a person and his life circumstances. For the contractor and the auctioneer, there are always two weights and two measures, depending on whether they are dealing with someone who can be useful or with someone of no use; and they easily forget today what yesterday was the object of all their attention.

The contractor and the auctioneer have studied, like no one else, the flexibility and rigidity of the spine. They are attentive, self-satisfied, and big spenders when things are moving along. On the other hand, they are brusque, inattentive, and impolite when they have nothing to hope for. If power is being exercised by a friendly acquaintance, the contractor is always disposed to make concessions to the public promptly because he knows that farther down the road, the contract will be improved to his advantage. But if those who can help him are not in power, the contractor proves to be very zealous of the law, very particular about the fidelity of contracts, and a true idolizer of judicial power, which he considers to be a sure protection against all inequity.

Social Parasites

A world of parasites establishes itself on every organism, and when it is not destroyed, it ends up sooner or later killing off even the healthiest body. In Lima there are two branches in this category, which day by day sap huge amounts of wealth and must be curtailed, at least if one wants to save Lima from the most serious illness that has ever afflicted it. These parasites could end up destroying the life of the city if it does not subject them to strict control and unless the atmosphere breathed by this unhealthy element is not treated in time.

Beggars and *sinvergüenzas* (scoundrels) are the tangible expressions, the objectification or individuation of the mistakes, flaws, and failings of all the inhabitants of Lima. They are our own creations, living testimony to all our faults and the spoiled offspring of all the evil that has earned our applause, all the wickedness that has enjoyed our tolerance, all the injustice that has relied on our complicity. Beggars and scoundrels are, respectively, the victims and the executioners whom society has produced via all the acts carried out in its hidden corners, outside moral law. In a certain sense, beggars and scoundrels represent the sanctioning of social crimes, and they are thus the index of the state of public health. The beggar represents the last stage of personal expiation, subject to all the consequent privations as well as to occasional alms that barely suffice to partially nourish an exhausted and sick body and a soul that has sunk low and must still suffer greatly in seeking to regain the level it lost.

The scoundrel represents the opposite type in terms of the comforts of life. He lives without working and is always happy; incapable of eking out a living, he steals it day after day. And he strolls along unmoved, looking down arrogantly on the imbecile or with insolent scorn at the sons of labor, something he has never experienced. Always hanging around on street corners, in cafés, and in sinful places, the wretch is unaware that he is only a step away from begging or the penitentiary. Without ever worrying about tomorrow, lacking the slightest notion of dignity, duty, or any morality, alien to all religious sentiment and scarcely distinguishable from an animal in his appearance, the scoundrel worries only about having money to spend, let it come from wherever it may. He makes the tailor and the barber the only gods in his cult, certain of finding with their help a "decent outward appearance," because it would not be fitting for a spirit lacking ideals and a heart without virtue to want anything else.

The scoundrel can be found among all social classes. In wealthy families, he spends his time squandering his parents' money and corrupting society with his flatteries and the glitter with which he surrounds himself. In families of middling position, he busies himself with snatching from his mother and sisters whatever they possess whenever they have it, obliging them to suffer the greatest deprivations so that he can treat himself to all kinds of amusements. In poor families, one so often sees the mother and sisters of the scoundrel spending whole nights sewing from dusk until dawn until they become consumptive, and scarcely feeding themselves—all to earn a few coins with their arduous labor in order to be able to meet the expenses run up by the scoundrel's vices.

It is necessary, in sum, that everyone know that if more people die each year in Lima than are born in the city, it is almost entirely because scoundrels devour so much and produce nothing. And because they are so numerous, the income earned by men who do honest work does not go far enough to maintain everyone. The deficit translates into poor nutrition that carries to the grave those who die from hunger in the guise of tuberculosis. These victims ought to have lived and added to the natural growth of the population, but they could not because their persons became fodder for scoundrels—a necessary evil arising from the lack of guidance in the state, the city, the school, and the home.

Industry

With rare exceptions, it can be said that among us industry—commerce, agriculture, and all other forms—revolves mainly around monopoly and usury, with competition and credit playing little part in the game of stimulating industry in the city. Each business owner is concerned above all with being the only one, or at least with reducing the competition as much as possible. And each capitalist is concerned above all with obtaining as interest on his capital "the greatest possible gain," the current rate being 3 and 4 percent or as much as 10 percent per month (with the loan companies).

To achieve their aim, industrialists and capitalists solicit and obtain the intervention of the authorities. Industrialists ask for strong import tariffs to close the door to similar products from abroad, while farmers, manufacturers, and the like worry a lot about this approach. Capitalists ask that civil laws be revised to the point that debtors have no judge before whom to defend themselves. The capitalists' ideal is that the creditor's simple presentation would be sufficient for the debtor to hand over everything he has and all he owns. Here the interest penalties are 3 percent per month (1 or 2 required by law), with the result being that a debt more than doubles in two years and thus the mortgaged security is not enough to cover even the fees. The loan companies, except for "special cases," auction off goods after six months, regardless of the value of the pawned item. The gas and water companies, without any judicial or administrative proceeding whatsoever, proceed to shut off the services for any farm that gets behind in payment or resists arbitrary increases in its rates. The so-called Banco Hipotecario [Mortgage Bank] takes upon itself the auctioning of the farm that falls behind in paying the quarterly interest. Fiscal tax collectors set up guards at the mere presentation of a bill, in case it is not paid promptly. Everything, everything is efficient and quick. He who must, pays or dies. Thus, usury ordains it and thus it is done. Unfortunate is the person in Lima who has no dread of credit. In matters large or small, whoever uses this terrible instrument of exploitation can be sure of complete ruin.

The mistaken policies established in Peru over credit have done more harm than all the revolutions and all the bad governments combined. Those erroneous policies have utterly perverted national customs, weakened the laws, ruined property, wrought public misery, and ultimately created a way of perceiving and thinking that must be fought to the end if we wish to save the individual, the family, and the state from soon succumbing to being devoured by usury. Genuine credit lives off trust and takes an interest in the progress of the debtor, not in his ruin. Usury, on the contrary, flourishes where trust is lacking; and like hyenas who feed on dead bodies, usury lives off poverty and disgrace, which it encourages with its bold plundering.

And while usury wreaks its destructive work, the spirit of monopoly does not lag behind. We are not talking here about a question of producing better articles and offering them at a better price. It is solely a matter of obliging the consumer to buy the goods available, however shoddy they may be, thus guaranteeing the highest price that can be gotten. First, the protectionist system is invoked, asking in its name that import tariffs be set up in such a way that the foreign product suffers an enormous surcharge. This leads to its price being raised much higher than that of the so-called national article, even when the latter is expensive and poor in quality, as happens whenever protection is relied on.

The monopoly industries in Lima constitute a group that is the most powerful and the most difficult to destroy. Among them are the so-called established import houses, financial backers, and lenders and collectors on whom all industrial activity in Peru depends. Those companies—few in number but powerful in influence among all circles, all agents of the press, and all centers of national life—make up a vigorous core that is accustomed to making laws or vetoing them without anyone realizing it. This nucleus thus makes and unmakes what best suits its interests with no other motive than getting its hands on all the national wealth. When these companies find it convenient to make their influence felt, they may call themselves the "Chamber of Commerce." And when it suits them to keep their anonymity, they may assume names like "property, right, justice, civilization, wealth" and others no less appealing in their literal sense. But among those in the know, these words have a technical meaning that is well understood only by them.

Those companies have amassed precise and detailed knowledge of all industrial activity in the republic. Indeed, they could compile a set of statistics that would be hard for the government to match. With commercial precision, they know from top to bottom the costs of production and the profits of all Peruvian industries and sales centers, and whatever else on the subject that might interest them. Endowed with combined capital operating in unison and based in Europe, they trade in Lima with capital one hundred times as effective, obtaining 99 percent of what they lack thanks to their profound knowledge of the country, its practices and customs, and the vices and virtues of its social classes—in sum, of everything that can lead to the success of their peerless industry.

These established firms constitute a great suction pump that pulls toward itself all the national wealth as soon as it is produced. And after setting aside a small portion in order to continue favoring the manufacturers, these companies send the remainder to Europe in the form of very good merchandise, bought here at the maximum discount imaginable and sold there at the best prices and in very legitimate pounds sterling. Using this amazing system, they have managed to take much more money out of Peru than in the Spaniards' time and yet without provoking similar uprisings of Indians, protests, or anything of the kind. This commercial approach has the advantage of being less costly and more peaceful, leading the victim along of his own volition, with that smiling air that always accompanies fools—and every man is one when he forgets that he has a role to play in this world.

Such an individual finds himself in possession of a sum that his parents left him as his inheritance and that he knows how to work, within the limits of the small amount of capital that he possesses. With these funds, this capital, and his own personal aptitudes, such an individual can live comfortably in his own social class and can also capitalize each year a sum large enough to assure an even better future. But our man has no commercial or economic education, and his entire intellectual background on the subject boils down to newspaper articles that fall into his hands occasionally. In such papers, he has read all those paeans that are commonly written about the wonders of credit. And without further reflection, he launches down the dangerous slope, mortgaging, of course, his entire inheritance to obtain borrowed capital in order to set up machinery or expand his crops on a large scale, changing, of course, his readily sold crops for cotton, sugarcane, or something else that may be easy to export. After many steps, letters of introduction, displaying of property titles, and so on, the happy moment arrives at last for our man to be presented to the head of an established firm and to formulate his aspirations specifically. The head of the firm deigns to descend from the heights of his financial position to receive the new slave who solicits such a coveted status. And after arrangements, discussions, and the like, our budding entrepreneur succeeds in signing the contract of his ruin, which he nevertheless believes will be nothing less than his greatest good fortune.

Right away, the financing company advances him funds at a moderate interest rate, in some cases, a mere 6 or 8 percent—in gold, of course—so that the rate of exchange falls wholly on the debtor. He, however, is obliged to return the sum received in dividends payable with the proceeds of the funds, at a fixed price, stipulated in advance, or to hand over these products on consignment to the financing company, in either case fixing a minimum for the amount of the remittances to be paid during the year. To ensure fulfillment of the contract and in order to follow "a simple formula," it is agreed that the debtor will pay fines, interest penalties, et cetera and that he will be charged commissions, differences of exchange, reductions, damages, and other "similar little charges." And with things arranged thus, our poor capitalist rushes off down the tortuous path of the man of great enterprise. The poor devil does not know that very soon he will wind up on the street, as poor as the last of his employees. The fixed price, the assigned accounts, the little charges, and the agreements according to a simple formula create a wondrous mechanism with inexorable consequences. In vain will our man work from six to six and make every kind of effort imaginable. The numbers will be arranged in a thousand combinations in the accounts, and when all is said and done, after long years of arduous labor, he will find himself thrown off the estate and owing millions, without ever being able to account for how or why a matter in which he believed he saw his supreme chance ended so badly.

Unfortunate is the man in Peru who sets himself up to work with borrowed capital. [Moreover,] the monopoly of capital is so powerful here that the government itself has fallen victim to it, and on such a grand scale that all the national wealth in guano and nitrates evaporated in this cauldron, feeding the corruption and vices of an ignominious past that— let us hope—we will never forget.

After the big firms come the monopoly enterprises set up by laws and contracts—like the railroads, the incorporated tax-collecting companies, those providing municipal services, gas, and light, the trusteeships of convents and brotherhoods, and the like—whose steady earnings are based (some more and some less) on levies and countless abuses exercised at all hours on the inhabitants of Lima. These monopoly enterprises have agents everywhere: at given times, they have managed to be the government, the congress, the judicial power, the municipality, and whatever other forms have been best suited to bringing their deals to fruition, whatever the cost.

And if all this were not enough, we see every day that for these enterprises there is no judge or authority whatsoever standing between them and the consumers of their services. The enterprise presents its bill and one is forced to pay without discussion, without delay, cost what it might. The government itself has less power over the pocketbook and the health of the city than the individual who owns any one of the favored enterprises, whether by virtue of laws or special contracts that are abided by more or less according to each case.

After the favored industries come the industries established in the normal way, with enough capital and directed by experts who are knowledgeable about the business and the region. Here are the business owners of a certain importance, the manufacturers, farmers, mine owners, and experts who have no debts and pledges and attend only to their own capital and to their own ordinary profits, which result naturally from a business subject only to economic laws. In this group, one finds the real bees of the hive, and without them no wealth whatsoever would be produced. Above them are the executioners and below them, the indebted victims of the feast: that is to say, the small industries and the emerging industries that I am going to examine.

With the remnants of industries that prospered and flourished during the guano and nitrate eras and in other instances with tiny amounts of capital managed by older manufacturers or by operators or knowledgeable businesspeople, diverse smaller establishments of commerce, industry, and artisanal manufacturing have been formed. They eke out a sad, hand-to-mouth living from one day to the next, loaded with debts and pledges that they attend to laboriously, sacrificing the last cent of their daily earnings. In many cases, these smaller manufacturers discover that they must divest themselves little by little of the few tools of the trade they possess. And thus, they find themselves being slowly devoured by creditors until they end up in the street asking for handouts, men who in any place less choked by usury, monopoly, and fiscal control would have prospered rapidly, to the immense gain of their families and the country where they were born. For many, it would be enough to save them if their creditors would limit themselves to taking only a portion of their income and not the capital itself with which they work!

The small manufacturer will reap no benefit from his habits of order and thrift, his love of the work, and his expertise in the area he manages. Nor will he be helped by his honesty proved over many years, his habit of fulfilling his pledges, or the few funds that he salvaged from the wreckage, hoping to use them to work and improve his situation. Usury, monopoly, and fiscal control will drown him without relief. Credit will not come to his aid because there is none here. In the end, there will be no law of equity for the payment of previous obligations or for large changes due to forces beyond his control. Nothing will avail him, and he is doomed to die because pariahs have only the right to die.

The one group of manufacturers not yet discussed is the poorest of all, the most abandoned. In this group are all the men who, knowing how to make something for profit, have only a tiny sum of capital—rarely as much as a few dozen *soles* and hardly ever more than a hundred. These individuals deal in portable businesses, work as artisans, or join one trade or another. They are the ones who provide the small items needed most in life, and their profits are scarcely enough to be reckoned, a wage earned each day after hard labor and running all the risks they undertake on their own account.

And all that has been said here is so accurate and unexaggerated that anyone who has lived in Lima in the last twenty years can verify how many of those numerous peddlers of an earlier time have disappeared, the ones who sold all the little necessities of life. One's own experience also confirms how much more expensive and scarce these articles have become as well as how much public poverty has grown, along with the city's death rate. But none of this matters: the auctioneers and contractors get rich fast, and thanks to them we have capital, which is available for loan at 10 percent per month.

What has been said up to now makes it possible to see that in Lima, the favored industries enjoy a prosperous status and those established by regular means have their existence assured, while the small industries and the budding ones succumb and perish. The first two types possess, beyond their basic conditions of existence, social influence, the press, and political institutions entirely at their service; and favored by such powerful elements, nothing opposes their advancement and continuing development. The last two categories have none of these advantages, and being short on capital as well, they inevitably lead a sickly existence, winding up sooner or later (with rare exceptions) going bankrupt or out of business, their managers swelling the hordes of beggars or joining the ranks of first vice and then crime.

The Family

In contemplating Lima from the perspective of the family, it can be said that the entire city is nothing more than a single family. Such an entity has not evolved sufficiently among us to organize itself into the immediate unity of the social body, as is already happening in the big cities. In those populous centers, the family consolidates into the father, the mother, and the minor children. All the others remain separate from this nucleus and maintain with it only bonds that are purely social and more or less limited, according to the degree of prosperity of various members. With the family defined thus, the head of the household knows the extent of his obligations; and within the limits of his capacity to produce wealth, he chooses the social level that fits his means and lives in that manner calmly and in an orderly way, setting aside savings and fulfilling his obligations toward the woman who cast her fate with him and toward the children that [they] brought into the world. In this kind of family, poverty intrudes only when the father of the house is a man of vices or when special circumstances have left him unfit for work.

In Lima, however, things do not go this way. The nuclear family just described does not end with the minor children. All the children, their grandparents, uncles and aunts, and their relatives are also part of the family. And thus, it turns out that the head of this tribe, however much he may work, can never obtain enough income by honest means to support so many people. Here, more than anywhere else, lies the ongoing cause of poverty in Lima and the political corruption of certain men. For each individual who works, there are ten idle ones who live at his expense— now by this means and later by some other but never by their own efforts.

IN CONCLUSION, THE potential of individuals in this city is very encouraging, but effectiveness in action leaves everything to be desired. With the elements that we have in Lima, it is possible to climb very high on the road to glory, grandeur, and well-being. But today, for the time being, we remain very far from those elevated heights that gratify patriotism.

8

Buenos Aires in the Early Twentieth Century*

Juan Alvarez

Translated by Sharon Kellum

The idea of the "primate city"—a disproportionately large national capital dominating an extensive hinterland by preempting functions and energies from smaller towns—recurs frequently in the literature on Latin America. The development of Buenos Aires in the past hundred years furnishes the classic example of such a city. Since 1880, Buenos Aires has functioned as a highly active export-import center, shipping to Great Britain and other industrial nations the beef and wheat produced on the fertile plains of the Argentine pampa. Today, the city's metropolitan area contains about one-third of Argentina's population.

Juan Alvarez, in his classic work Buenos Aires, *analyzed the ways in which the city had come to dominate the nation: as a port for overseas commerce, as an industrial center, and as the seat of the national government. He concluded with a proposal for creating new urban systems to offset the economic and political power of the capital.*

As a port, Alvarez noted, Buenos Aires had garnered the lion's share of Argentina's international trade, relegating other port cities such as Rosario or Bahía Blanca to minor roles. He emphasized the effects of the centralized railway network, most of the lines of which converged on Buenos Aires, and of discriminatory freight rates that facilitated the sale of European manufactured goods in the interior, to the detriment of local industry. Although Alvarez advocated government regulation of the rail companies, he failed to deal with the problem of export dependency: Argentina's railroads had been built largely by foreign entrepreneurs to serve the needs of foreign businesses, and because the export of

From *Buenos Aires* (Buenos Aires: Editorial Cooperativa Ltda., 1918), 21–190 passim.
*The editors express their gratitude to Bainbridge Cowell, Jr., for his assistance in editing this chapter and preparing the introductory note.

agricultural products constituted the most dynamic sector of the Argentine economy, that sector determined the shape of the transportation system.

Much of the nation's industry also centered in and around Buenos Aires. Alvarez, recognizing the determinative power of culture and habit, showed why Argentine industrialists had to live and work close to the center of government bureaucracy—only through personal influence or bribery could they ensure policies favorable to their enterprises. Industrial growth, however, was limited. More recent research has shown that large-scale industries in the city between 1880 and 1930 consisted of food processing for export and the manufacture of light consumer goods for the domestic market. These factories represented only a tentative, incipient industrialization, unbalanced in composition because of the demands of the export economy. Interior towns such as Córdoba or Tucumán had little hope of industrializing because northwest Argentina had permanently lost its main export market—Upper Peru (modern Bolivia)—at the time of Independence.

In discussing the role of Buenos Aires as the national capital, Alvarez noted the presence of tens of thousands of government officials as well as bankers, entrepreneurs, lobbyists, and petitioners. Continuing the vice-regal tradition, residents of the city enjoyed the best public services and educational facilities in the land. Significantly, he pointed out that government banks tended to concentrate their investments in Buenos Aires, in effect siphoning off wealth from the provinces.

Alvarez's suggestion to redress the balance between Buenos Aires and the other Argentine cities stands as an early example of modern regional planning. According to his proposal, two networks of cities would bypass Buenos Aires entirely, utilizing existing railways. Each would include a seaport (such as Bahía Blanca) tied to one or more interior centers (such as Mendoza). This model went far beyond previous schemes for canal digging, connecting the interior with the Pacific coast by rail, or moving the national capital—ideas bandied about for decades by Argentine planners and thinkers.

Juan Alvarez—lawyer, historian, university professor, federal judge, and eventually attorney general of Argentina in the 1930s—spent much of his life in the port of Rosario. His numerous publications included an economic history of Santa Fé and a book on the development of Rosario. Throughout his writings, he championed the cause of the provincial cities versus the overweening metropolis, thereby anticipating present-day dependency theory. In his work on Buenos Aires, however, Alvarez failed to address two fundamental conditions that had powerfully affected Argentina's development: the structural distortions in the Argentine economy produced by reliance on agricultural exports, and the domination of city and countryside by a small elite of merchants and ranchers whose monopoly of land and native capital discouraged immigrants from settling in the interior. The result was the continued concentration of the *country's political and financial power in Buenos Aires and a distorted process of modernization. Alvarez touched on these topics elsewhere, most notably in* Estudio sobre las guerras civiles argentinas *(1914).*

The Terms of the Problem

Nature endowed Buenos Aires with a benign climate and an enviable location at the mouth of a great river system surrounded by fertile land. Starting off with these elements, we have made the city into a great commercial and industrial center, a market for the fruits of the land, the final destination of all our transportation routes by land and sea, and the arrival station for the large numbers of immigrants who come to us from abroad. Here we have the political, educational, artistic, and religious center of the country. Here too is a city of luxury, pleasure, and play served by admirable hotels, racetracks, clubs, theaters, and recreational establishments.

As a result of all this development, population and wealth are distributed in an unusual way in Argentina. Gathered in an area slightly larger than 7 square leagues [about 21 square miles] are 1.5 million inhabitants, who represent more than one-third of all the employees of industry and trade in Argentina, along with 47 percent of the commercial capital and 30 percent of investments in manufacturing. The value of all the real estate owned by the state amounts to 585 million pesos, two-thirds of it within this small radius. Located here are the main port and military installation as well as 300 million gold pesos in the Caja de Conversión, which contains most of the national bank reserves. The rest of the Argentine population, businesses, capital, and means of defense are scattered irregularly across 118,000 square leagues [113,110 square miles].

As it turns out, Buenos Aires is not well located to serve as the focal point of the national economy because it lies at one extreme of the territory. As an industrial center, the city is too far away from the forests, waterfalls, and oil wells that could supply it with fuel. This situation translates into an enormous permanent loss incurred by transporting via Buenos Aires the foreign goods consumed in the interior as well as the Argentine products required by the big city. If the inhabitants of Buenos Aires lived closer to the areas that produce wine, sugar, and tobacco, our protectionist policies could free up the great sums that we are currently paying to the stockholders of the foreign railway companies that transport these goods over long distances.

As for the import trade, the disadvantage of locating the great national storehouse at one edge of the country is evident in view of the navigable waterways, each one twenty-eight to thirty feet deep year-round, that can carry cargo upriver four hundred kilometers into the interior. [This raises a] striking difference regarding freight rates given the fact that sixty miles of land transportation costs more than six thousand miles of transportation by waterway. If European goods had to go inland from the coast to reach the great center of consumption and had to pay for long stretches of shipment by rail, we could support industries in the interior without needing to protect them excessively.

Buenos Aires costs the Argentine republic dearly. The configuration of our country is such that from Salta to Tierra del Fuego, foreign trade could be organized with a minimum of railway freight charges by following perpendicular lines to the sea or to a navigable river. But with the city transformed into a storehouse, port, metropolis, and manufacturing center, railways are required to run hundreds of kilometers diagonal to or parallel with the coast through barren land, at a pure loss. Some areas escape paying this penalty, to be sure, but others are cut off without connections because the system oriented toward Buenos Aires has no ready outlet to a closer port. These railways, the natural enemies of interior ports that could shorten routes, create competitive rates to take cargo away from interior ports and to discourage oceangoing vessels. The discounted rate is made up for by increasing rates on other routes, and hence the country pays the railway companies to maintain a system that runs contrary to the nation's well-being. As a result, anyone living in Salta who decides to conduct important business cannot reach the great Argentine market without traveling nearly three thousand kilometers by rail.

Similar waste and hardships are produced by the administrative procedures of the federal authorities, given that the capital's inconvenient location also reflects its difficulties in the political system. In bygone days, more than a few uprisings counted among their elements of success their great distance from the central government. Moreover, the luxurious ambience of the present-day city is not very fitting for the political needs of a modest republic of eight million inhabitants. In attracting more than 1.5 million of them, Buenos Aires forms a disturbingly centralizing political core in the machinery of federal government. The city has not even managed to get its own municipal government organized in stable form. And because Buenos Aires is the model for other Argentine communities, the municipal system in the country operates in a state of perpetual adjustment. Finally, the accumulation in the city of more people than those attracted to it naturally has produced an excess of workers who fight desperately to displace each other and who stir up misery, strikes, and violence.

The census of 1914 attributed to the city of Buenos Aires only those who had spent the night there hours before the count. Practically speaking, the city contains many more inhabitants, including the forty-six thousand residents of Avellaneda who are separated from Buenos Aires by only a bridge. The urban core fans out beyond the official perimeter, extended by electric trolleys and rapid trains that carry thousands of individuals employed in the city back to the outskirts to sleep. La Plata itself lies today no farther from Buenos Aires in travel time than Belgrano did when it was incorporated into the municipality. The real number of inhabitants of our federal capital must hover around two million, that is to say, one-fourth of the national population.

The Great Overseas Port

Until the first third of the eighteenth century, the meager trade maintained with Spain by the areas around the Río de la Plata was concentrated in the anchoring point of Buenos Aires, not only because the king had ordained it but also because this was the only populated place where oceangoing vessels could stop. During the eighteenth century, several towns began to emerge along the coast of Uruguay and on the previously uninhabited route between Buenos Aires and Santa Fe. Little by little, however, this maintaining of the old state of things without adapting to new developments gave rise to increasingly bitter complaints and then to wars. Finally, around the middle of the nineteenth century, the rivers were opened to world trade, about the time that paddle wheelers began to be practicable.

Today, looking back from the perspective of several decades, the formation of new population centers at these and other points in the country is clearly desirable for exportation. But in terms of imports from abroad, progress seems almost paralyzed. Statistics confirm that in 1873 Buenos Aires received 83 percent of all imports and sent in return some 75 percent of all Argentine exports. Forty years later, Buenos Aires's share is 80 percent of imports and 35 percent of exports. Thus, four decades later, the ships come closer and closer to the point of production to load our goods, but first they unload in Buenos Aires the foreign goods brought over to pay the producers. These goods are then redispatched to their destination from the great urban center.

Now let us consider agriculture. Each tenant farmer [*colono*] produces on his small farm many tons of grain of equally good quality. They are likely to be sold in one contract to the traveling agent of a foreign-owned buying house, who in a few days can assemble the entire cargo for a transatlantic ship. To warehouse it in the granaries, simple chutes extending from the high ground are sufficient. Without incurring excessive expenses, any supplier can finance buying agents in the countryside and additional buyers for railways that rely on storehouses in the stations. The procedure is not much different with respect to cattle products, except for the greater difficulty of loading.

The import trade differs. A good port for unloading is lacking, and the customhouse exercises more careful vigilance, becoming more bothersome due to the wide range of the products. Meanwhile, each tenant farmer, far from consuming a quantity of similar items at once, needs them in such variety that no single industry can produce them as a whole. In addition, the tenant farmer's consumption is spread out over the year. Lacking practical know-how, he is not in a position to place orders directly with the overseas traders. Moreover, the tenant farmer's need to obtain credit to settle up accounts when bringing in the harvest adds to the situation a lack of landed collateral that obliges anyone who advances him money to keep a close eye on it.

Clearly, such surveillance cannot be carried out by the traveling agents of each foreign-owned industry. It is more practical to organize things so that a kind of general agent, who is set up in a regular office and can offer on credit and in small amounts as many articles as the producers need and who takes upon himself the risks of debt collection, is established near the tenant farmers. Thus, the permanent warehouse keeper has arisen among us. But the supply of articles of each kind that this warehouseman needs is also small; and because his solvency depends absolutely on the success of the harvest, he too cannot be watched from a distance. Foreign traders thus prefer to come to an agreement with only the large importing houses in the great trade centers of the country, thereby avoiding the need for a branch office at each point of consumption. Importers distribute their products among the retailers, who disseminate them to consumers. Such a system prevents a city lacking strong commercial networks and capital from importing directly from abroad what is needed by the region served by that city. A major commercial center is also a market where goods can be taken in search of a buyer. Here one finds the banks and the interested parties for all kinds of cargo and transport. If capital is not accumulated in these sites, they will not develop into large entrepôts, nor will they emerge as such without an integrated railway network whose rates can be controlled.

Considering the matter from another angle, maintaining a customhouse system that is a remnant of the old port monopoly aggravates the problem. Free navigation of the rivers still does not mean actually being able to set up operations of commercial interchange at any point along the coast. Only certain places (the ones designated as major customhouses) afford ample storage for imported goods, while in other locations (the minor customhouses), ships are able to unload and store cargo only for a few days. It is common to arrange for the unloading of goods for which duties have been paid at a particular minor customhouse, as long as the interested parties pay out of their own pockets the cost of posting a guard. Otherwise, along any river or bank in the country where a vessel is found docked, public treasury officials must inquire into the reason for this abnormal occurrence and arrest the presumed lawbreaker if they suspect an attempt to operate at an unauthorized stop. Such a commercial system promotes the formation of ad hoc railway networks, whose owners have an interest in blocking new authorizations of foreign ships in domestic waters. [Sadly] for those merchants who do not live in a place designated as a major customhouse, it is advisable to give up on direct foreign trade. Their businesses are stocked instead from the center where duties are collected, and they [must] pay extra railway charges.

Along a seacoast with extended beaches, the Atlantic provides a deep harbor accessible to vessels of great tonnage a few kilometers south of Bahía Blanca. This locale, directly accessible from abroad, is more than six hundred kilometers from Buenos Aires and is thus a site that might well serve much of the abundant region now monopolized by Buenos Aires. Similar circumstances apply to the provinces of Cuyo. When the port of Buenos Aires had a depth of sixteen feet, the one in Bahía Blanca already had a natural depth of thirty. It still offers that capacity today, without major dredging, which makes it the ideal site for a great import center. And has the city developed over the course of forty years?

Absolutely. Bahía Blanca is a prosperous city that is full of life, but it has not succeeded to any appreciable degree in attracting customers away from Buenos Aires. During the ten years between 1904 and 1913, the docks at Bahía Blanca unloaded a yearly average of 3.2 percent of national imports, and no trend toward increasing that percentage has been noted.

Why is this happening? Because the natural bay and the wealth of the surrounding area are not enough to divert currents of trade already established in another direction. Needed in addition are port facilities, storehouses, sound capital, and (perhaps more than anything else) a policy prohibiting railway rates that discount the long runs unfairly at the expense of the short ones. Bahía Blanca represents a typical case of lack of facilities and highlights the drawbacks of entrusting the management of the ports to individual railroads.

The Manufacturing City

Many factories of recent creation are operating in Argentina, but they are not distributed across the territory in proportion to wealth, size of area, or number of inhabitants. The new factories prefer instead to occupy a few hectares near government offices in the national capital, where they form a small manufacturing zone.

Excepting those who produce food or build houses (whose occupations prevent them from clustering together in one location), the census yielded this finding: of the 188,000 individuals employed in manufacturing, only 84,000 find work outside the municipality of Buenos Aires. Hundreds of plants operate on the outskirts of the city, extending it even further, and thus our metropolis brings together the majority of Argentine factories. This phenomenon is even more striking if we recall that this herding together at one extreme of the territory came only a short time after the disappearance of various major manufacturers that had been operating in the provinces. The disappearance and ruin of many textile factories that had earlier operated successfully outside the capital are undeniable facts. This phenomenon can be observed to a lesser extent in other kinds of industries: tanneries that produce shoe soles, leather factories, embroidery and needlework factories, and silversmithies.

It is no secret that competition dislodged the old Argentine textile factories when railroads and transatlantic ships brought inexpensive products from European factories in contact with the consumers in this country. Nor is it a secret that we waited until free trade had ruined our established manufacturers to become rabid protectionists. But why is today's protectionism bringing the old industries back to life in Buenos Aires and not in the provinces, where they prospered before? How can it be explained that the new factories chose to start up their enterprises in precisely the location most accessible to the competition from foreign industry?

The new industrial managers obtained a lot of cheap labor in Buenos Aires that was not available elsewhere. During the last third of the nineteenth century, Argentina needed foreign immigrants to transform its cattle-raising areas into agricultural settlements, and, as usual, the country attempted to make the change with great haste. Before the required lands and houses were ready, Europe began to send us shiploads of men, many of them completely unfamiliar with farm labor. Steamships, which evoked memories of the old slave ships, were dedicated to this traffic.

The immigrants transported in this manner arrived in Buenos Aires, the destination of their journey, dazzled by the creature comforts of the big city but lacking money and pressed to find work immediately. Barely off the ship, they accepted the wages offered to them at the dock. Men with families, illiterates who had never ridden a train, preferred out of ignorance a sure wage to the uncertainties of farm life in unknown places. In Buenos Aires they stayed.

The influence of the factories of Buenos Aires was felt even by those who found employment in the countryside. Each time a drop in grain prices showed that agriculture was not as profitable as had been thought, many of the men who had gone out to make *colonias* (settlements) out of the estancias (ranches) saw the demand for their labor shrink perceptibly. With bad harvests, the extraordinary wages also ceased. How to provide work for the extras? In order to prevent them from leaving Argentina, we hastily invented industrial occupations in the city. This modus vivendi, which was tolerable as a temporary means, has gradually solidified and created vested interests. Our first two periods of excessive protectionism followed the crises of 1873 and 1890, coinciding with the times when the largest numbers of immigrants were returning to their countries of origin.

The policy initiated in 1890 shows unmistakably the tendency to employ immigrants in the big city. It was easier to crowd them by any means into existing houses in the vicinity than to provide each family with a small farm, fencing, a well, a dwelling, seeds, livestock, tools, and credit. The historic law of minimum effort was fulfilled once again.

During the intense periods of the industrial transformation of Buenos Aires, our customhouse mechanism was so complex, haphazard, and confusing that almost none of the new manufacturers could feel certain of maintaining any protection if they were located far from the federal capital (the seat of offices in charge of granting such protection). It was necessary to monitor at close range the maintenance of high duties on foreign products as well as the discounts on raw materials being imported. And the process was exacerbated by crazy fluctuations in paper currency that impeded any serious effort at calculating the value of wages.

The volatility of tariffs during this period and their obvious favoritism reflected the constant lobbying by manufacturers in congressional anterooms, the office of revenues, and the finance ministry as they negotiated steps toward indispensable changes of categories. Operating behind the applications swarming in the congressional record were influences, frauds, and deceptions. Clearly, one had to be close by, within reach of the telephone, to avoid having payoffs be ineffectual during any of the annual revisions of the customs laws. Any particular type of industry could arise in the interior only after the same kind of business in Buenos Aires had become strong enough to constitute respectable interests. But at that time, nearly all the country's customers belonged to the factories in the capital.

If one admits that a 10 percent profit determines the investment of capital in a certain sense, imagine what little sense of security manufacturers far from the seat of government could feel about their businesses when the tax rates were fluctuating from one year to the next by 50 to as much as 200 percent. I deplore the scant interest that Argentine capitalists showed in looking for profitable investments in the new industries. Still, one must wonder whether the men of the country, who were familiar with the twists and turns and dangers of the system, did not choose wisely in dedicating themselves to promoting cattle raising and farming.

[Moreover,] a new set of cogs has appeared in the complex machinery [that affects industry]. It is now the customs inspector who decides what sum the state will demand on the contents of any particular package. This official, who is not always trained to resolve the thousand technical problems that arise in practice, can be lazy in reviewing the contents or show himself amenable to a bribe. The persistence of smuggling and fraud in the port of Buenos Aires demonstrates that little trust can be placed in the protection of Argentine tariffs by those who do not closely scrutinize this latest grinding of the tariff mechanism's gears. And this new approach, which is constantly encouraged by the import dealers of the great metropolitan center, has become yet another hindrance to establishing industries in the interior that are not found in Buenos Aires.

[Finally,] the railroad's influence in creating great centers at its terminal points cannot be doubted. Railway freight charges have contributed a great deal to the industrial development of Buenos Aires. The special railway rates between the port of Buenos Aires and those in Rosario and Concepción del Uruguay keep the oceangoing vessels in Buenos Aires and also hinder the development of coastal trading by artificially reducing overland freight charges. Thus, the interior has gradually been diverted from using the docks in Rosario. Since the presidency of Bartolomé Mitre (1862–1868), this port has been the interior's natural means of communication with the outside world, and yet this rich Mesopotamia, surrounded by water, has been forced to seek a port outside its territory.

Some rates take arbitrariness to the absurd and inflict grave damage on the national economy. Such is the case with Mendoza, cut off from trans-Andean traffic by an unimaginable system: for certain items, transport between Mendoza and Los Andes in Chile is more expensive than that between Los Andes and Buenos Aires via Mendoza, a trip a thousand kilometers longer. The rates on river transport are usually uneven as well and reveal the lack of effective government control. At times they replicate the example of Mendoza and Los Andes: the great distance traveled results in lower railway cargo rates.

The convergence of the three factors studied—labor, proximity to the government as a prerequisite for success, and special rates on transport—explains why foreign capital has preferred Buenos Aires for investments in industry. Moreover, the state authorities failed to correct that orientation and in some cases even favored it by dedicating much of the money available in the official banks to the metropolis.

The Seat of Government: The Source of Employment

The nature of the federal capital attracts people to Buenos Aires by various means, the most direct being the residence of the government, as dictated by the constitution. In interpreting these provisions, it has been assumed that in addition to the basic executive, legislative, and judicial powers, the headquarters of all administrative offices and many of the offices themselves must remain in Buenos Aires permanently.

Fifty-three thousand persons employed by the government implies about 250,000 residents living on the government payroll, an extraordinary number in comparison with the total counted in the census of 1895, when Buenos Aires had less than 10,000 public employees. Thus, the capital alone absorbs almost as many government dependents as the rest of the country, including provincial and municipal employees. And this figure does not take into account the personnel of foreign embassies, legations, and consulates.

Beyond the many who are obliged by their jobs to live in Buenos Aires are numerous others who headquarter there to be near the government. This second form of attraction to the capital brings together many financial agents and representatives of banks, insurance companies, and other enterprises whose boards of directors need to be in direct contact with the public authorities. For such reasons, the administrative bureaucracies of several railway companies previously operating in the interior have been transferred to Buenos Aires, dragging along with them hundreds of families. There are also those who, without abandoning their permanent residence in other places, go to Buenos Aires frequently to arrange governmental, political, or financial matters. They form a floating population that is always being replenished, and, as patrons of hotels and other services, these frequent visitors swell the number of workers needed in the city.

A third form of attraction to Buenos Aires results from the official preference given to those who deal directly with the high powers of the state. To appreciate this advantage, simply compare the quantity and quality of schools, police, and public assistance agencies in the nation's provinces with those at the disposal of the city of Buenos Aires. These services are as federal as the metropolis, and even when the government itself determines their distribution, the beneficial effect of personal contact with top officials is indisputable.

[The construction boom has also attracted people.] Since 1880 enormous sums have been spent on endowing the capital with permanent public buildings, and their construction has provided jobs for many workers. In a curious persistence of old monarchical attitudes, we take pleasure in ensuring that those buildings are monumental. Just as the king was the prime resident and the city where he resided was therefore preferred over all others, we now think that Buenos Aires as the capital has the right to the same advantages. We consider it just and normal that the city's public buildings, walkways, and institutions are more impressive than those of the rest of the country. And the offices and officials of Buenos Aires generally enjoy higher rank and better salaries for equal work. This concept cannot be imputed more to one party or locality than to another. Rather, it constitutes a kind of conviction, maintained among creoles out of custom (because things have been done this way since the times of the viceroy) and among foreigners because almost all of them come to us from monarchical countries. Official favor in turn attracts population: outsiders looking for grandiose sights, students seeking the great university or great library, landowners seduced by a city of luxury.

A Solution for the Problem

Having established the various artificial causes that have allowed Buenos Aires to enhance its natural advantages and thus attract great masses of population, it is logical to admit that if one diverted the same factors to other locations, they would take along with them much of the migratory flow. Three cities of a certain importance exist in the republic—Córdoba, Tucumán, and Mendoza—each with its own products of major consumption and industrial capacities and each one situated so that it can compete with the market of Buenos Aires in distance and freight rates within a certain radius. Argentina also has two deepwater natural ports [Rosario and Bahía Blanca], the locations of which offer unique advantages: the first is found where the deep waters of the Paraná come closest to the western part of the republic; the second is defended by fortresses and has excellent circumstances for serving as a new entrance to the country, thus avoiding the drawbacks of the Río de la Plata as the only port and Buenos Aires as the obligatory gatekeeper. These five cities are linked to each other and the rest of the interior by railroads leading away from the Río de la Plata. Thus, they could serve as channels for two trade routes between the coast, the north, and the west, specifically the integrated routes of Bahía Blanca-Mendoza and of Rosario-Córdoba-Tucumán. The matter then becomes one of accelerating their growth while slowing that of Buenos Aires. Such is the solution I propose.

Of course, even the most well thought-out procedures will not prevent differences in development. Rosario, with 250,000 inhabitants, may soon reach 500,000 or more because even without official assistance, the city is doubling its population every fourteen years. Córdoba, with the motor power of its waterfalls and being the center of a region rich in agriculture, livestock production, and mineral exploration, will grow rapidly as long as the factories it can sustain are protected. Bahía Blanca, despite its admirable possibilities, still has only fifty thousand inhabitants. Mendoza, somewhat larger but bounded by cliffs to the west, can with the railway become our great export center for the Pacific, the market for Cuyo, Neuquén, part of the pampa, and the Río Negro. It is here that the wool from the Andean valleys should be woven. Mendoza is already producing wine, fruit, and cattle and will produce olives on a large scale if properly attended. The hundred thousand inhabitants of Tucumán enjoy a more extensive geographic reach because the northern part of the republic sends its products to the coast and to the interior. Tucumán can corner the market on the cotton and tobacco industries and on the growing and processing of herbs and rice, given that more than a thousand kilometers now separate the planting beds from the factories. These industrial possibilities—when added to the sugar and alcoholic beverages that Tucumán is already processing and its production of winter vegetables and tropical fruits—show that the city offers excellent prospects for becoming the great industrial center of the north.

In terms of ports, if the trick lies in maintaining in favor of Buenos Aires a policy that differentiates according to river depths and commodities, then what is called for is the elimination of all new expansion or deepening of the capital port except when justified by the zone that it should reasonably serve. All other commodities should be conceded as appropriate to Rosario, Bahía Blanca, and any other port. Foreign vessels must transport as much cargo as possible directly to the interior without making an earlier port of call in Buenos Aires, whether they travel via the island of Martín García or via Paraná de las Palmas.

It is also desirable to adopt a definitive policy on the issue: maintain three or four large overseas ports that are well equipped rather than one enormous port and many inadequate ones. Large vessels will never go to the latter because they lose time with every successive unloading and transfer. Even with enough cargo for five medium-sized ships bound for other such small ports, it will always be more convenient for the shipowner to transport cargo at one time from one place and then distribute the products in smaller boats. Large vessels must be able to get to the interior and a large trade center there. Also, immigrants will board a large ship directly because they always prefer its speed and the comforts of the trip that it can offer. A lack or shortage of docks, cranes, and sheds involves delays that transatlantic ships will not tolerate.

To promote the rapid growth of Córdoba, Tucumán, and Mendoza, at least three initiatives are required: making them major customhouses; providing them with labor and capital; and establishing favorable railway rates. The same measures should also be applied to Rosario and Bahía Blanca. Having a customhouse in Córdoba (which had already been tried by the king in the early seventeenth century) has often seemed an advisable solution, and various laws since 1869 have mandated its creation. Unfortunately, the executive branch never acted on them—at times to avoid placing the public treasury within reach of possible revolutionaries, at other times, out of fear of smuggling or without explaining the reason. Anyone who has read what I have written here about the influence of the major customhouses on the development of the import trade will not doubt the advantage of opening such offices in the three trade centers in the interior. The system fits our practices because land transport in boxcars is currently allowed on runs as long as the one from Chile to Buenos Aires by way of Bahía Blanca.

Nevertheless, all efforts to establish commercial storehouses in the interior will fail as long as railway rates are kept in their current form. They must be revised. It is possible that foreign manufacturers might organize in such a way that the foreign railways in Argentina could form an integrated unit that would prefer to transport the products of their own countries, thus ruining ours. Railway rates, if not attended to, can neutralize the effects of the customhouse tariff.

With regard to capital, as long as the Banco de la Nación is overflowing with deposits and the Banco Hipotecario [Mortgage Bank] continues to be able to issue certificates, there will be little difficulty in getting capital to the five cities within the system. Official banks determined the success of the sugar and wine industries, and thus we are operating in familiar territory. Moreover, legislation can divert toward the interior capital funds that do not come into the country via the official banks.

Regarding labor, three measures are necessary: closing the hotel for immigrants in the capital and prohibiting provision of any shelter or employment for new arrivals there; setting up five large hotels with placement offices in the interior cities discussed; and organizing a railway service direct from the port of Buenos Aires to these hotels for immigrants who get off in these cities. Labor and capital also require technical schools. Accordingly, the provincial and municipal authorities of the respective cities should liberally sponsor scholarships at such schools.

THEORETICALLY SPEAKING, IF the location of the national government in Buenos Aires becomes an insurmountable obstacle to balancing the country's development, then what is indicated is nothing less than the elimination of that difficulty by moving the capital out of Buenos Aires. This measure would compensate for the natural advantages that today favor the coast of the Río de la Plata. Practically speaking, however, the prospect of such a transfer might cut too deeply; surely many Argentines would think it better to leave things as they are if they have to be remedied at that price.

[Of course,] left unanswered in all this would be the old question asked by the Argentine congress: where to transfer the capital? Should we wish to maintain the present-day metropolis in Buenos Aires, the beneficiary of various artificial factors, it is illogical to eliminate all such factors. The city can maintain its first rank by leaving the capital there and transferring elsewhere the other factors that perpetuate the current [political-economic] imbalance. Taking all the advantages away from Buenos Aires would amount to destroying the work that we have lovingly brought to fruition. It is fine for the city to remain the capital without aspiring to hold onto everything. But if the first decision makes the second impossible, it would be appropriate to transfer governmental influence elsewhere during the time strictly necessary to develop the new plan. Once the plan was implemented, the seat of government would be returned to Buenos Aires. Let us not forget that it is always good to settle our differences with the past.

9

The Transformation of São Paulo[*]

Gilberto Leite de Barros

Translated by Gerald G. Curtis

Gilberto Leite de Barros's A cidade e o planalto: Processo de dominância da cidade de São Paulo *began as an essay entitled "Aspectos sociais e econômicos do isolamento de São Paulo no período colonial," written under the direction of a leading Brazilian historian, Sérgio Buarque de Hollanda, at the Escola de Sociologia e Política de São Paulo in 1951. In the sixteen years that elapsed between that essay and the publication of* A cidade e o planalto, *Leite de Barros studied the process by which the city of São Paulo, emerging from the isolation of the earlier colonial period, came to dominate the hinterland of South Central Brazil. He himself characterizes his work as social history. He uses sociological and economic models, such as "modernization theory," to add interpretative dimension to his study, but subordinates these to the historical theme of the emergence of the city of São Paulo as an administrative, economic, and social center in the late eighteenth and the nineteenth centuries.*

The early chapters of Leite de Barros's lengthy book describe the sixteenth-century settlement of São Paulo de Piratininga, as it was then known, the slave- and gold-hunting expeditions (bandeirismo) *of the sixteenth and seventeenth centuries, the ethnic mix of the colony, and the decline of the* bandeirante *tradition in the early eighteenth century. During that century, because of its proximity to the gold and diamond mines of central Brazil, the São Paulo captaincy, long ignored by the Portuguese authorities, attracted increasing attention from the overseas metropolis. The administrative elevation of São Paulo from* vila (town) *to* cidade (city) (1711), *its new status as a bishopric (1745), and the restoration of its administrative autonomy from the capital, Rio de Janeiro (1765), reflect the heightened interest of the Portuguese monarchy.*

From A cidade e o planalto: Processo de dominância da cidade de São Paulo, lv. in 2t. (São Paulo: Livraria Martins Editôra, 1967), 164–613 passim.

[*]The editors express their gratitude to Darrell Levi for his assistance in editing this chapter and preparing the introductory note.

Unlike many traditonal historians of São Paulo, Leite de Barros sees the eighteenth century not as a decadent interval between the bandeirante epoch and the future prosperity of the coffee cycle, but as a period of economic, political, and social preparation for later developments. He describes at length the administration of Captain-General Luis Antônio de Sousa Botelho Mourão, the Morgado de Mateus (1765–1775), who was dispatched to São Paulo by the Marquês de Pombal to institute reforms to make the captaincy better serve the interests of the mother country. As Leite de Barros's narrative makes clear, Luis Antônio de Sousa's administration had something of the flavor of a sixteenth-century conquest, as the rationalistic representative of the Crown sought to tame the unruly and independent Paulistas and make them into productive servants of Portugal.

A second stage in the growth of São Paulo was marked by the independence of Brazil in 1822 and the promulgation of the Constitution of 1824. This period witnessed the city's bureaucratic rationalization and its increasing control over its hinterland. A third stage may be dated from 1850, when the development of the coffee economy served to consolidate the hold of the city over the planalto despite the fact that the urban-rural demographic ratio actually declined. Finally, after 1870, with the development of an efficient railroad system, with massive European immigration, and with an influx of European styles, ideas, and machines, São Paulo became the locus of an embryonic metropolitan economy, presaging its emergence in the twentieth century as the foremost concentration of capital and industrial might in Latin America.

In his introduction, Leite de Barros notes that although São Paulo, as an outpost in the sertão, occupies a unique position in Brazilian municipal history, it also has many features of universal interest to the growth of cities. Perhaps chief among these is the development of an urban mentality. In analyzing the evolution of this mentality, Leite de Barros places major emphasis on the "rational," "modernizing" roles of the planter, the mule trader, the bureaucrat, the merchant, and the law student, in opposition to the "instinctive reaction" of the bandeirante and the traditional rural patriarch. The growth of a city, he implies, must not be measured solely by physical, political, and economic transformations but also by the creation of an infrastructure of urban ideals, beliefs, and practices. In his conclusion, Leite de Barros broadens his scope and proposes that the São Paulo urban experience and its by-product of regional integration may offer a solution to present-day Brazil's need for balanced and effective national economic integration.

Dom Luis Antônio de Souza, the Morgado de Mateus, governed the captaincy of São Paulo from 1765 to 1775. His administration marked the beginning of a new cycle of Paulista history, a cycle of fruitful labor, of progress, and of social, economic, and political organization. It was a period in which the incipient Paulista patriarchal system, weak during the first two centuries of colonization, was greatly strengthened. During this auspicious period of the regime's history, the Paulistas became more aware of themselves and much more familiar with the territory covered by the captaincy. Boundaries with the other captaincies were fixed, points of economic production in the plateau region were gradually defined, and the city founded by [Manuel de] Nóbrega* began to consolidate its hegemony over the other surrounding urban clusters.

In 1765 the Morgado de Mateus ordered the first demographic census in São Paulo, which recorded 899 homes with 1,748 men and 2,090 women for the parish of São Paulo. The city itself was comprised of 392 homes with 648 men and 867 women. In the economic census, we found 204 references to property belonging to the family heads of the 392 homes in the city and 212 references to those of the 507 homes which formed the surrounding neighborhoods. The most distinctive fortune inventoried was 28 *contos* [one *conto* was equal to one thousand *mil-réis*] and the most modest, 25 *mil* and 600 *réis* [2.56 percent of one *conto*].

Owners of small general stores must have been numerous since it was customary at the time to find slaves among the retail merchants. There were six sales clerks listed and only four students. A wayfarer was spoken of who perhaps was a traveling salesman. Among liberal professionals we found three surgeons and a few specialists in law. Among the "craftsmen in mechanical trades," as they were termed at that time, tailors predominated (13), followed by carpenters (11), cobblers (8), hairdressers (5), goldsmiths (3), painters (3), masons (2), blacksmiths (2), miners (2), and cutlers (2).

It was a difficult task for the Morgado de Mateus to congregate the relatively small plateau population around the towns and villages and also to stimulate the people to engage in steady work. Once the Morgado, a man of lively intelligence, had established himself in the land, he soon became aware of the principal traits that comprised the Paulista character: the natural distrust and apprehensions that accompanied living in a virgin forest; the dissatisfaction and feeling of impotence in the presence of overwhelming natural conditions; and the consequent uncontrolled aggressiveness in prescribed day-to-day activities. They were completely ignorant, noted Dom Luis Antônio, of "the usefulness of owning private property, which parents may leave their children, . . . to those who live on

---

*Nóbrega was the leader of the Jesuit missionaries who established the first European community in the sixteenth century at the site of Piratininga, the Indian village that later became São Paulo.

a piece of cleared and planted land which is incapable of satisfying basic needs and which lasts no more than a year before it is exhausted." The *reinóis* themselves, those recently arrived from Portugal, would no sooner settle on the plateau than they succumbed to the force of the environment, blending with little resistance into the sluggish, unambitious local life-style. On one occasion the Morgado expounded on the *reinóis* who had just arrived: "They fill themselves with vices because of the ease of living in this country, and they never settle down."

The population was sparse, especially in the urban districts. "In these lands there are no people and for that reason there is no one to serve the State," the Morgado pointed out. No one would marry unless there was the assurance of a dowry, and for that reason men and women generally cohabited, producing illegitimate children and increasing the already excessive number of *mamelucos* [the offspring of a white and an Indian] and mulattoes. The latter were bastards without any particular trade who would end up roaming through the rural regions, giving the government the false impression of an idle character, of the "Iniquitas Sodomas-Otium ipsius," according to Dom Luis Antônio's expression. The Paulistas worked grudgingly; "a Paulista peasant," noted Arouche Randon in 1788, "worked two to three months in a year."

In spite of a basic attitude of disbelief among the populace in regard to any progressive initiative on the part of the Crown, the Morgado de Mateus began an effective campaign of political, economic, and social organization in the captaincy of São Paulo, seeking to correct the general disorder that existed in the systems of transportation, market supply, public health care, instruction, and the police. "I speak not of the difficulties of rousing the new inhabitants, for some are unwilling, others ask for things we don't have, some weep, while others hide; for all this can be overcome. I speak of the many whims and desires that we must reconcile in order to achieve something so fair and necessary and for which my strength is insufficient. Nor is it possible for me to compel them." He was referring to the negligence on the part of the powerful with respect to the economic progress of the land; those "city councilmen, or rather," the Morgado observed, "the Republicans who, neglecting the economic situation of the lands which should be their responsibility, direct their attention with too much zeal to the general government of the captaincy which does not concern them."

On July 3, 1767, the Morgado referred to the "republicans who were accustomed to governing the land in their own way" with inordinate excesses, and to the "hidden Jesuits who it seems to me are still here." The inhabitants of the captaincy who were not nobles, republicans, or gentlemen of sizable possessions had no other alternative than to subject themselves to the rich and powerful, unable to exercise a trade of their own. In that connection, the Morgado pointed out: "Except for very few mulattoes who employ their trades, the rest are all lords or slaves who serve these lords. These *senhores* are obliged to have slaves of all occupations, for none is perfect. Any craftsman who comes from the kingdom, sets himself up after a short time as a lord; he buys slaves, teaches them, passes on to them his trade and then collects the daily wages that they receive. The price of these craftsmen goes up greatly and no one can get any work done."

The problem lay in the low cultural standard of a people who had settled a region that was remote from the other centers of the country, situated on a plateau where access to the sea became almost impracticable. Still, the captain-general did not back away from the obstacles that stood in the way of fulfilling the mission entrusted to him by the Marquês de Pombal [Portugal's great imperial reformer]. In skillful fashion he was able to subdue the ill will of the powerful, enforce without hesitation the law that forbade the formation of so-called mobile sites, and plan and establish new settlements comprised of about fifty inhabitants each. He himself affirmed: "I established order among the populace, founded once again many colonies, and I am fortifying the navy, all without funds, because the local office of the purveyor does not have the wherewithal for assured payments."

With regard to the military sector of his administration, the Morgado specified that he had raised "troops in spite of all the opposition on the part of the free heathen who are accustomed to living in the woods without any type of submission or good breeding." In the area of the economy, finally, he strove to stimulate the production of sugar, rice, and other crops and to encourage the merchants to set themselves up next to the settlements, grouped at different points in the captaincy. The greatest impediment in regard to production lay in the difficulty of finding a vessel in which to ship the merchandise, for those that touched at Santos were only interested in loading gold, leaving "the land poorer than it had been before."

The city of São Paulo became more closely connected to the area that surrounded it, extending its economic influence to distant areas of the captaincy. As a result a lively rivalry began to emerge between the capital and the other settlements located along its borders. It was a healthy rivalry, a stimulus to progress, dynamically favorable to the whole plateau region. As the ecologist N. S. B. Gras points out, "The rivalry between the city and the country is more apparent than real." In truth, one depends upon the other and it is this "interdependence which explains the relationship between the city and the rural area."

In the São Paulo of the 1700s the economic system that developed was based on two occupations that stood out among the rest: that of the farmer or planter and that of the drover. The opportunity to become a progressive farmer or an active mule trader meant the promise of better days for the man from São Paulo, stimulating him to think of the future and to build his savings. The transformation associated with these particular business activities signified a change in values, in standards of behavior and mentality. Farming came to symbolize a stable profession that enhanced a man's position. It clothed him in nobility and dignity, brought him close to the land, obliged him to become a traditional patriarch.

The drover, a professional who became a common fixture on the Paulista plateau in the second half of the eighteenth century, also contributed toward stimulating the economic system of the captaincy inasmuch as he was the agent for the circulation of wealth. A man with his "house in his saddle pack," he assumed the role of a liberal transportation entrepreneur, an introducer of civilizing habits, a dreaded visitor of urban gatherings, and the bearer of truthful news as well as rumors, serving as newspaper and mail carrier. Drovers often spent the night on a plantation and took orders from the plantation house ladies for costume jewelry and fine cloth without the latter bothering to inquire about current prices in the cities. Those from the lower classes did not appreciate the drover but they tolerated him; in their opinion he represented a class whose members were slaves to money, traffickers and avaricious.

At the beginning of the nineteenth century the Paulista farmer became a leading element in the economic system of the captaincy. He began to earn money, grew accustomed to spending it on consumer goods, and learned to reinvest or save part of the profit from his agricultural activities. Used to taming the uncultivated fields and the forests that covered the hills of his plantation, the man from the interior began to look straight in the face, with the defiant attitude of a fighting cock, the proud man from the city, especially the ones who lived in the capital of the captaincy. As a result, the differences between the capital and the interior, between urban and rural elements, between the politically, economically, and socially dominant city and the country dominated by that city became more and more accentuated.

~ The municipal administration did not disregard the beautification of the city when São Paulo became a provincial capital upon Brazil's elevation to the status of a kingdom in 1815. Day by day, hour by hour, the small Piratiningan village was being progressively transformed. A series of municipal ordinances came one after another during the transitional phase from rural to urban as virgin nature was violated and transferred piece by piece to urban boundaries in the form of wood, stones, sand, and clay. The processes employed in the opening of streets, in the rerouting of streams and rivers, in the demarcation of lands, in the sanitation of mud flats, were improved, becoming more and more technical. Instead of building houses unwittingly on top of enormous ant hills, locations were chosen meticulously, and great care was exercised in taking measurements beforehand. Alongside crooked alleys, which were fetid and dark— Camargos Alley, Trashpile Alley—broad, airy streets appeared, such as Artillery Street and São José Street. The rivers, which once had posed a challenge to artificial urban symmetry, began to undergo diversions through systems of canals constructed along their courses.

As the physical transformation of the city went forward, its spirit lost some of its former luster. The city wall became conspicuous because it restricted the freedom and familiarity that local citizens enjoyed as they moved through the streets. In 1812 the council approved a mandatory street vendor's cry for those selling flour, beans, and corn; it also determined that they should bring two measures, a quarter and a half-quarter to guarantee the reliability of the transactions. Firm recommendations were brought forth that no rocks be left in the streets "or anything else that might create a hindrance to traffic." People were no longer allowed to let pigs run loose outside their pens, nor let them stretch out sluggishly in the middle of public roads, and one rarely heard bleating kid goats cornered by dogs. The owners of the latter were obliged to observe legal restraints imposed on their pets, "leading them about with leather muzzles." Otherwise, the dogs might be put to death and the owners fined 6,000 *réis*. In the meantime, people were no long allowed to leave out on the sidewalks such things as hoes, harnesses, and the various tools used in their work.

~ The first half of the nineteenth century demonstrated the prestige of the Paulista *chácara*, a type of country dwelling on the outskirts of town that was preferred by the well-to-do. On the *chácara* such an individual could regale his spirit during the twilight of quiet evenings, stretched out in the relaxation of a soft hammock that swayed in measured and peaceful rhythm. In his country house he rested his eyes on the high crowns of mango trees or on the thick branches of jaboticabas. The *chácara* represented a kind of suburban branch of the plantation, a midway point between rural and urban environments. It gave one the sensation of being in the city while at the same time not completely away from the farm and the backcountry.

The Paulistas who comprised the patriarchal order, *bandeirante* style, began to enjoy the fruits of relative comfort on such *chácaras*. There they could invite their friends, visitors, and those with whom they did business. The house on the *chácara* served as dwelling, office, and even chapel, for the owner solemnized on his lordly mansion religious rites similar to those practiced by the opulent masters of the "big houses" on the sugar plantations.

It is well to point out that the preference for the *sobrado*-type [two storey] construction was closely linked to the parallel development of urban activities such as those related to commerce or small industry, with commercial activities exercised more intensely in the port cities. Thus, in Santos the use of the *sobrado* was even more widespread and grew even faster than in the Paulista capital.

In São Paulo the *sobrado* was generally constructed on the principal streets; it had two storeys, was for the most part somber and even had a sad look about it. Constructed with mud walls and covered by concave tiles, it appeared almost white in color. Some, however, appeared yellow, "straw yellow or pale pink," according to [the North American missionary traveler] D. P. Kidder, who referred to the balconies as "favorite spots" not only for comfortably observing sunrises or sunsets but also for viewing processions. With regard to such balconies, [German travelers] J. B. von Spix and C. F. P. von Martius noted that those in São Paulo, in contrast with those in Rio, maintained a railing.

～ Commercial interchange in that period established its axis in the Paulista capital. Traders coming from the south crossed through it as well as those from the seaports who were heading for the interior to sell recently imported products. [The French naturalist, Auguste de] Saint-Hilaire, referring to the makeup of the population of the *bandeirante* capital, emphasized the fact that, along with functionaries of all kinds, workmen, owners of urban houses, ranchers who did not live on their ranches, and a large number of retail merchants were conspicuous. Items sold by the merchants included fabrics, food products, tools, odds and ends, wine, Negro slaves, and especially beef cattle. The herds, according to [English traveler] John Luccock, were driven to Rio de Janeiro, a distance of seven hundred miles. Saint-Hilaire, in whose opinion the dominant position of the Paulista capital as a point of convergence for the flow of commerce could not be justified, confirmed, nevertheless, that the Piratiningan village was preparing day by day to take on the recent surge of progress in the country. He observed that in São Paulo there were "some houses which were truly wealthy" and that in the center of town there were "well-stocked and well-ordered stores" with as rich an assortment of merchandise as that in the stores in Rio de Janeiro. There was no disguising the dominance of the city founded by Nóbrega over the rest of the plateau territory. São Paulo shone as the regime's social center par excellence, its political nucleus, economic fortress, and religious conglomerate.

With the promulgation of the Brazilian Constitution of 1824, an organized bureaucracy began to emerge with the usual government entities designed to serve traditional business and civic needs. These bodies included assemblies, general councils, inspectorships, ministries of police, and certain technical departments. As an effect once again of the structural changes taking place, the provincial capitals began to prepare themselves in terms of urban development to comply with the duties which attended their becoming seats of administration. During this period, Brazilian towns would gradually change from backward communities, quiet and peaceful republics whose streets and public squares constituted special preserves belonging exclusively to the citizens, to organized confederations of extended families, grouped institutionally around the constitutional State.

After 1822 the city of São Paulo began to enjoy exceptional prominence as a social and political center. In the capital, Paulistas debated political topics while groups buzzed about a particular nomination or the dismissal of ministers or presidents—a sure sign that the nation was gradually becoming politicized.

The bureaucracy began taking shape during the administration of the first president of the province of São Paulo, Lucas Antônio Monteiro de Barros [1824–1827], and expanded as public power gradually infiltrated the various sectors of society. Lucas Antônio soon had to confront the difficult task of controlling the abuse of power on the part of regional bosses. In addition, he had to determine whether or not entities of public administration were competent. He had to decide on the extent and diversification of rights and privileges belonging to public functionaries while avoiding conflicts between them. He was also obliged to define the powers of the city councils and to eliminate as far as possible their habit of resorting to [increasingly] powerful republicans for help in the delivery of public services. Finally, it was his duty to delineate the limits of clerical intervention in social institutions, especially in regard to the family and education. These were all complex and intricate charges, but they proceeded from the imperatives of the law.

The cultivation of coffee spread throughout the interior of the *bandeirante* province beginning in the middle of the nineteenth century. From 1825 to 1850 this expansion was slow, limited to the narrow confines of the Paraíba Valley. But after that period planters extended their activity to the areas of Campinas and Piracicaba, and in the last quarter of the 1800s, to Ribeirão Preto and adjacent areas. This movement, rapid and widespread now, caused an appreciable displacement toward the interior on the part of many who had first settled in the major urban centers, especially in the capital.

According to statistics collected by Marechal Daniel Pedro Müller, the province of São Paulo had 326,902 inhabitants in 1837 while the capital city had 21,933. The population of the capital represented approximately 7 percent of the total for the province, a rather small proportion that would change little until 1886, as shown by statistical data gathered at the time by order of the president of the province. Of the 1,221,394 total for the province, only 47,697, less than 4 percent, lived in the capital. The population in the capital had gone up only slightly during that fifty-year interregnum although the total for the province had increased greatly. According to an observation by Pierre Monbeig in relation to this period of Paulista history, "until 1870 progress was still slow. The slow pace of urban evolution [was] caused by the evolution of agriculture. The cultivation of sugarcane fail[ed] to show substantial progress and [was] relegated to an inferior position by the cultivation of coffee. The mid-nineteenth century was the period during which coffee made its deep penetration into Paulista territory. The capital kept itself apart from the coffee rush and its commercial bustle but the march of coffee would soon create more favorable conditions for urban development."

As the plantations became less autocratic, depending more and more upon urban commercial houses and financial establishments, their owners began to acquire more respect for the law and authorities. The justice system and the police, organized now on rational foundations, no longer allowed the large landowner to dictate his own laws while defying the State or attempt to judge by himself the squabbles and disagreements on his estate. The owners of sugar mills or coffee plantations in the nineteenth century were simply unable to maintain the long list of powers that the patriarchs of bygone days had exercised for two or three centuries.

The surge of progress that took place in the middle of the nineteenth century due to the cultivation of coffee on the Paulista plateau hastened the expansion of the city of São Paulo. Professional craftsmen of different kinds began to appear in the *bandeirante* capital, people who contributed with their specific activities to the development of more impersonal and indirect human relations. Paulista citizens began to depend upon a greater number of people, a phenomenon that marked a revolution in lifestyle and prevailing moral values.

In the city the strength of tradition gradually diminished as other values related to science and technical know-how grew in importance and took their place. There was more schooling in the city than in the country, more conviviality, more social breeding. Everything changed in the city. There was less religiosity and more of a practical spirit based on economic motivations. There was less conformity and more resistance to adversity; less honesty and more lack of trust in one's fellowman; less decorum, more exhibitionism; fewer authentic friendships, more fleeting acquaintances; fewer firm handshakes, more cordial embraces; less personal identification, more anonymity; less peace of mind, more restlessness; less good health, less hygiene, and more promiscuity, more illness, neurosis, misery, crime, vagrancy, and abandoned children.

~ As the nineteenth century advanced, among the elements that influenced the process of disintegration within the partriarchal Paulista family none was more important than the *bacharel*, the prospective law graduate. The latter entrenched himself in the garrets of urban society and undermined prevailing patriarchal practices whenever possible with his insatiable revolutionary spirit. We should explain at the outset that the Paulista law student during those years belonged to none of the legitimate sociological groups in the city. Certainly his group of students constituted no recognizable division or unit of the city. He was neither republican, alderman, nor bureaucrat. He did not represent a majority of the population nor even a fifth or sixth thereof. He represented a colorful, decorative facade, but one of a temporary nature only. Still, the law student made up part of a revolutionary group that constantly challenged the folkways and mores acclaimed by the local populace. The *bacharel* obeyed no established standards of conduct and always sought to place himself at the very edge of social control.

The São Paulo merchant, along with the *bacharel*, became the direct adversary of the patriarch in the struggle for social dominance, and played an important role in the period of rapid social evolution that began after Independence. He contributed to the circulation of money in many hands; he was active in the exchange of merchandise, carrying out transactions that brought him knowledge of new techniques, prestige, and the air of a well-traveled individual. He participated in the spread of progressive ideas and motivated change in the sense that his principal role was that of selling to all kinds of customers, thus helping to undo a system of rigid social stratification. The merchant was a professional whose appearance marked the economic evolution of a society as it surpassed the simple production phase of development. The merchant identified with the true urban man, for as his occupation grew in importance, there was a parallel development of the monetary economy, based first on money and later on credit. He gradually transformed the prevailing economic mentality, using money in place of bartering in kind. He no longer tallied goods for the purpose of trading them but instead began to calculate their monetary value. There-fore, he worked toward changing the concept of property, once consid-ered primarily as the land necessary to sustain life through the cultivation of subsistence products, and now as surplus property that might be accu-mulated as part of one's inheritance. As the German philosopher Oswald Spengler observed, when a city changes into a "money market and value center," the businessman "ceases to be an instrument and becomes the sovereign of economic life."

One could identify the embryo of a metropolitan economy through-out the city of São Paulo in the final quarter of the nineteenth century. During those years the largest city on the plateau already had its nose turned up with respect to the surrounding communities as its sphere of influence spread over the region. São Paulo was positioned on the crest of a wave of economic expansion that would break out over the plateau in the next century and result in bold achievements in the areas of agricul-ture, commerce, and industry.

After the opening of the first railroad lines, São Paulo exercised even more control over the plateau, firming up its position as the cultural, po-litical, social, and financial capital, and, in time, the industrial capital of the *bandeirante* province. The human conglomeration founded by Nóbrega, located at the juncture of the Tietê and Tamanduateí Rivers, represented the channel for the distribution of provincial agricultural prod-ucts to other regions. The framework for the circulation system on the plateau had been established; what remained was to produce and promote the flow of the respective products. Santos was the outlet to the sea. São Paulo was the main beam in the framework with support from Sorocaba and the Paraná area in the south. Campinas represented the other support toward the west looking toward the hinterland, from the valley of the Moji-Guaçu to the Rio Grande on the borders of Minas Gerais.

The principal result of São Paulo's consolidation as the center of the plateau railroad system was the stream of people that began to flow to-ward the city, making use of the convenient transportation. Beginning in the 1870s there was a great increase in the population of the *bandeirante* urban area as a result of those who abandoned the interior and headed for the capital, motivated by their desire to become a part of the urban pro-fessional scene. In addition to the already mentioned substitution of ur-ban for rural activities, a capitalistic class began to emerge as well as a greater contingent of women in the liberal professions. São Paulo was an easily accessible capital, a fairly large city that was opening up to take in immigrants of disparate nationalities on their way to the plateau: Italians, Portuguese, Spaniards, Germans, Frenchmen, Englishmen, Russians, Austrians, Belgians, Swiss, Danes, and Swedes. In 1897 the number of

Italians in the capital was greater than that of Brazilians by a two-to-one margin, an index that served as an unmistakable demonstration of the social change operating in the city.

The population of São Paulo increased substantially during the final phase of the empire and the first years of the republic. In 1890, São Paulo had a population of 64,934; and in 1893, 129,409. The social countenance of the city underwent a rapid metamorphosis with the addition of several nationalities to the Paulista social aggregate. There were inevitable clashes as men of various cultures and statuses came together, almost all in search of accommodation and assimilation into the new culture of their chosen homeland. [French journalist] Max Leclerc noted in 1890: "The city of São Paulo is developing with extraordinary speed for an interior city; there is nothing fictitious, however, in that growth fever." And as he saw Paulistas at work, he added: "We are persuaded to have faith in their industry."

Despite the hostilities and cultural clashes accompanying the arrival of the immigrants, we must recognize how much of a useful nature these settlers brought to São Paulo and to Brazil. How much technical knowhow they introduced, how much cultural blending, how much change in mentality, in standards of conduct. How much curiosity in regard to what was new accompanied them, how much reexamination of the cultural resistance of native peoples and of newcomers as well. How much assimilation took place and how much re-creation of values and concepts of life!

The city that had changed little for half a century, from the time of the proclamation of Independence until 1870, was now in a state of constant flux. Improvements similar to those in the imperial capital, Rio de Janeiro, were introduced, such as animal-drawn streetcar service, initiated on October 2, 1872, on tracks that departed from Rosário Square "at the Java Café," as Carl von Koseritz noted. Rail service to Santo Amaro was inaugurated in 1885, inasmuch as the Iron Rail Company of São Paulo had already constructed a line from Carmo Square toward Brás on July 1, 1877. Journalist von Koseritz felt in 1883 that "the city" possessed "abundant water" and pavement "throughout most of its extension, but only on the main streets does the pavement consist of paving blocks as in Rio. The other streets are still done with irregular stones and the sidewalks are made of large slabs of granite."

Along with the urban transfiguration itself, there was also a restructuring of police services since the government had been unable to suppress riots and other disorders. The urban milieu is typically characterized by an exaggerated individualism, by people eager to defend their own life-styles, and for that reason misunderstandings are common in the city and not always resolved peaceably.

During the government of President Laurindo de Brito, work on holy days and Sundays was forbidden, and the Urban Company, later called the Civic Guard, was organized with a fire department made up of twenty men. In 1882 the Capital Fire Department was formally constituted.

During the period from 1886 to 1940, there was a tendency for the city to expand into the intermediate zone between the center of town and the periphery. At the beginning of the present century, however, the center became more marked as an area of retail trade and high finance. At the same time, residential areas were encroaching into the intermediate zone. This zone, which blended into the center, would go through a period of transition during the first three decades of the twentieth century.

As development continued, one could discover many ecological aberrations in downtown São Paulo at the beginning of the century. In the block between Líbero Badaró and Formosa Streets certain functionally antagonistic elements continued to exist. "In front of the D'Aurea shoestore," noted Cícero Marques, there was "a butcher shop. A butcher shop on Líbero Badaró Street!" Just a bit farther was "the popular dentist, D. G. Salério. Next door to Salério, was a hardware store. Farther down, a women's Shooting Gallery where svelte young ladies competed in tourneys." Even farther down the street was the Little Market of São João (Post Office Square), "a shed with no aesthetics, dirty, foul, irritating to the pituitary with odors rising from decomposing debris." Thus, the downtown area was beginning to take shape, but it was not yet clearly defined. And it would, in fact, become defined only during the third decade of the present century when, after pushing out toward other areas that included residential clusters, wholesale businesses, open-air markets, and military posts, the city center would begin to subdivide into well-defined areas.

It will fall to the Piratiningan people to play an important role in the arduous task of redressing the country's lack of harmonious growth. "São Paulo built up during the last century," states Tristão de Athayde, "the largest concentration of capital in Brazil. Its mission in the twentieth century is to take the lead in a rational organization of its labor and an intelligent distribution of its accumulated capital. A period of accumulation should be followed by one of distribution." "The development of São Paulo," Professor C. A. de Carvalho Pinto affirms, "may not be interpreted as a privileged local phenomenon, for it has an objective of national transcendence—the implantation of an evolutionary process that will extend through the various regions of the country. The historical drive of *bandeirismo*, the outward push of the *bandeirantes* from São Paulo, is a permanent feature of the Brazilian dynamic. Formerly it was a matter of territorial integration. Now, in the twentieth century, it has to do with the integration of national unity. The new generation of Paulista leaders, businessmen, intellectuals, and workers has the duty to struggle against underdevelopment in order to share with their Brazilian brothers and sisters the conquest of a better and more worthy life for all our people."

Exhortations such as these, aimed at the Paulistas, urging them to fulfill an integrative destiny in Brazilian history, may appear high-sounding, but they are inspired by realistic expectations. The economically favorable geographic location of São Paulo, set in an area of Brazil where the mild climate favors agricultural development, situated as well at the gateway of the vast central plateau of the continent—a location that enables it to function as an important valve for the national economic system—has clearly provided benefits to the city throughout the historical process of Brazil. However, it is neither fitting nor even relevant to examine here the favorable conditions characteristic of the Paulista region in contrast with those of other parts of the country. Brazil in and of itself is already a continent that can be compared politically, as Júlio de Mesquita Filho affirmed in a memorable address, to an empire whose colonies find support within its own borders. Whatever the picture, the diagnosis of the regional disparities in the country, of the subdivision of Brazils within Brazil, and of the lack of integration of the regions, has already been made; the task now is to hasten the application of the recommended therapy.

10

Another São Paulo*

Carolina Maria de Jesus

Carolina Maria de Jesus was an unlikely Brazilian literary celebrity. Born out of wedlock in 1914 in the impoverished back country of Minas Gerais, at the age of 23 she migrated to the industrial metropolis of São Paulo in search of work. As her daughter narrates in this selection, she did not prosper. Eventually, she made a shack of pieces of lumber, cardboard, and tin in the favela (slum) of Canindé, where she supported herself and her three illegitimate children by collecting scrap paper and metal to sell. Despite her meager schooling, she had acquired a great love for writing from her mother and maternal grandfather, and she kept a diary for most of her years in the favela. When that diary was published in 1960 as Quarto de despejo *(Room of garbage), it sold ninety thousand copies within six months—at that time, the best-selling book in the history of Brazilian publishing. In short order, the volume was translated into thirteen languages and sold in forty foreign countries.[†]*

Such an improbable publishing phenomenon was largely a matter of timing. In the late 1950s and early 1960s, Brazil was riding a wave of optimism. Jucelino Kubitschek had won the presidency in 1956 on promises of more jobs, hospitals, and teachers, and rapid development of industry, agriculture, and infrastructure. Part of becoming modern—"fifty years' progress in five," promised Kubitschek's campaign slogan—involved a new spirit of openness and social responsibility. Brazil showed its brighter side to the world in cinema, music, sports, and in the

From *Child of the Dark: The Diary of Carolina Maria de Jesus*, trans. David St. Clair (New York: The New American Library, 1962), 20–22, 24, 34–35, 37–39, 41–42, 45–48, 52, 55–56, 61–62, 112, 124–25, 128–29, 137, 158. Oral histories courtesy Robert M. Levine.

*The editors express their gratitude to Timothy Henderson for his assistance in editing this chapter and preparing the introductory note.

†Biographical and much historical information has been culled from Robert M. Levine and José Carlos Sebe Bom Meihy, *The Life and Death of Carolina Maria de Jesus* (Albuquerque: University of New Mexico Press, forthcoming).

dazzlingly modern architecture of its brand new capital city of Brasília. Democratic harmony was showcased in official visits from Cuban revolutionaries Fidel Castro and Che Guevara, even as the regime invited in foreign capitalists with equal warmth. The publication of the diary of a black woman from São Paulo's slums seemed the last bit of evidence that Brazil was finally truly modern. It said, symbolically at least, that denying society's ills was a kind of political immaturity that Brazil had gone beyond.

Unfortunately, acknowledging society's ills was not the same as curing them. The Kubitschek regime, whose massive development projects plunged the country into debt and hyperinflation and paved the way for unprecedented corruption, did nothing to develop the country's archaic system of monocrop agriculture, which monopolized land and underemployed the landless. The rural poor, unable to survive and neutralized politically by a strong tradition of landowner hegemony, flocked to the great metropolises of Rio de Janeiro and São Paulo. But the safety valve of migration only redistributed the problem: the countryside continued in crisis, even as those who found no niche in the urban economy were often, like Carolina, obliged to live in improvised shanties in favelas like Canindé.*

Carolina's diary is a bleak, laconic, and often monotonous litany on the themes of hunger, violence, prostitution, delinquency, alcoholism, filth, and the perfidy of hypocritical politicians. It presents a landscape where the flamboyant facade of modernity only masks a sordid reality, the "cheap stockings underneath." In her stormy relations with fellow favelados, casual sexual liaisons, dutiful acceptance of drudgery, and frequent expressions of despair, Carolina seems almost a textbook example of what anthropologist Oscar Lewis described as "the culture of poverty," a state of anomie brought on by rapid social change. According to this view, as traditional societies break down, their members have no choice but to haunt the margins of the capitalist order, absorbing values and mores that constantly assure them of their own inferiority.†

Indeed, in many respects, Carolina's diary shows us the inconsistent and perjorative message of the dominant society as it is reflected and reshaped by the seemingly weak and alienated culture of the Canindé slum. She sings the praises of her own blackness and Afro-Brazilian heritage even while she disparages such traits in others. She heaps scorn on politicians and their unfeeling system even as she goes to great lengths to register to vote and acts as a champion of legality and order within the favela. She is full of praise for "the poor" in the abstract, yet finds her

---

*Elisa P. Reis, "Brazil: One Hundred Years of the Agrarian Question," *International Social Science Journal* 124 (May 1990): 160–61.

†Oscar Lewis, "The Culture of Poverty," in *Anthropological Essays* (New York: Random House, 1970), 67–80.

own impoverished neighbors intolerable and wishes only to distance herself from them.

Nevertheless, Lewis's "culture of poverty" remains a crude tool for analyzing the dynamic and complex reality found in Brazil's (and Latin America's) slums and shantytowns. Subsequent writers, for example, have drawn our attention to the emergence of voluntary associations and other coping strategies amid the great poverty. In the process, they have cautioned against the application of overwrought models and grand theories to a diverse urban landscape. *

Notorious for her headstrong and irascible temperament, Carolina Maria de Jesus steadfastly refused to be a representative of anything. No matter. Those on the left lauded her as a courageous survivor and chronicler of poverty but were put off by her reluctance to be a revolutionary. She made an equally poor ally for Cold War liberals, who wanted to see in Carolina's tale a sobering portent ("discontent breeds Communism," warned the book's English translator in his preface†*). But if leftists had to work hard to extract from her story some revolutionary hope, liberals were likewise hard-pressed to find in her a real revolutionary threat. Meanwhile, conservatives regarded her variously as a distasteful climber, a possible subversive, and a potential national embarrassment.*

Ultimately, like any intimate observer, Carolina was at once part of her surroundings and apart from them. She described herself as "the poet of the garbage dump, this idealist of the favela, a spectator." In giving us "the poor," including herself, as both reality and abstraction, she reminds us that slum dwellers are not hypothetical entities, but individuals in a specific time and place—in this case, the prosperous industrial city of São Paulo at a time when its favelas were only just coming into being. The dichotomies she depicts in her diary—the rural-urban imbalance, poverty amid affluence—have in fact become much more acute. In the late 1940s, when Carolina went to live in Canindé, there were fifty thousand favelados in the city; today there are at least four hundred thousand. Moreover, as her son remarks, their problems with drugs, pollution, violence, and crime are far more dire than what was faced in Carolina's day.

Sadly, Carolina was unable to sustain her overnight success, especially after the military takeover of 1964, when her books were removed from bookstores. Eventually, she lapsed back into poverty, though never as extreme as that of the favela. She died in 1977 and was buried in a paupers' cemetery. Today, in Brazil, she is largely forgotten.

---

*See, for example, Janice E. Perlman, *The Myth of Marginality: Urban Poverty and Politics in Rio de Janeiro* (Berkeley: University of California Press, 1976), and Nancy Cardia, "The Social Movement in Favelas in São Paulo: A Psycho-Social Approach" (Ph.D. diss., London School of Economics, 1990).

†St. Clair, translator's preface to *Child of the Dark*, 9.

The excerpts from Carolina's journals that follow for 1955, 1958, and 1959 are intended to be representative of the diary as a whole. We have interpolated with these selections excerpts from a series of interviews with her adult children—Vera Eunice de Jesús Lima and José Carlos de Jesús (Zé)—interviews that were carried out in 1991 and 1992, respectively. The children's remarks are included in the hopes of contributing some new details to Carolina's engrossing story and providing another perspective on her complex personality.

Vera

"Like many poor people from northern Brazil, my mother went to the big city to better her life. It was the only way.

"Well, it's clear that her first months in São Paulo were even more difficult. She didn't know anyone; she had never left her small town; and now she had gone right to one of the largest metropolises in the hemisphere. But in time, living virtually without food, things began to improve. She got work as a maid, washing the floor in a restaurant, cleaning dishes, and if you do well enough the boss asks you to come back. In this way, things improved for her. Suddenly, even rich families were willing to hire her!

"My mother had her good moments in those days. She had to work a good deal but on her breaks she could read and write. And there's more: my mother began to have boyfriends! Her preferences were odd: she didn't like to be involved with [native born] Brazilians, especially Bahians. And if he was black, get out! She wouldn't go near Bahians or blacks, even as friends.

"It was like that in the *favela*. We didn't have any better financial conditions than the others but few people got along with her. With men she was involved with, the situation was worse. Not just anyone would do: he had to be a gringo!

"Do you know that each child had a different father? It was because of these romances that she began to lose her jobs with the families who had hired her. They didn't like it when she went out at night during the week; she came in at all hours. When she became pregnant, then, it was the last straw. The families liked her but they preferred to hire single women, childless. The well-off people don't want the expense. It's incredible, but it is reality.

"Only my mother didn't accept such things. In no way! She left jobs before she was fired from them. If her employers grumbled, she found another job and left right away. Her life was hers! But with children, things were looking bad for her. One small child, a second, and my mother no longer gets anything. She ends up going to the *favela*.

"The *favela* is the first thing that I remember. It was where I was born. Everything was dirty, filthy, and every shack was overcrowded. During the night there always was some kind of commotion outside."

Carolina, 1955

July 18 I got up at 7. Happy and content. Weariness would be here soon enough. I went to the junk dealer and received sixty *cruzeiros*. I passed by Arnaldo, bought bread, milk, paid what I owed him, and still had enough to buy Vera some chocolate. I returned to a Hell. I opened the door and threw the children outside. Dona Rosa, as soon as she saw my boy José Carlos, started to fight with him. She didn't want the boy to come near her shack. She ran out with a stick to hit him. A woman of 48 years fighting with a child! At times, after I leave, she comes to my window and throws a filled chamber pot onto the children. When I return I find the pillows dirty and the children fetid. She hates me. She says that the handsome and distinguished men prefer me and that I make more money than she does. The only thing that does not exist in the *favela* is friendship.

My kids are not kept alive by the church's bread. I take on all kinds of work to keep them. And those women have to beg or even steal. At night when they are begging I peacefully sit in my shack listening to Viennese waltzes. While their husbands break the boards of the shack, I and my children sleep peacefully. I don't envy the married women of the *favelas* who lead lives like Indian slaves.

I went to collect paper and stayed away from the house an hour. When I returned I saw several people at the river bank. There was a man unconscious from alcohol and the worthless men of the *favela* were cleaning out his pockets. They stole his money and tore up his documents. It is 5 P.M. Now Senhor Heitor turns on the light. And I, I have to wash the children so they can go to bed, for I have to go out. I need money to pay the light bill. That's the way it is here. Person doesn't use the lights but must pay for them. I left and went to collect paper.

July 19 In the *favelas* children of 15 stay out as late as they want. They mess around with prostitutes and listen to their adventures. There are those who work and those who just drift. The older people work. It's the younger ones who refuse to work. They have their mothers who pick up fruits and vegetables that fall from the street markets. They have the churches who give them bread. They have San Francisco Church that once a month gives away necessities like coffee and soap.

They go to the fish market, pick up fish heads, anything they can find. They eat anything. They must have stomachs of reinforced concrete.

Sometimes I turn on the radio and dance with the children; we pretend we're boxing. Today I bought candy for them. I gave each one a piece and felt them looking at me a bit differently. My João said: "What a good mother!"

July 20 At this moment I can't give my children a decent house to live in, so I try to give them decent food.

They finished breakfast and I washed the dishes. Then I went to wash clothes. I don't have a man at home. There is just me and my children, so I can't relax. My dream is to be very clean, to wear expensive clothes and live in a comfortable house, but it's not possible. I am not unhappy with the work I do. I am used to being dirty. What disgusts me is that I must live in a *favela*.

Vera

"Soon after I was born, during the 1950s, my mother began to write her diary. During her sleepless nights she would take a used notebook and write down things that had happened. She wrote about the people in the *favela*, about the police, who had been fighting, who died.

"Audálio Dantas, a journalist, discovered my mother. He entered our lives at the end of the decade of the 1950s. Audálio had gone to the opening of a little park in the *favela*; but it had been taken over by troublemakers and vagrants, who set out to break the swings and other things placed there before the children could even play there once! My mother called the police, and the press found out, and Audálio showed up. The bums were in the park, with my mother on the other side of the fence shouting loudly: 'I'm going to put you in my book!'

"This is what struck the attention of the reporter. He asked to read the notebooks, picked out the most legible pages among her pages and pages of diary notations, novels, and poems among her big collection of paper, and took them away to read. He came back later and told my mother that a newspaper would help her publish her diary."

Carolina, 1958

May 15 On the nights they have a party they don't let anybody sleep. The neighbors in the brick houses nearby have signed a petition to get rid of the *favelados*. But they won't get their way. The neighbors in the brick houses say: "The politicans protect the *favelados*."

Who protects us are the public and the Order of St. Vincent Church. The politicians only show up here during election campaigns. Senhor Candido Sampaio, when he was city councilman in 1953, spent his Sundays here in the *favela*. He was so nice. He drank our coffee, drinking right out of our cups. He made us laugh with his jokes. He played with our children. He left a good impression here and when he was candidate for state deputy, he won. But the Chamber of Deputies didn't do one thing for the *favelados*. He doesn't visit us any more.

I classify São Paulo this way: The Governor's Palace is the living room. The mayor's office is the dining room and the city is the garden. And the *favela* is the backyard where they throw the garbage.

The night is warm. The sky is peppered with stars. I have the crazy desire to cut a piece of the sky to make a dress.

Zé

"Exactly when we moved to Canindé, the *favelas* were appearing in the city. My mother observed this, and wrote about it. Obviously, there always was poverty, but the *favelas* were something new. The person who 'institutionalized' the *favelas* was the former mayor of São Paulo, Abrão Ribeiro. He had invited the president of Portugal to the city and because of that São Paulo had to be cleaned up. Construction projects were undertaken, the holes in the roads paved, garbage removed. The mayor had the police get all the beggars off the streets. There wasn't one left! They just gave the people some wood and ordered them to build the shacks. In the end he moved everyone who was homeless to the outskirts of the city: the beggars, the criminals, the prostitutes. At the edge of the Tietê River, when the river was still halfway clean, you know."

Vera

"What did he do? He ordered everything cleaned; he repaired the public squares, they filled in the holes in the streets, and ended up sending the police to get rid of the beggars! One by one, they took them off the street and stuck them on vacant pieces of land, like Canindé was. The poor people couldn't sleep in the street without waking up in the police station; there it was worse: bad treatment, assaults. Whether men or women or even old people, anyone who was poor, so these people built shacks with wood from crates, cardboard, old cans, and the *favelas* began to grow.

"Every month new families arrived: father, mother, children. They found the least undesirable spot they could find and suddenly another shack appeared; from night to day the population grew. One hovel smaller than the next and filled with more people. I still remember these images, a little place to live, with floors of beaten earth, a stick of furniture in the corner, a table, the rest crates and tin. From this came the name *Quarto de despejo* (The garbage room), my mother's most famous book. The garbage room because it was the place to throw the things no one wanted.

Canindé *favela* was like this, a space to forget the people who weren't worth anything anymore."

Zé

"My mother even 'thanked' the mayor in a poem that was published in the paper:

> I admire Abrão Ribeiro
> He mixed the people together
> Like pigs in a pigsty."

Carolina

May 19 There have been people who visited us and said: "Only pigs could live in a place like this. This is the pigsty of São Paulo."

I'm starting to lose my interest in life. It's beginning to revolt me and my revulsion is just.

I washed the floor because I'm expecting a visit from a future deputy and he wants me to make some speeches for him. He says he wants to know the *favelas* and if he is elected he's going to abolish them.

The sky was the color of indigo, and I understood that I adore my Brazil. My glance went over to the trees that are planted at the beginning of Pedro Vicente Street. The leaves moved by themselves. I thought: they are applauding my gesture of love to my country. I went on looking for paper. Vera was smiling and I thought of Casemiro de Abreu, the Brazilian poet who said: "Laugh, child. Life is beautiful." Life was good in that era. Because now in this era it's necessary to say: "Cry, child. Life is bitter."

I went on so preoccupied that I didn't even notice the gardens of the city. It's the season for white flowers, the predominating color. And in the month of May the altars must be adorned with white flowers. We must thank God or Nature, who gave us the stars that adorn the sky, for the flowers that adorn the parks and the fields and the forests.

At 8:30 that night I was in the *favela* breathing the smell of excrement mixed with the rotten earth. When I am in the city I have the impression that I am in a living room with crystal chandeliers, rugs of velvet, and satin cushions. And when I'm in the *favela* I have the impression that I'm a useless object, destined to be forever in a garbage dump.

May 20 The morning was damp and foggy. The sun was rising but its heat didn't chase away the cold.

I opened the window and watched the women passing by with their coats discolored and worn by time. It won't be long until these coats, which they got from others, and which should be in a museum, will be replaced by others. The politicians must give us things. That includes me too, because I'm also a *favelado*. I'm one of the discarded. I'm in the garbage dump, and those in the garbage dump either burn themselves or throw themselves into ruin.

The women that I see passing are going to church begging for bread for their children. Brother Luiz gives it to them while their husbands remain home under the blankets. Some because they can't find jobs. Others because they are sick. Others because they are drunk.

Sometimes families move into the *favela* with children. In the beginning they are educated, friendly. Days later they use foul language, are mean and quarrelsome. They are diamonds turned to lead. They are transformed from objects that were in the living room to objects banished to the garbage dump.

For me the world instead of evolving is turning primitive. Those who don't know hunger will say: "Whoever wrote this is crazy." But who has gone hungry can say: "Well, Dona Carolina. The basic necessities must be within reach of everyone."

May 21 Who must be a leader is he who has the ability. He who has pity and friendship for the people. Those who govern our country are those who have money, who don't know what hunger is, or pain or poverty. If the majority revolt, what can the minority do? I am on the side of the poor, who are an arm. An undernourished arm. We must free the country of the profiteering politicians.

Yesterday I ate macaroni from the garbage with fear of death, because in 1953 I sold scrap over there in Zinho. There was a pretty little black boy. He also went to sell scrap in Zinho. One day I was collecting scrap when I stopped at Bom Jardim Avenue. Someone had thrown meat into the garbage, and he was picking out the pieces. He told me: "Take some, Carolina. It's still fit to eat."

He gave me some, and so as not to hurt his feelings, I accepted. I tried to convince him not to eat that meat, or the hard bread gnawed by the rats. He told me no, because it was two days since he had eaten. He made a fire and roasted the meat. His hunger was so great that he couldn't wait for the meat to cook. He heated it and ate. So as not to remember that scene, I left thinking: I'm going to pretend I wasn't there. This can't be real in a rich country like mine. I was disgusted with the Social Service that had been created to readjust the maladjusted, but took no notice of us marginal people. I sold the scrap at Zinho and returned to São Paulo's backyard, the *favela*.

The next day I found that little black boy dead. His toes were spread apart. The space must have been eight inches between them. He had blown up as if made out of rubber. His toes looked like a fan. He had no documents. He was buried like any other "Joe." Nobody tried to find out his name. The marginal people don't have names.

Zé

"Did you ever see people starve to death? Well, I did, and I saw people die while they were eating, eating rotten stuff! They died poisoned. People know that the food's rotten but hunger is stronger than reason. So then the guy doesn't have any notion he can die. He doesn't have any notion about anything! At least he dies with his belly full. I just think that's the end of the road!"

Carolina

May 22 The children eat a lot of bread. They like soft bread but when they don't have it, they eat hard bread.

Hard is the bread that we eat. Hard is the bed on which we sleep. Hard is the life of the *favelado*.

Oh, São Paulo! A queen that vainly shows her skyscrapers that are her crown of gold. All dressed up in velvet and silk but with cheap stockings underneath—the *favela*.

May 27 It seems that the slaughterhouse threw kerosene on their garbage dump so the *favelados* would not look for meat to eat. I didn't have any breakfast and walked around half dizzy. The daze of hunger is worse than that of alcohol. The daze of alcohol makes us sing but the one of hunger makes us shake. I know how horrible it is to have only air in the stomach.

The Radio Patrol arrived. They came to take the two Negro boys who had broken into the power station. Four and six years old. It's easy to see that they are of the *favela*. *Favela* children are the most ragged children in the city. What they can find in the streets they eat. Banana peels, melon rind, and even pineapple husks. Anything that is too tough to chew, they grind.

May 30 More new people arrived in the *favela*. They are shabby and walk bent over with their eyes on the ground as if doing penance for their misfortune of living in an ugly place. A place where you can't plant one flower to breathe its perfume. To listen to the buzz of the bees or watch a hummingbird caressing the flower with his fragile beak. The only perfume that comes from the *favela* is from rotting mud, excrement, and whiskey.

May 31 Saturday—a day that always drives me crazy because I have to arrange for something to eat for both Saturday and Sunday. I made breakfast using the bread that I got yesterday. I put beans on the fire.

When I was washing the beans I thought: today I feel like Society—I'm going to cook beans! It seemed like a dream.

I got some bananas and manioc roots at a shop on Guaporé Street. When I was returning to the *favela*, a lady at 728 Cruzeiro do Sul Avenue asked me to throw a dead dog into the Tieté and she would give me five *cruzeiros*. I left Vera with her and went. The dog was inside a bag. The woman stood watching my "*paulistana*" steps. That means walking fast. When I returned she gave me six *cruzeiros*. When I received the money I thought: now I've got enough to buy some soap.

I arrived in the *favela*; I don't think I can say I arrived at my house. A house is a house. A shack is a shack. The shack, as much interior as exterior, was dirty. That mess disgusts me. I stared at the yard. The rotting garbage was stinking. Only on Sundays do I have time to clean.

I asked a woman that I saw for the first time: "Are you living here?" [She replied:] "I am, but pretend I'm not, because I can't stand the place. This is a place for pigs. But if they put pigs in here they would complain and go on strike. I always heard people talk of the *favela* but I never dreamed it would be a place as loathsome as this. Only God has pity on us."

June 8 All I know is, whatever is cursed, the *favelado* gets. When we moved into the *favela* we went to ask for water from the brick houses. Dona Ida Cardoso gave us water. Thirteen times she gave us water. She told us she'd only give us water on weekdays; on Sunday she wanted to sleep late. The *favelado* is not a donkey but he was vaccinated with donkey's blood. One day they went to get water and didn't find the public spigot turned on. So they formed a line at the door of Dona Ida and everybody shouted: "I want water for the baby's bottle. My God, what are we going to do without water?"

They went to other houses, beating on the doors. Nobody answered. Nobody showed up to wait on them, so as not to listen to: "Could you give us a little water?" I carried water from Guaporé Street from the place where I sell paper. Others carried water from the Social Service in bottles.

One Tuesday afternoon Dona Ida's mother-in-law was sitting, resting, and she said: "Somebody should send a flood to wipe away the *favela* and kill those nuisances. There are times when I'm furious with God for putting poor people on earth. All they do is annoy others."

Zé

"Society discriminated against slum people much more in the 1950s. Walking into a bank, a store, even a school was more difficult. You had to have money, because appearance was paramount in those places. On the other hand, poor people were not feared, as they are today. Any ragged kid in the street is seen as a thief. We were mischievous, not criminals; we represented no threat to society. People gave charity to the less fortunate without being afraid, and an unemployed father was respected by upper class people. We made the rounds of houses asking for food, but it wasn't just food they would give us. No! They'd give food, clothes, an old bicycle, used toys. I never heard of people talking about kids who stole, just a little fruit, not very much, just kid things. And people who lived in the slums weren't as poor as they are now."

Carolina

June 5 I have now observed our politicians. To watch them I went to Congress, a branch of Purgatory, for it's the head office of the Social Service, in the Governor's Palace. What I saw there made me gnash my teeth. I saw the poor go out crying. The tears of the poor stir the poets. They don't move the poets of the living room, but they do move the poet of the garbage dump, this idealist of the *favela*, a spectator who sees and notes the tragedies that the politicans inflict on the people.

June 9 I was lying down when I heard children's voices shouting they were showing a free movie in the street. I didn't believe what I heard and decided to go and see. It was the health department. They came to show a film to the *favelados* on how snails transmit anemic disease. They told us not to use the river water. That young snails grow up in that water. Even the water, instead of helping us, it contaminates us. Not even the air we breathe is pure, because they throw garbage here in the *favela*.

They asked the *favelados* to build bathrooms!

June 16 I wrote plays and showed them to the directors of circuses. They told me: "It's a shame you're black."

They were forgetting that I adore my black skin and my kinky hair. The Negro hair is more educated than the white man's hair. Because with Negro hair, where you put it, it stays. It's obedient. The hair of the white, just give one quick movement, and it's out of place. It won't obey. If reincarnation exists I want to come back black.

The white man says he is superior. But what superiority does he show? If the Negro drinks *pinga*, the white drinks. The sickness that hits the black hits the white. If the white feels hunger, so does the Negro. Nature hasn't picked any favorites.

November 1 I found a sack of corn flour in the garbage and brought it home for the pig. I am so used to garbage cans that I don't know how to pass one without having to see what is inside.

Today I'm going out to look for paper but I know I'm not going to find anything. There is an old man who is in my territory.

Yesterday I read that fable about the frog and the cow. I feel that I am a frog. I want to swell up until I am the same size as the cow.

I see that the people are still thinking that we must revolt against the price of necessities and not just attack the transportation company. Dr. Adhemar told the newspapers that it was with an ache in his heart that he signed the raise agreement [to increase bus fares]. Someone said: "Adhemar is mistaken. He doesn't have a heart." [And:] "If the cost of living keeps on rising until 1960, we're going to have a revolution!"

December 25 XMAS DAY. João came in saying that he had a stomach ache. I knew what it was for he had eaten a rotten melon. Today they threw a truckload of melons near the river.

I don't know why it is that these senseless businessmen come to throw their rotted products here near the *favela*, for the children to see and eat.

In my opinion the merchants of São Paulo are playing with the people just like Caesar when he tortured the Christians. But the Caesars of today are worse than the Caesar of the past. The others were punished for their faith. And we, for our hunger!

In that era, those who didn't want to die had to stop loving Christ.

But we cannot stop loving eating.

Vera

"Most of the things I remember about the *favela*—the garbage, the violence, the hunger—still are nightmares for me. That is how I see the *favela*, as a nightmare following me. I still remember that school was the only source of food for us during the day. We did have food, but at least once a week we went without.

"These days I still awake sweaty during the middle of the night. For a child, especially, the *favela* experience is traumatic! I never have been able to blot it out. Some nights I have nightmares; I dream that I have returned to that suffering, chaos, and misery. This is the reason that I still feel sorry for people who live in *favelas*. If I you haven't lived in one, you can't imagine what it is like."

Carolina, 1959

January 4 In the old days I sang. Now, I've stopped singing, because the happiness has given way to a sadness that ages the heart. Every day another poor creature shows up here in the *favela*. Ireno is a poor creature with anemia. He is looking for his wife. His wife doesn't want him. He told me that his mother-in-law provoked his wife against him. Now he is in his brother's house. He spent a few days in his sister's house, but came back. He said they were throwing hints at him because of the food.

Ireno says that he is unhappy with life. Because even with health life is bitter.

January 5 It's raining. I am almost crazy with the dripping on the beds, because the roof is covered with cardboard and the cardboard is rotten. The water is rising and invading the yards of the *favelados*.

January 6 I got out of bed at 4 A.M., turned on the radio, and went for water. What torture it is to walk in water in the morning. And I catch cold so easily! But life is like that. Men are leaving for work. They are carrying their shoes and socks in their hands. Mothers keep the children inside the house. They get restless because they want to go out and play in the water. People with a sense of humor say that the *favela* is a sailors' city. Others say it is the São Paulo Venice.

January 7 Today I fixed rice and beans and fried eggs. What happiness. Reading this you are going to think Brazil doesn't have anything to eat. We have. It's just that the prices are so impossible that we can't buy it. We have dried fish in the shops that waits for years and years for purchasers. The flies make the fish filthy. Then the fish rots and the clerks throw it in the garbage and throw acid on it so the poor won't pick it up and eat it. My children have never eaten dried fish. They beg me: "Buy it, Mother!"

But buy it—how? At 180 *cruzeiros* a kilo? I hope, if God helps me, that before I die I'll be able to buy some dried fish for them.

April 29 Today I am out of sorts. What saddens me is the suicide of Senhor Tomás. The poor man. He killed himself because he was tired of suffering from the cost of living.

When I find something in the garbage that I can eat, I eat it. I don't have the courage to kill myself. And I refuse to die of hunger!

I stopped writing the diary because I got discouraged. And I didn't have time.

May 1 I got out of bed at 4 A.M. I washed the dishes and went to get water. There was no line. I don't have a radio so I can't listen to the parade. Today is Labor Day.

May 2 Yesterday I bought sugar and bananas. My children ate a banana with sugar because I didn't have any lard to cook food. I thought of Senhor Tomás who committed suicide. But if all the poor in Brazil decided to kill themselves because they were hungry, nobody would be left alive.

Vera

"With the money the publisher, Francisco Alves, deposited for my mother, Audálio bought a brick house for us. It was a mansion for someone from the *favela*, with running water, a refrigerator—rich things! Even more delicious was the neighborhood: Santana, an upper-class district! The sidewalks seemed to shine with cleanliness. There were big houses there, the families of important people, new cars; I even remember about the school we attended. The students were clean and wore new shoes. They brought lunches from home, [and there were] chairs, pencils, chalk, erasers.

"The beginning was a dream but after a few months the four of us were truly fishes out of water. The house felt to us like a prison! The neighbors blamed us for things and complained. In the *favela* it was easier; no one bothered about the poverty of the others. In Santana we learned about prejudice.

"My mother was unable to stand seeing a beggar in the street asking for money, cold, in the rain. She didn't accept that. The rich people didn't understand this; they didn't know what it was to be cold and wet. They go to restaurants, ask for lots of food, and throw out what they don't eat. If she saw someone in the street having trouble, she would stop everything to take that poor person into our house. Our house! My mother took everyone in. The result was that the neighbors complained, and the reporters wrote about it in the papers. In Santana we didn't have peace in life.

"We had a good deal of bad luck then. The house was filling up with beggars; the police and the reporters didn't leave us in peace. My brothers were often separated from my mother because of her trips. In the *favela* we had always stayed together. This was weakening our sense of being a family. My mother became more impatient. Now she never had privacy. Even on Sundays people would come asking for help: a job, a truck, food, a bus ticket, get a relative out of jail, asking her to do everything. People came from far away, very far away! They arrived in the early morning and lined up to ask for things She became known as the Favela Queen. Audálio couldn't stand her extravagances and complained, with reason. She was spending our money on others. If she had it, my mother spent it."

Zé

"I had a regular childhood, just like any other slum kid in São Paulo. At that time, the old *favelas* were miserable but there was solidarity among their residents. They were not as violent or as marginal as they are today. In Canindé, if someone got sick, the neighbors would go to our shack to lend money, and they even loaned money to buy medicine. My mom was like that, too. This was a great difference. Carolina, my mom, acted like a security guard in the *favela*. If there were fights in the middle of the night, a man beating his wife, she would send my brother João to take care of us and then leave to call the police. She would file a complaint and file the papers. The slums used to be like that: one needs something and the other helps, understand? I think that thirty years ago there was a lot more solidarity among the poor than among the rich.

"Life was healthier in the *favelas* in those days. Boy, was it! We'd go to school, have a snack in the afternoon, and then come back. My friends and I would go out to 'run the market' [*correr feira*]. This is what all the little slum kids did, grabbing fruit on the sly, stealing sweets, and, on top of everything, earning tips carrying packages. We'd build a little car out of a box and ball bearings to carry the groceries or we'd pick up boards and leftovers to sell later. We'd end up spending the day out of the house. My mom would [be] picking up refuse with Vera on her back and João and I would take off around here. Everything would end up in a soccer game, naturally.

"What I liked least was going to school. They did have good quality public schools with competent teachers, but people who lived in the slums suffered all kinds of prejudice when they went to school. But children played without danger, more jobs were available, you could feed your children.

"Because of this I believe that *Quarto de despejo* today is a book that is more and more relevant. I wish it weren't, but it is! It would be better if things had been different, but Brazil preferred to silence my mother's message to opening its eyes. Now what we see out of the window is a sea of garbage [and] misery on the outskirts of the cities, misery on the bus, misery in downtown, misery, misery, misery!"

Carolina

August 13 What I have noticed is that nobody likes the *favela*, but they need it. I looked at the dread stamped on the faces of the *favelados*.

11

Mexico's Megalopolis[*]

Jonathan Kandell

When La Capital, *Jonathan Kandell's "biography of Mexico City," appeared in 1988, one reviewer took the author to task for approaching his subject with a "reporter's instincts"—that is, for seeking "balance," a "human touch," and a "ray of hope amid the despair." "Maybe it is too late," the critic lamented, "to do anything other than watch the biggest city in the world slowly poison itself."[†]*

Of course, balance and optimism are not normally pejorative terms. But such are the feelings stirred up by Kandell's subject that the reporter/historian was attacked merely for hinting at the possibility of a silver lining. To its detractors (and even to a few admirers), Mexico City is a nightmare, a monster out of control. It is home to some twenty million people, nearly a quarter of the country's population. An average square kilometer contains 5,494 human beings, the highest demographic density of any city in the world.[‡] And it just keeps growing. According to experts, the city should have a population between twenty-six and thirty million by the year 2000, and by the year 2060 its resource requirements will be twice what they are today, even if current decentralization programs enjoy success beyond anyone's wildest expectations.[§] The city is also the scene of an unprecedented ecological catastrophe, both natural and human in origin, that has driven venerable experts to despair while long-time residents take it all in stride, reading the day's air pollution index in the same perfunctory way that other people glance at the weather forecast. As if that were not enough, Mexico City is also the seat of a ruling

From *La Capital: The Biography of Mexico City* (New York: Henry Holt and Company, 1988), 485–87, 506–8, 528–29, 551, 554–66, 568–75.

[*]The editors express their gratitude to Timothy Henderson for his assistance in editing this chapter and preparing the introductory note.

[†]David Frum, "Ruin," *Commentary* 87, no. 4 (April 1989): 68–70.

[‡]Alberto Navarrete Jiménez, "México, el décimo primer país más poblado del mundo," *El Nacional*, July 28, 1990.

[§]Sara Lovera, "Tendrá el DF 26 millones de habitantes en el año 2 mil," *La Jornada*, March 19, 1992.

party that, in its overcentralization, corruption, authoritarian pretensions, and frequent ineptitude, seems nothing less than the political reflection of that unwieldy urban behemoth.

Mexico City has been the center of political, economic, and cultural life in the country since long before the arrival of the Spaniards (see the Soustelle selection in Chapter 2). But the systematic concentration of power, resources, and population is largely the consequence of a deliberate development strategy that grew out of the conjunction of internal conflicts and global trends. The Mexican Revolution of 1910–1920 was a massive and violent social upheaval. Its immediate cause was a political crisis occasioned by the end of thirty-four years of dictatorial rule. Its more profound inspiration was the anger of the rural poor at abysmal and worsening conditions in the countryside. Popular outcry led to an ambitious program of agrarian reform that effectively ended the centuries-long dominance of the land-hungry hacienda. But no sooner had the rural poor been granted land than economic priorities shifted and their land began losing its worth. World War II made essential manufactured imports scarce and gave the developing world incentive to replace imports with domestically produced goods. The mammoth one-party government born of the revolution—the Institutional Revolutionary Party, or PRI in its Spanish acronym—not only constituted itself as the sole conduit and terminus for popular demands but also awarded itself unprecedented power in economic decision making. Native industrial enterprises were shielded from foreign competition through import duties and licensing. The "economic miracle" spawned by this initiative was impressive indeed, earning praise from all quarters and the emulation of other poor countries. Most of that miracle was centered squarely in Mexico City, the economy's engine; as the countryside became a low priority for policymakers, rural people began flocking to the capital at the rate of hundreds per day.

And they kept coming, even after it became apparent that the city's industry could only absorb a fraction of them. As Kandell demonstrates in his portrait of one of those migrants, Roberto Jara, the pull of industry was not their only incentive. Nor even was it that pull combined with the push of rural poverty. There were subjective factors at work, too. The lure of the city had become part of the culture. Many equated the big city with civilization, and the government helped to confirm that prejudice by making it the epicenter of Mexico's intellectual and cultural universe. Not only was it the site of the country's only prestigious universities, but it also seemed that nearly all literate life was centered there. By the early 1980s, for example, only twelve of the country's thirty-one states could boast even a small public library. For people like Roberto Jara, the city*

*Carlos Monsiváis, " 'Just Over That Hill': Notes on Centralism and Regional Cultures," in Eric Van Young, ed., *Mexico's Regions: Comparative History and Development* (San Diego: Center for U.S.-Mexican Studies, 1992), 248.

meant getting ahead in life, a challenge which only the incorrigibly lazy and provincial would shirk.

Jonathan Kandell, who covered Latin America for the New York Times *before becoming assistant foreign editor for the* Wall Street Journal, *grew up in Mexico City. In the sections of his hefty book excerpted here, he gives the reader a lively tour of the Federal District since the 1940s, years during which it grew from a charming city of 1.5 million souls to a monstrous megalopolis of nearly 20 million. He employs personal portraits and dramatic episodes to elucidate the city—its charms as well as its horrors. Indeed, in spite of everything, the city does continue to have its charms. Readers will need to decide for themselves if it deserves the qualified admiration of Kandell or the unmitigated disgust of some of his critics. Ironically and paradoxically, it probably deserves both.*

[D uring its] golden decades (1940–1970) the Mexican capital enjoyed world renown as a pulsating, modern metropolis that managed to preserve rich remnants of its colonial and Indian heritage. Factories, commerce, and service jobs sucked in hordes of rural migrants who swelled Mexico City's population from 1.5 million inhabitants in 1940 to 8.5 million in 1970. Many of the wealthier residents retreated to the semirustic neighborhoods on the southern outskirts, where industrial fumes and traffic exhaust had not yet poisoned the crystalline skies nor obscured the snow-wreathed volcanoes and purple mountains encircling the Valley of Mexico. In communities like San Angel, Mixcoac, and Coyoacán, nostalgia could be indulged without foregoing the amenities of modern life. Asphalt dissolved into cobblestone streets where the clip-clop of horseshoes and the squeak of peddlers' carts were as familiar as the rumble of automobile tires. As they had for centuries, artisans and vendors, each with their patented musical ditty or whistle, hawked their wares from house to house: woolen rugs and serapes with brightly woven Indian designs; parrots, parakeets, and exotic songbirds; honeycakes, preserves, and gelatins; charcoal-singed corn-on-the-cob sprinkled with cheese; slices of succulent *jícama* and radish smeared with lemon juice and chili. Sprawled over leafy plazas a short walk from most residences were the Indian marketplaces offering a cornucopia of vegetables, fruit, flowers, tortillas hot off the griddle, live chickens, and freshly laid eggs.

These vestiges of a slower-paced traditional life, however, were being overwhelmed by Americanization. The tourist trade emerged as the largest industry in Mexico and spearheaded an American economic and cultural invasion. Ciudad Satélite, on the northwest outskirts of Mexico City, grew into a huge, middle-class suburb of cookie-mold houses patterned after postwar communities in southern California and Long Island. Throughout the capital, fast-food outlets serving hamburgers, hot dogs, and pizza vied with taco stands. Baseball crowds rivaled those at bullfights and soccer matches. Supermarkets stocked their shelves with Kellogg's Rice Krispies, Campbell's soups, Coca-Cola, Heinz catsup, and Van Camp's Boston baked beans. Neon signs flashed a lexicon of U.S. corporate names: Ford, General Motors, Chrysler, Zenith, General Electric. Blue jeans became the uniform of the younger generation, rich and poor. A hit parade of rock 'n' roll competed with Mexican *corridos* on the radio. "Ozzie and Harriet," "Leave It to Beaver," "Mannix," "Dragnet," "The Lone Ranger," and many other American television series had a loyal following. Hollywood relegated Mexican films to the more decrepit movie houses. Even Christmas became Americanized: in department stores, adoring youngsters sat on the lap of a red-coated, white-bearded Santa Claus; at home, stockings were hung over the fireplace, and gifts were piled under fir trees festooned with pulsing lights and cotton snow fluffs. Only the more tradition-bound families continued to stage *posadas*, the Nativity processions commemorating the nine-day journey by Mary and Joseph from Nazareth to Bethlehem.

This architectural, economic, and cultural metamorphosis of Mexico City was presaged by an eventful shift in political power. The provincial revolutionary generals ceded the government to an urban middle-class elite. Flocking to the metropolis for law degrees, which became their passports into the high bureaucracy, this new generation of politicians made the city their permanent residence, the locus of their entire careers, and the prism that refracted their vision of the rest of the country.

Revolutionary slogans continued to exalt the ideals of land for the rural dispossessed, living wages for the proletariat, and a determinant voice for the state in economic affairs. But the rhetoric masked a growing alliance between politicians and Mexico City-based entrepreneurs, who shared the conviction that wealth had to be amassed before it could be distributed. And so, Mexico embarked on an era of unbalanced growth. Explosive urbanization, particularly in Mexico City, contrasted with the torpor of the countryside. Rampant consumerism among the more affluent classes coexisted with social neglect of the disadvantaged majority. Corruption greased the wheels of commerce and industry, but also diverted potential benefits for the poor. Peasant and labor organizations were effectively excluded from policymaking and the upper rungs of politics.

Mexico City was a beacon for the ambitious poor. Between 1940 and 1970 more than four million people left their homes in the countryside to establish themselves in the capital. They were part of a massive migration that transformed Mexico into a nation with an urbanized majority as early as 1960. The migrants were expelled from the countryside by prolonged droughts, the inability of ejidos [communal farms] to sustain families, the mechanization of private farms, and the growing population resulting from health care improvements that cut mortality rates of infants and adults. Taken together, these factors led to a spectacular 74 percent increase in the number of landless agrarian workers between 1940 and 1960.

Besides being pushed out of agriculture, the migrants were pulled toward Mexico City by the communications revolution—radio, films, and newspapers reaching into the most isolated rural zones—that evoked an advanced, remunerative, and exciting way of life as an alternative to the static poverty of the countryside. This vision was both a reality and a mirage. By 1960 the average family income in the capital exceeded by 185 percent the average for the nation as a whole. Jobs were more plentiful, and there was a greater possibility for wives and children to supplement the earnings of male heads of households. The metropolis also offered more access to running water, electricity, cooking fuel, medical clinics, schools, movies, sports events, and other entertainment. But these advantages were vitiated by economic inequalities that were greater in Mexico City than in the rest of the country.

The deficiencies of life in the metropolis began with housing. In the 1940s and 1950s most migrants settled first in the old downtown tenements abandoned generations before by the middle class. Over a third of the population dwelled in these *vecindades*, many of them constructed during the Porfiriato [1876–1910]. In *The Children of Sánchez[: Autobiography of a Mexican Family* (1961)], the classic study of Mexico City's poor during the 1950s, Oscar Lewis evoked a typical *vecindad*. It was located in Tepito, a tough neighborhood a ten-minute walk north of the Zócalo [the city's central plaza]. This warren of rutted streets and dusty alleys enclosed small factories and warehouses, tiny shops, public baths, run-down cinemas, overcrowded schools, foul-smelling saloons and *pulquerías*, wooden stands selling soups and tacos, and the open-air thieves' market where stolen and used goods could be purchased at a bargain price. Once the lair of the underworld, Tepito was now populated mainly by artisans, vendors, factory laborers, unskilled workers, waiters, office clerks, messengers, and porters. The average income per capita was somewhat less than $20 per month.

Casa Grande, the *vecindad* described by Lewis, sprawled over an entire square block and housed seven hundred people in its two-storey tenements. The two narrow entrances to the *vecindad*'s alleyway were guarded by ceramic statues of the Virgin Mary and high gates which were locked at night. Residents returning home in the late evening had to pay the janitor a small toll to have the gates unlocked. In the daytime, Casa

Grande's four courtyards were alive with dogs, cats, and caged songbirds, and an assortment of farm animals—turkeys, chickens, pigs, goats—that were slaughtered on festive occasions. Children played in these courtyards to avoid the heavily trafficked streets. Women used the public faucets to wash their laundry, which was then hung on clotheslines that crisscrossed the tenements. Vendors wandered through until the late afternoon when teenagers took charge of these enclosures for their soccer games. At night, the men played card games over upturned wooden boxes. And on Sunday evenings, the courtyards were reserved for outdoor dances.

A family of up to a dozen members crowded into each windowless one-room dwelling, aired only by the door opening onto a courtyard or the alleyway. Parents and favored children claimed the bed, while the rest spread themselves out on straw mats. Odors were overpowering and inescapable: from the tiny toilet only half-closeted near the doorway; from the exposed kitchen area; from the animals in the courtyards. In these cramped dwellings, tempers flared and family violence easily erupted. Sexual tensions mounted, and incest between half brothers and sisters and fathers and stepdaughters was not uncommon. There was no privacy in Casa Grande, not even in its public bathhouse, where women were constantly being spied upon by male children and adults.

In the mid-1950s monthly rent for a one-room apartment in Casa Grande was under four dollars. The basic diet consisted of coffee, tortillas, beans, and chili, supplemented by meat perhaps once a week. Recent arrivals from the countryside still used tortillas to scoop up their food; more "citified" residents relied on spoons. The possessions of the poor were meager. Besides the bed and mats, furniture consisted of a table and several wooden chairs, and a large dresser shared by the entire family. Clothes were worn a week or more before being laundered. Half the residents used gas stoves, serviced by tanks in the courtyard. The rest depended on kerosene ranges or charcoal braziers—the mainstay of the peasant kitchen. A measure of Casa Grande's relative affluence compared to nearby tenements was the presence of modern luxury items: almost 80 percent of tenants had radios, more than half sported wristwatches, and 20 percent owned televisions.

While the urban poor could on occasion reveal a boundless faith in religion, their expectations from the temporal world were set much lower. For them, the only thing miraculous about the Mexican economic miracle was finding employment that enabled them to survive. There were never enough jobs in industry, commerce, or services to meet their demands. And the huge pool of labor created by successive waves of new migrants to Mexico City ensured that salaries would remain inadequate.

~ [In the past two decades,] office and apartment towers, shopping malls, freeways, middle-class residential projects, and gigantic squatter settlements of the poor have obliterated most of what was identifiably "Mexican" in the urban landscape. Traces of the Indian heritage are preserved only in the museums. Architectural remnants of the colonial past are confined to a few blocks in the center and tiny cul-de-sacs in outlying neighborhoods. Long known as a city that encourages walkers, the capital has become daunting for people who try to get about on foot. They must persevere through a gauntlet of cars illegally parked across sidewalks, traffic lights designed for sprinters, a maze of pedestrian overpasses that tests even youthful stamina, and noise levels that often reach ninety decibels—the equivalent of standing next to a jackhammer.

Political, social, economic, and ecological forces have conspired to make the capital increasingly unmanageable, overpopulated, unproductive, and insalubrious. With twenty million people, Mexico City has become a true megalopolis, the greatest urban concentration in history. It sprawls over 950 square miles, about three times the area of New York City. More than three million motor vehicles slow traffic to the pace of the horse-and-buggy era. Every day, automobile exhaust and industrial fumes spew twelve thousand tons of pollutants into the atmosphere, provoking uncounted thousands of premature deaths and thickening the once azure skies to a yellow-gray opacity that veils both distant mountains and nearby skyscrapers. The ground can be as deadly as the air: ten thousand lives and hundreds of buildings were claimed by the monster earthquake of 1985.

Supergrowth has robbed Mexico City of economic logic. The logic behind urban industrialization was that cities offered "economies of scale" conducive to the rapid growth of enterprises: a pool of skilled labor and managerial talent; a concentration of investment capital; a large market for industrial and consumer products; transportation and communication facilities; and a geographic compactness that made for a more efficient use of energy, water, and sewage networks. From 1940 to 1970, [Mexico City's] powerful industrial muscles tugged the rest of the country forward. As the twentieth century comes to a close, however, the Mexican capital is being borne on the unsteady shoulders of the hinterland. Because of monumental government subsidies for public transportation, food, health facilities, education, fuel, water, and other essential services, Mexico City is absorbing more from the nation's economy and contributing less. The political elite has discovered that it is far easier to stimulate the growth of the city than to bring it under control; easier to encourage industrial concentration than the dispersal of factories; easier to attract rural migrants than to expel them back to the provinces; easier to build and centralize a huge federal bureaucracy than to reduce and scatter it across the country.

~ [Yet even as the city's economy languished, rural people continued to migrate to the capital.] It is not necessary to travel far from Mexico City to discover the causes of [the] massive provincial exodus. In the state of Morelos, just south of the capital, hundreds of people make the move every day, hoping to repeat the relative success of individuals like Roberto Jara, a peasant-turned-factory worker. Jara, born in 1955, is a native of Villa de Ayala, a small Morelos community steeped in revolutionary lore and the ideals of agrarian reform. It was there that Emiliano Zapata unfurled his Plan de Ayala in 1911 calling for the distribution of land to Mexico's peasants. Jara's maternal grandfather rode with the hero.

Decades of peace in Morelos transformed the people, the economy, even the landscape. Eventually, however, the ancient mismatch between people and resources reasserted itself. There was not enough land to accommodate a new, far more populous generation of peasants. Some of these rural youths were fortunate to find employment in nearby factories, commercial establishments, and hotels. Others spent part of the year as temporary farm workers in the United States. But most were drawn to Mexico City, the great lodestone for half the rural migrants who abandoned the Mexican countryside during the postwar decades.

Roberto Jara was a stocky, moon-faced fifteen-year-old when he decided to move to Mexico City in 1970. He was the youngest of five children. After his father died, the eldest son inherited the ejidal plot and encouraged his siblings to find a livelihood elsewhere. Roberto needed little prodding. Two cousins, who had migrated to the capital, returned periodically to Villa de Ayala and beguiled him with tales of money, women, and big-city adventures. They barely mentioned the noise, pollution, and tenements where a dozen people slept side by side in windowless rooms.

The cousins were *albañiles* (unskilled construction workers) and arranged a job for Roberto with the labor contractor who employed them to build houses in wealthy neighborhoods. One of his cousins also invited him to stay temporarily in his *vecindad* in Tepito. Roberto did not get along with his cousin's wife, however, who complained there was barely enough space in their single-room apartment for her two children, her husband, and herself. So Roberto bedded down at the building sites where he worked, returning to Tepito only during those weeks between the end of one construction assignment and the beginning of another.

Within three years of arriving in Mexico City, Roberto had a family of his own. He met his common-law wife, Hortensia, at a construction site in Coyoacán where she sold tacos and soft drinks to the work crews. When she became pregnant, they moved into a one-room tenement Roberto had rented in his cousin's *vecindad*. Through another relative, Roberto also found a steadier, higher-paying job as a mixer in a cement factory in Azcapozalco, a grimy industrial district in northern Mexico City. And from his fellow factory workers, he got the idea to take up residence in Ciudad Nezahualcóyotl, the huge slum ten miles east of downtown Mexico City.

"Neza"—as residents call it—is the largest of the working-class settlements that have mushroomed mainly beyond the eastern and northern outskirts of the capital. As recently as 1957 it had only ten thousand people. Yet when Jara moved there in 1974, Neza had added a startling one million inhabitants. And with more than three million residents in 1987, it had become the fourth most populous city in the nation. More than half of the inhabitants were refugees from the teeming downtown slums of the capital. The rest had migrated directly from rural zones.

It is easy to see why the poor found living space in Ciudad Nezahualcóyotl. Neza is an ecological wasteland spurned by middle-class and affluent Mexicans. Sprawling over the partially dried bed of Lake Texcoco, its earth is so saline that hardly a tree or shrub grows in the community. And because it is located at the very bottom of the Valley of Mexico, Neza becomes a natural tub during the wet season. The rains accumulate in stagnant pools, mix with raw sewage, and seep into wells, polluting the drinking water. An overpowering smell of organic waste saturates the air. Some of it emanates from the shrinking remains of Lake Texcoco, which receives piped sewage from Mexico City. There is also the stench from the enormous open-air garbage dump that creates a no-man's-land between the lake and the eastern periphery of the slum. In the dry season, dust and fecal particles swirl up in the winds, spreading airborne gastrointestinal diseases.

Many of the migrants settling in Neza during the 1960s were forced to pay developers who claimed to have title over the land. But in subsequent years, new arrivals insisted that the entire zone belonged to the state because it occupied land that had once lain below Lake Texcoco. Squatting became the most usual way to take possession of property. Developers and corrupt municipal officials sent the police to dislodge the invaders. But in the early 1970s, President Luis Echeverría, taking a more benign and populist view, sided with the squatters. The government expropriated the disputed properties and sold them to occupants at prices well below market value, with payment terms stretched over five to ten years.

Roberto Jara was a beneficiary of this new policy. Arriving in Neza in 1974, he squatted on a plot of land close to the garbage dump and erected a shack from corrugated tin, wood, and cartons. He "hijacked" electricity by stringing a wire from his home to the closest utility pole. Every day, Hortensia used a public faucet down the block to fill buckets that supplied the household with water for washing and drinking. As soon as the state government "regularized" Jara's title to his property, he built a sturdier two-room house with cinder blocks bought at a discount from a government agency. In 1977 the Jaras' dwelling was legally connected to the municipal electricity grid and water system. By then, he had convinced his two cousins to move to Neza, a few blocks from his home on adjoining lots which he had claimed for them. "I wanted to show my gratitude for all they had done for me," said Jara. "If it had not been for them, I would still be a peon back in Villa de Ayala."

In the dozen years since Jara settled there, Neza has gained a solidity that often confounds an outsider's preconceptions of what a Third World shantytown should look like. The stench of sewage and rubbish is still inescapable. In the new outlying districts, flimsy shacks still rise along dusty, unpaved roads where mangy dogs rummage through garbage heaps. But slightly older neighborhoods have two-room cinder-block houses built by their residents in the mold of Jara's home, with television antennae sprouting from their roofs. Their streets are asphalted and relatively clean. On the larger avenues, there are stores of every sort, although they do not sell the luxury or higher-quality goods available in downtown Mexico City and the shopping malls of its affluent districts. At the government-run CONASUPO stores, food and other basic necessities can be purchased at subsidized prices. An outdoor market, running along the avenue that marks the boundary between Neza and the capital, serves as a permanent bazaar for the community's underground economy. Unlicensed peddlers sell used clothes, motor vehicle parts, fresh and cooked foods, household goods (new, used, or stolen), candies, razor blades, and every variety of hardware. Barbers shave and shear their customers while they sit on wooden chairs in full view of passing cars and strollers. Back inside Neza proper, young men and children battle over scuffed balls on dusty soccer fields. At night, spectators of all ages jam into theaters that screen mostly kung-fu movies and insipid Mexican melodramas about loyal servants helping their wealthy employers survive a family crisis. Even more popular is the local sports palace—one of the few buildings higher than two storeys—where masked wrestlers heave each other across a wilting canvas ring.

On workdays, most residents rise before dawn. Jara is out of the house by 6:00 A.M. He catches a bus that drops him in front of the subway station on the outskirts of Neza, boards the packed train to Azcapozalco, and, emerging there, takes another bus to his factory—altogether a ninety-minute journey that still costs less than a nickel, thanks to the heavily government-subsidized transportation system. His factory job pays about twice the official minimum wage, ranking Jara near the top of Neza's thoroughly proletarian hierarchy. Urban industrialization may have been the magnet that drew rural migrants to Mexico City, but most of them had to settle for marginal, nonfactory occupations. In Neza, less than a quarter of adult males are industrial workers. It is far more usual to be a construction laborer, a street peddler, or a messenger or porter for offices and stores in the capital.

Among women, the most common professions are domestic servants, seamstresses, and vendors of tacos and sandwiches. Children under ten years old are sent into the streets of the capital to hawk gum and candy, wipe the windshields of cars stalled by traffic lights, or openly beg. Jara's wife, Hortensia, works at home as a seamstress, earning somewhat less than a third of her husband's salary. Two of her children are in the local elementary school and have not been required to contribute to the household income. The oldest son, a teenager, is apprenticed to an electrician.

Jara is bitter over the inflation of recent years, which has cut deeply into his purchasing power. "We used to have meat as often as we wanted," he says. "Now, once, twice a week, and only chicken. Otherwise, it's tortillas and beans, beans and tortillas. New clothes, a new bed—forget it." For him, the causes of the persistent economic crisis are clear: "Those politicians who can't stop stealing, union leaders who won't fight for their people, *patrones* [employers] who send their money out of the country."

But whatever the deficiencies of life in Ciudad Nezahualcóyotl, Roberto prefers it to the countryside he left behind. He barely disguises his contempt for peasants who "lack the courage" to move to the city. "They have no ambition," he says. "Even the ones who have land are lazy. Give them a few pesos, and they drink pulque and chase after women. They resent people who work hard—they try to pull them down."

Hortensia chides him about his own drinking bouts and infidelities. She is thinner, darker, and less ebullient than her husband, and, with creases on her face and gaps between her teeth, she looks almost ten years older than he. Occasionally, she visits relatives in her native Veracruz town of Tierra Blanca and once lingered there with her children for several months when Roberto took up with a younger woman. She has fantasies of buying a small mango and papaya orchard in Veracruz and retiring there

someday with her husband. "But in the city, the children have more opportunities," she concedes. "If we took them to Tierra Blanca, they would
only be back here a few years later looking for jobs."

The sudden appearance of so many migrants in Mexico City and other
urban centers has made it necessary for the political elite to find strong
local leaders who can act as liaisons between the government and these
mushrooming communities. Most often, these local bosses, called caciques, emerge at the very moment a new slum is born. They are leaders
of the squatters who invade an uninhabited strip of land on the urban
periphery. To draw the attention of the public authorities, they initially
display an irksome militance—banners with antigovernment slogans, noisy
demonstrations, even a willingness to clash with the police. But once the
government concedes recognition to a cacique, he becomes an uncondi-
tional supporter of the PRI. It is a pretty straight deal, really: the municipal authorities grant legal deeds to the squatters, and slowly extend basic
services like running water, electricity, sewage canals, and garbage disposal to the new community, and, in return, expect the cacique to deliver
the vote; the cacique convinces his followers that he was instrumental in
obtaining these benefits, and he expects the municipal authorities to allow him great leeway in maintaining his local political hegemony and
extracting personal financial gains from his community.

The most notorious and powerful of Mexico City's slum caciques in
recent years was Rafael Gutiérrez Moreno, the so-called garbage czar.
Until his death in 1987, Gutiérrez was the boss of thousands of
pepenadores, the scavengers who live and toil in the huge refuse dumps
on the capital's periphery. Through intimidation and persuasion, he gouged
a fortune from this caste of virtual "untouchables" and molded them into
a voting bloc that elected him to Congress.

Pollution, poverty, and politics wind together like a single strand in
Mexico City's garbage industry. Most of the five million tons of refuse
collected in the capital in 1987 were delivered to compacting plants or
incinerators. But about 1.5 million tons a year are handled by the lowly
pepenadores, who sift through mammoth dump sites for the food, glass,
metal, plastic, paper, fabric, and wood wastes that are sold for reprocess-
ing in factories. This primitive recycling of garbage, often carried out
illegally by small businesses that are unsupervised by the municipal authorities, poses serious health hazards to the population at large. Discarded
livestock fodder from these dumps is transformed into vegetable lard;
rotted fruit wastes end up flavoring soft drinks; decayed animal corpses
are ground into saugage meat; car grease is reprocessed into cooking oils;
and bones are pulverized into soup concentrates. The garbage, in its un-

processed form, is even deadlier for the *pepenadores*. The wastes pollute their water and air, spreading gastrointestinal and respiratory ailments that reduce their life expectancy far below the city's norm. And for their eight- to ten-hour workdays, the *pepenadores* earn less than the legal minimum wage.

Gutiérrez himself was a product of this environment. He spent his childhood as a *pepenador* at Santa Cruz Meyehualco, a garbage dump on the eastern outskirts of Mexico City, where he was born in 1942. As a teenager, he was ambitious and lucky enough to escape the refuse heaps and become a sanitation truck driver, the next rung up the labor hierarchy of the garbage industry. In his early twenties, he had figured out the shadowy links between trade union affairs, municipal government, and party politics. By 1965 he had been elected president of the union representing Mexico City's *pepenadores*. He also held several minor posts in the PRI, mainly involving tasks as a bodyguard. Even more important, he had found his political godfather in Benjamín Carpio, head of the city's sanitation department, who acted as a go-between for Gutiérrez and his future wife. (As usual in Mexican politics, personal ties helped cement a political relationship.)

In the early 1960s the *pepenadores* of Santa Cruz Meyehualco, which had become the city's largest dump, organized a cooperative to bypass intermediaries and sell their sifted garbage directly to businesses that recycled it. Carpio, the municipal sanitation chief, was earning a considerable income as an intermediary in the garbage trade and vehemently opposed the cooperative. He found a willing ally in Gutiérrez, who in the guise of union organizer purported to be acting against the cooperative in the true interests of the *pepenadores*. In the prolonged conflict that ensued, the sanitation department withheld garbage from Santa Cruz Meyehualco, fights broke out between supporters of the cooperative and those who backed Gutiérrez, and a few *pepenadores* were killed. By 1965 the cooperative had disintegrated, and the bulk of income from the resale of the dump's refuse was going to Carpio and Gutiérrez. To further reward Gutiérrez for his loyalty, Carpio agreed to give him absolute control over Santa Cruz Meyehualco.

In the next two decades, an avalanche of garbage flowed into Santa Cruz. After being thoroughly scavenged, the refuse piled up in three hundred-foot mounds, foul-smelling and smoky from the natural combustion of the decomposing wastes at their bottom. The dump site expanded until it covered all but a tenth of the community's land. Despite the cramped residential space, the local population doubled, roughly keeping pace with Mexico City's demographic increase. Rural migrants, wanted criminals, and Santa Cruz's own elevated birthrate swelled the numbers of *pepenadores* to about five thousand. And Gutiérrez—"Rafael," as everyone called him—dictated their lives.

He unquestionably had a benevolent side, although he was quick to claim credit for any favors bestowed on his people. Thus, when the municipal government constructed seven hundred homes for the *pepenadores* of Santa Cruz, Rafael decided which families would occupy them. And he earned the gratitude of the new homeowners by arranging to have them pay part of their mortgages with garbage instead of cash. He sponsored local soccer teams, supplied the uniforms, and built four playing fields, which he named the Rafael Sports Center. He constructed a church and a large cross overlooking the dump site. He personally handed out gifts to all youngsters on Children's Day, and to their parents on Mother's Day and Father's Day. Once a year, he organized a pilgrimage to the shrine of the Virgin of Guadalupe on the northern outskirts of the capital. And every January, he hired buses to transport virtually all five thousand *pepenadores* to Acapulco, where they received free accommodations and meals for a week. He also claimed to instill in his people a sense of pride and class consciousness by festooning Santa Cruz with catchy painted slogans, like "We *pepenadores* are also Mexicans," and "Land for the peasants who till it, garbage for the *pepenadores* who sift it."

But no amount of charity or demagoguery could obscure the misery that Gutiérrez helped perpetuate among the garbage scavengers. According to estimates in 1979, he and his henchmen syphoned off more than half the income made by the *pepenadores* of Santa Cruz Meyehualco. Put another way: while the average *pepenador* collected less than three dollars daily, Gutiérrez and his aides raked in more than fifteen thousand dollars a day.

All refuse that entered and left Santa Cruz was under Gutiérrez's control. Every morning, sanitation trucks lumbered through the dump site's sole gate under the watch of armed guards. After the garbage was unloaded, the *pepenadores* sifted out the valued wastes, collected them in sacks, and delivered them to Gutiérrez's foremen. The foremen weighed the refuse on scales that automatically subtracted ten kilos from each load, allegedly on account of extraneous material and dirt mixed in with the recyclable rubbish. After being baled, the sifted garbage was trucked to businesses under contract to Gutiérrez. The *pepenadores* were not allowed to sell their pickings to anybody except the cacique and his assistants and were prohibited from leaving the dump with rubbish in their possession. To reduce discontent, Gutiérrez occasionally rotated rights to the choicer garbage—for example, aluminum and tin refuse that commanded higher prices—among the *pepenadores*, who vied with each other to be known as Rafael's men of confidence.

Gutiérrez constantly sought to strengthen his political clout in the government and the PRI. He ingratiated himself with [politicians] by turning out his *pepenadores* for political rallies of every sort. He dressed his men as peasants or factory workers or in their own *pepenador* uniforms and trucked them by the hundreds to May Day parades, demonstrations on patriotic holidays, and to the airport to welcome visiting foreign dignitaries or the nation's president returning from a trip abroad.

By 1979, Gutiérrez himself had become politically prominent enough to run as his district's "alternate" legislator (a largely superfluous post created by the government to reward a rising politician, allowing him to automatically replace an incumbent legislator who is forced to step down because of illness or a new political assignment). At the convention in the National Auditorium where the PRI formally unveiled its legislative candidates that year, Gutiérrez both fascinated and appalled his political colleagues and journalists. Dark glasses, an enormous scar along the right side of his jaw, and the glitzy, powder-blue suit draped over his short, barrel-chested frame gave him the classic aura of a gangster. Six armed bodyguards made him seem even more sinister. When his name was called out by the master of ceremonies, the floor erupted with chants of "Rafael! Rafael!" from hundreds of *pepenadores*. As soon as the assembly ended, Gutiérrez took out a fat roll of pesos from his money belt, gave it to one of his aides, and, within earshot of journalists and other politicians, instructed him: "Take this for the press and tell them who it came from, huh? Photos, articles, I want everything." When the election results a few months later announced the usual PRI landslide, Gutiérrez had his "alternate" seat in Congress.

By the mid-1980s, Gutiérrez, still in his early forties, had lived a rags-to-riches story that was hardly ever supposed to occur in Mexico. In a system that increasingly ignored "mass politics" in favor of bureaucratic expertise, he had fashioned one of the strongest grass-roots followings, and among the sort of constituents whom political analysts claimed to be beyond the reach of the PRI. He had become a considerable power broker in the official party and municipal government, courted by elite politicians who were embarrassed to socialize with him but anxious to tap his extravagant bankroll and solid bloc of votes.

The dark fable ended abruptly in 1987. A *pepenador*, who claimed his wife had been raped by Gutiérrez, fatally shot him. Assassinations of politicians usually fan rumors of Machiavellian plots, but Gutiérrez was so notorious for his uncontrolled sexual appetite that no other version surfaced in the press or political circles. And soon after his death, women who announced they were his common-law wives and scores of his alleged children and grandchildren filed claims to his fortune, which reputedly reached tens of millions of dollars.

Whatever their moral deficiencies, caciques like Rafael Gutiérrez have played a crucial stabilizing role in Mexico City and elsewhere in the country. They have been buffers between a burgeoning underclass and the political elite. In this respect, caciques are comparable to trade union leaders, with whom they often act in concert. While trade union leaders exercise power over workers in their places of employment, it is the caciques who wield influence in the communities where laborers and their families reside. Moreover, with only a third of Mexican workers enrolled in unions, the caciques are able to claim political leadership over vast numbers of the urban poor who are untouched by the labor movement.

~ As the 1980s unfolded, the government continued to demonstrate its political acumen in coping with the possibility of social unrest in Mexico City's shantytowns. But the megalopolis was being tested on a more unexpected front: its potential devastation by natural and man-made environmental accidents. [Early in the morning of September 19, 1985, an] earthquake, measuring 8.1 on the Richter scale of 10, unleashed shock waves that were felt as far away as Houston, about eleven hundred miles from the epicenter. Coastal towns in Michoacán and Jalisco, only fifty miles from the quake's origin, were relatively resistant to the tremors because their solid rock, geological foundations diminished the shaking of buildings on the surface. But the quake was devastating for Mexico City. The muddy sediments of the Aztec lakes under its central district reacted like a bowl of gelatin that magnified and multiplied the vibrations of the shock waves.

The intense tremors began at 7:19 A.M., and continued for almost three full minutes. With their voices and images shaking, television newscasters informed viewers of what was already apparent to them—and then abruptly went off the air. In the downtown neighborhoods, electricity was cut and faucets ran dry as underground water mains and copper cables snapped. Throughout much of the capital, telephones went dead. The streets undulated like a rolling sea, bucking motor vehicles until their engines stalled. Subway riders were plunged into claustrophobic darkness and continuously heaved against each other. Commuters fortunate enough to be caught waiting in the stations scurried up to the surface. There they found an urban landscape that seemed under intense bombardment. Buildings swayed and buckled, showering pedestrians with bricks and mortar, crumbling upon their foundations or exploding in fireballs. Thousands of people lay buried in their ruins. Those who escaped the entombment gave miraculous accounts of their survival.

The locus of the greatest mayhem was the Tlatelolco public housing project. A fourth of its 103 buildings—home to lower-income and middle-class families—were severely damaged. "My seven-year-old daughter and I were rushing through breakfast before I took her to school on my way to work," said a government employee, who lived with his family in a fourth-floor apartment in one of the buildings. "All of a sudden the shaking began. Trying to calm my daughter, I shouted for my wife to join us. We embraced tightly. Only by pretending to protect them could I control my terror. Things fell all around us and the windows shattered. After what seemed an eternity, the trembling stopped. We were alive. I said to my wife: 'Let's get out of here before it begins again!' She turned her head slowly to the window. 'Oh my God, look!' she said. 'The people in the Nuevo León building!' And we saw that massive cement structure collapsing like a castle of cards."

María Gutiérrez, a housewife living on the sixth floor of the Nuevo León, had just dropped her teenage daughter at school and was driving her car into the building's parking lot. Her three youngest children and her mother-in-law had stayed behind in the apartment. "As I got out of the car, I could see my home, everybody's homes, the entire building being ripped apart. Walls, windows, everything crumbled. And I could not get there. My three little kids were inside."

There were about three thousand residents in the block-long, thirteen-storey Nuevo León, and almost half of them were trapped, dead or alive. As soon as the *temblor* ceased, hundreds of people from the adjoining buildings began a desperate search through the ruins for survivors. "There was so much dust that we had to cover our faces with handkerchiefs, and bystanders were shouting that there would be an explosion because of all the gas in the air," said Tito Montalbán, a nineteen-year-old Politécnico student. "But the screams and cries from the people buried under the rubble were too much to bear. We just kept digging until our hands bled without giving a thought about whether we would be blown up."

Ambulances arrived within minutes. Unable to handle all the victims, their drivers begged the owners of private cars and pickup trucks to help transport the injured. The closest major hospitals were at the National Medical Center. With twenty-five buildings, it was the biggest facility of its kind in Latin America and experienced in dealing with large-scale catastrophes. But the ambulances had to be waved back: the earthquake had devastated the medical complex, too. Virtually all its buildings were damaged, among them the General Hospital, and the separate structures specializing in traumatology, pediatrics, oncology, and gynecology and obstetrics ceased to function. The Cardiology Hospital, the pride of national medicine, had collapsed, killing seventy physicians, nurses, and other employees. Throughout the medical center, several hundred patients were fatally crushed or smothered, and more than three thousand had to be evacuated. "When we ran out of litters, we used bed sheets to carry them out," said a doctor at one of the hospitals. "We just lay the patients on the pavement, and attended them there. I kept screaming to the hospital workers not to go back into the building because the stairwells were so unsteady that they shook with every step. But they wouldn't listen. They just kept going back for more patients."

Almost as soon as the ground stopped trembling, the political aftershocks began. Throughout the capital, ordinary Mexicans railed against their government for its ineptitude during the emergency. On paper, at least, a well-conceived plan existed in the Interior and Defense ministries to rapidly mobilize security forces and other government personnel in the event of a massive earthquake. Several thousand troops and policemen were, in fact, rushed to zones of greatest damage. But most of them merely cordoned off the sites, instead of plunging ahead with excavation and rescue work. When government workers finally began digging out the victims, it was apparent that their picks and shovels were woefully inadequate. Private contruction companies sent bulldozers into the worst-hit neighborhoods, but the government, anxious to project a nationalist image of self-reliance, declined relief offers from abroad during the thirty-six hours that followed the quake. Foreign equipment and expert personnel were eventually welcomed, though the crucial time lost probably doomed many victims who suffocated or bled to death before they could be reached under the rubble.

The vaunted organizational talents of the PRI were nowhere in evidence. The party's labor and agrarian wings, which on numerous occasions had convoked hundreds of thousands of trade unionists and peasants for political rallies, failed to mobilize anybody to aid the earthquake victims. Nor did the caciques play any visible role. Instead, the volunteers who converged on the disaster sites were citizens reacting spontaneously to the emergency. They came from slums, middle-class projects, and wealthy neighborhoods, private and state universities, public and parochial schools. Forming themselves into brigades, they shoveled and clawed for survivors under the mass of concrete and steel. Small, wiry men, known as *topos* (moles), burrowed through narrow tunnels and crevices to rescue the injured and retrieve the dead. Thousands of other volunteers dispensed medicine, food, drinking water, clothes, and tents. The size and fervor of the volunteer effort surprised many of those involved, who had never thought of themselves as civic spirited. They responded despite government entreaties that the public remain at home or at least avoid visiting the disaster zones. And they suspected that the government was wary of a citizens' movement which it did not control. Suspicion turned to anger when public officials seemed intent on downplaying the scope of the tragedy.

Only thirty-six hours after the great *temblor*, a second, lesser earthquake struck the city. Government leaders dismissed its effects as negligible, but at least a score of buildings were brought down by the new quake. It was also lethal for uncounted numbers of survivors still entombed in the ruins of hundreds of structures knocked down earlier. Throughout the crisis, Mayor Ramón Aguirre and other officials released casualty and property damage figures that were consistently lower—far lower—than the estimates reported by journalists and relief workers. Their intention may have been to dampen panic and despair and to counteract exaggerated accounts in the foreign press that pictured a city wiped off the face of the map. (In fact, most of the earthquake damage was confined to a thirteen-square-mile zone, less than 2 percent of the megalopolis's surface area.) But for many citizens, especially those living in the devastated neighborhoods, the government appeared to be engaged in a perverse effort to belittle their losses. As a result, the authorities were not given enough credit for some of their solid successes in handling the emergency: food shortages were averted; epidemics were forestalled; electricity, running water, and telephone service were restored in the affected zones within days; and most of the city continued to function even in the immediate aftermath of the cataclysm.

Police and soldiers were special targets of public ire. In the ruins of the downtown building occupied by the attorney general's office, rescue workers found the corpses of prisoners bearing signs of torture. When the attorney general blamed the injuries on the earthquake, he was contradicted by several prisoners who had survived the quake and described being repeatedly subjected to electric shocks, beatings, and cigarette burns by their police interrogators. In Tepito and Morelos, poor neighborhoods devastated by the *temblor*, residents reported that police had looted their abandoned, shattered homes. In nearby Garibaldi Square, where hundreds of mariachis entertained tourists with traditional Mexican ballads, police were accused of stealing guitars, trumpets, and valuables from the ruins of the musicians' apartment building. At several temporary refuge sites, private donors bearing clothes, blankets, and food for the disaster victims were so suspicious of the security forces that they insisted on personally distributing the offerings to the needy. There were numerous complaints from people who were forced to pay bribes to claim the corpses of their relatives from temporary morgues. Bribes enabled clothing manufacturers to cross police cordons and rescue their inventory, machinery, and strongboxes from their wrecked downtown factories—in some cases, even before their injured and dead employees had been dug out of the ruins.

Many of the wounds of the 1985 earthquake have scarred over. Most of the seventy thousand people made homeless have been accommodated in new or repaired housing with the aid of the government. Predictions that the government would be politically vulnerable in the wake of the cataclysm have not come to pass. The small parties of left and right were unable to claim the loyalty of potential dissidents. The youthful volunteers who spent sleepless days and nights excavating the ruins for victims and generously aiding the survivors returned to home, school, and work. Only the passage of years will tell if they will look back on these experiences as a social or political awakening that changed the course of their lives. In the meantime, the regime has continued to display enormous resourcefulness in taming and co-opting its critics.

The widespread discussions and debates about the earthquake's long-term impact have at the very least heightened public consciousness that Mexico City lives on an ecological abyss—vulnerable not only to another killer *temblor* but also to catastrophes brought on by water shortages and worsening pollution.

[YET,] FOR ALL its problems, Mexico City continues to draw the rural destitute. A current (1987) employment rate of 12 percent and underemployment levels that may be twice as high would seem to be discouraging. But even if they are reduced to becoming bootblacks, street peddlers, and beggars, these agrarian refugees still feel they stand a better chance of surviving here than in the countryside. And sometimes, if the people don't come to Mexico City, Mexico City goes to them. The community of Cuauhtitlán, for example, existed for centuries in rural torpor twenty miles from the capital's center. Once considered the epitome of provincial backwardness—"Outside Mexico City every place is Cuauhtitlán" is an old saying—the town has recently become a flourishing industrial district and officially the northernmost limit of metropolitan Mexico City.

Cuauhtitlán has bequeathed to the modern inhabitants of Mexico City some of the bleakest annals from the ancient Indians, including the legend of the Fifth Sun, as the Aztecs called their last epoch. "It is also known as the Sun of Movement," stated the *Annals of Cuauhtitlán*, "and as the elders tell us, it will bring the shaking of the earth, and there will be famine, and thus we shall perish." But the Aztecs tempered such fatalism with a cyclical view of history that is still embraced by residents of the

Mexican capital in the present era of urban overdevelopment. Throughout its existence, the city has been scourged by war, social upheaval, plague, flood, earthquake. Yet the city has always reemerged, sometimes diminished by its ordeals, and sometimes catapulted to greater splendor.

Suggested Readings

Because of the city's centrality to Latin American society, the literature that touches on urban history is vast. Moreover, it cuts a wide swath across a variety of styles, disciplines, ideologies, and objectives. Interested readers will always do well to keep an open mind to the diversity of intellectual channels that depict and analyze urban life. The array of information includes chronicles dating back to the sixteenth century, descriptions written by observers traveling across Latin America at different times, and official documents depicting urban problems. Works of fiction, such as plays and novels, and essays known for their emphasis on the manners and life-styles of a given period can also be helpful; they create a literary genre known as *costumbrismo* (customs-oriented work). Of course, publications by historians and other social scientists, together with historical documents, represent a significant bibliographic resource.

In this section, we suggest titles that are accessible, approachable, and deal with some of the underlying issues of Latin American society across time and space. Thus, we will not be listing works along the categories of "colonial," "national," "nineteenth century," or other such temporally based classifications. Finally, the reader is encouraged to peruse the titles cited in several of the headnotes and listed in the notes that form part of Chapter 1. The majority of those works is not repeated here.

General

Overviews of Latin American cities can be found in volumes of collected essays in English such as Jorge E. Hardoy, ed., *Urbanization in Latin America: Approaches and Issues* (New York: Doubleday, 1975); and Richard P. Schaedel, Jorge E. Hardoy, and Nora Kinzer, eds., *Urbanization in the Americas from Its Beginnings to the Present* (The Hague: Mouton, 1978). An excellent and exceptionally comprehensive review of the state of the literature for the colonial era can be found in Fred Bronner, "Urban Society in Colonial Spanish America: Research Trends," *Latin American Research Review* 21, no. 1 (1986): 7–72. See also Louisa S. Hoberman and Susan M. Socolow, eds., *Cities and Society in Colonial Latin America* (Albuquerque: University of New Mexico Press, 1986), and Lyman L. Johnson and Socolow, "Urbanization in Colonial Latin America,"

Journal of Urban History 8 (November 1981): 27–59. An interesting typography of cities established in the conquest period is offered by Jorge E. Hardoy and Carmen Aranovich, "Urban Scales and Functions in Latin America toward the Year 1600: First Conclusions," *Latin American Research Review* 5, no. 1 (Fall 1970): 57–110. The perceptions of Latin American cities in the late nineteenth and early twentieth centuries were shaped by the camera lens. An unusual study of the construction of views dealing with Latin America through the photographic medium is presented in Robert M. Levine, "Images of Progress in Nineteenth-Century Latin America," *Journal of Urban History* 15 (May 1989): 304–23.

Portraits of Individual Cities

The list of books by modern historians portraying the social dynamics of a single city would begin with Richard M. Morse's study of São Paulo, *From Community to Metropolis*, 2d ed. (New York: Octagon Press, 1974), together with Irving Leonard's largely urban-centered *Baroque Times in Old Mexico: Seventeenth-Century Persons, Places, and Practices* (Ann Arbor: University of Michigan Press, 1959). Thereafter, fine single-city portraits include George Reid Andrews, *The Afro-Argentines of Buenos Aires, 1800–1900* (Madison: University of Wisconsin Press, 1980); Silvia M. Arrom, *The Women of Mexico City, 1790–1857* (Stanford: Stanford University Press, 1985); John K. Chance, *Race and Class in Colonial Oaxaca* (Stanford: Stanford University Press, 1978); Donald B. Cooper, *Epidemic Disease in Mexico City, 1761–1813* (Austin: University of Texas Press, 1965); Luis González, *San José de Gracia: Mexican Village in Transition*, trans. John Upton (Austin: University of Texas Press, 1972); Mary C. Karasch, *Slave Life in Rio de Janeiro, 1808–1850* (Princeton: Princeton University Press, 1987); and Jeffrey D. Needell, *A Tropical Belle Epoque: Elite Culture and Society in Turn-of-the-Century Rio de Janeiro* (New York: Cambridge University Press, 1988). Finally, various social and political dimensions of the nineteenth century related to the city of Buenos Aires are captured in two cross-disciplinary histories: James R. Scobie, *Buenos Aires: From Plaza to Suburb, 1870–1910* (New York: Oxford University Press, 1971); and Mark D. Szuchman, *Order, Family, and Community in Buenos Aires, 1810–1860* (Stanford: Stanford University Press, 1988).

Urban Politics

The political nature of the city is one of its essential characteristics. One of the few examinations of urban politics in the seventeenth century comes by way of Eduardo Saguier, "The Contradictory Nature of the Spanish-

American Colonial State and the Origin of Self-Government in the Río de la Plata Region: The Case of Buenos Aires in the Early Seventeenth Century," *Revista de Historia de América* 97 (1984): 23–44. The city of Lima is the focus of John P. Moore, who examines the changing role of municipal councils during the transition from the Hapsburg to the Bourbon administration in *The Cabildo in Perú under the Bourbons: A Study in the Decline and Resurgence of Local Government in the Audiencia of Lima, 1700–1824* (Durham: Duke University Press, 1966). A very different type of politics in Lima is analyzed by Henry A. Dietz and Richard J. Moore in their study of poverty-stricken residents taking up political action, *Political Participation in a Non-Electoral Setting: The Poor in Lima, Peru* (Athens: Ohio University Press, 1979). Another urban political regimen, based on democratic electoral contests, is the subject of Richard Walter, "Elections in the City of Buenos Aires during the First Yrigoyen Administration: Social Class and Political Preferences," *Hispanic American Historical Review* 58 (November 1978): 595–624. The political phenomenon of populism is not entirely the creation of the twentieth century, but conditions in the post-1930 period, especially the exploding process of urbanization, have certainly made it ripe for populist leaders. Robert H. Dix examines the nature of populism in "Populism: Authoritarian and Democratic," *Latin American Research Review* 20, no. 5 (1985): 29–52. The example of Peronism is given special attention within an urban setting in the very detailed and probing study by Daniel James, "October 17th and 18th, 1945: Mass Protest, Peronism, and the Argentine Working Class," *Journal of Social History* 21 (Spring 1988): 441–61. For a stimulating discussion of populism in Brazil that similarly stresses workers' initiatives in their dealings with the state, see John D. French, *The Brazilian Workers' ABC: Class Conflict and Alliances in Modern São Paulo* (Chapel Hill: University of North Carolina Press). Barry Carr provides an encyclopedic account of the rise and fall of "vanguard politics" in Mexico in *Marxism and Communism in Twentieth-Century Mexico* (Lincoln: University of Nebraska Press, 1992).

Urban Space

The use of urban space as a scholarly concept has been principally the domain of geographers, rather than historians. Two interesting titles are Charles S. Sargent, *The Spatial Evolution of Greater Buenos Aires, Argentina, 1870–1930* (Tempe: Center for Latin American Studies, Arizona State University, 1974); and Graciela Schneier, "Latin America: A Tale of Cities" [appears as "Tales of Cities: The Culture and Political Economy of Urban Spaces," in special issue of *International Social Science Journal* 42 (August 1990): 337–53].

Patronage

Personal ambitions in Latin America historically have been determined, to a great extent, by the use of connections and patronage. Regardless of one's social standing or racial category, from high officials to lowly laborers, patron-client relations have been essential for the advancement of goals. The Latin American city offers the most convenient venue for this most basic of rituals. Stephanie Blank, "Patrons, Clients, and Kin in Seventeenth-Century Caracas: A Methodological Essay in Colonial Spanish American Social History," *Hispanic American Historical Review* 54 (May 1974): 260–84, provides a means to study the mechanisms by which students of social relations can analyze the process. The vitality and fragility of networks required by members of the wealthy—or at least more comfortable—ranks of society is explored by John E. Kicza in "The Great Families of Mexico: Elite Maintenance and Business Practices in Late Colonial Mexico City," *Hispanic American Historical Review* 62 (August 1982): 429–57. For a more comprehensive and detailed study of commerce and connections, see his *Colonial Entrepreneurs: Families and Business in Bourbon Mexico City* (Albuquerque: University of New Mexico Press, 1983). A readily comparable study of a similar group at the southern end of the Spanish Empire is Susan M. Socolow, "Economic Activities of the Porteño Merchants: The Viceregal Period," *Hispanic American Historical Review* 55 (February 1975): 1–24, and the larger work, *The Merchants of Buenos Aires, 1778–1810* (New York: Cambridge University Press, 1978). An exceptional study of economic networks, recognized for its handling of several generations and the linkages with the expansion of political hegemony, is Maurice Zeitlin and Richard Ratcliff, "Research Methods for the Analysis of the Internal Structure of Dominant Classes: The Case of Landlords and Capitalists in Chile," *Latin American Research Review* 10, no. 2 (1975): 5–61.

Social Structures

The social structures of Latin American cities are examined in a wide-ranging set of titles, encompassing history, sociology, economics, and anthropology. The amount and type of attention the subject attracts can be gleaned from the ongoing work reported by William L. Canak, "City and Class in Latin America: Report on the 2nd Seminar of the Working Group on Latin American Urbanization," *Latin American Research Re-*

view 16, no. 3 (1981): 146–57. Known for the depth of his knowledge of both the legal and the behavioral aspects of the Spanish colonial system, Mario Góngora turns his attention to the urban social structure in "Urban Social Stratification in Colonial Chile," *Hispanic American Historical Review* 55 (August 1975): 421–48. A companion piece centered at the opposite pole of the Spanish Empire is Julia Hirschberg, "Social Experiment in New Spain: A Prosopographical Study of the Early Settlement at Puebla de los Angeles, 1531–1534," *Hispanic American Historical Review* 59 (February 1979): 1–33. Institutional settings offered convenient venues for members of a social or occupational group to cement ties and expand activities. A fine study of the relationship between institutions and socioeconomic practices is Anthony J. R. Russell-Wood, *Fidalgos and Philanthropists: The Santa Casa de Misericordia of Bahia, 1550–1755* (Berkeley: University of California Press, 1968).

Nineteenth-Century Brazil

Brazil's nineteenth century has come in for its share of analysis. For a view of the urban setting in the nineteenth century, there is the fine piece by Richard M. Morse, "Cities and Society in XIX Century Latin America: The Illustrative Case of Brazil," in *El proceso de urbanización en América desde sus orígenes hasta nuestros días*, ed. Jorge Hardoy and Richard Schaedel (Buenos Aires: Editorial del Instituto Torcuato Di Tella, 1969), 303–22. Historians have paid scant attention to domestic workers, an urban social group that historically represents a disproportionately large sector of the population and an overwhelming percentage of working women. Notable for its analysis of a group that leaves few traces of its own history is Sandra Lauderdale Graham, *House and Street: The Domestic World of Servants and Masters in Nineteenth-Century Rio de Janeiro* (New York: Cambridge University Press, 1988).

Mobility

Migration, both internal and international, has been a constant feature of Latin American society. Both the bases and the consequences of migration have yielded a good amount of scholarship. The colonial period constitutes the focus of David J. Robinson's collection of essays, *Migration in Colonial Spanish America* (New York: Cambridge University Press, 1990). Among the fine chapters is Ann M. Wightman, " '. . . residente en esta ciudad . . .': Urban Migrants in Colonial Cuzco," 86–111. Another essay, tightly focused and interesting for the institutional venue it explores, is Elsa Malvido, "Migration Patterns of the Novices of the Order of San Francisco in Mexico City, 1649–1749," 181–92. The Yucatán region shapes the interest of Nancy M. Farriss in "Nucleation versus Dispersal: The Dynamics of Population Movement in Colonial Yucatán," *Hispanic American Historical Review* 58 (May 1978): 187–216.

One of the pioneer studies of Mexican urban-bound internal migration in the nineteenth century is Alejandro Moreno Toscano and Carlos Aguirre, "Migrations to Mexico City in the Nineteenth Century: Research Approaches," *Journal of Inter-American Studies and World Affairs* 17, no. 1 (February 1975): 27–42. For the rural and urban settings of migration in the nineteenth century, see Donald Ramos, "City and Country: The Family in Minas Gerais, 1804–1838," *Journal of Family History* 3 (Winter 1978): 361–75.

The study of international migration to Latin America usually requires researchers to focus on the city, since the overwhelming majority of international migrants settled in metropolitan centers. Comparisons across borders of urban-oriented international migrations require a great deal of time and patient data-gathering skills, and while there are only a few such studies, they are valuable for the unusually wide perspectives they offer. See, for example, Bernard Wong, "A Comparative Study of the Assimilation of the Chinese in New York City and Lima, Peru," *Comparative Studies in Society and History* 20 (July 1978): 335–58; Carl Solberg, "Immigration and Urban Social Problems in Argentina and Chile, 1890–1914," *Hispanic American Historical Review* 49 (May 1969): 215–32; Herbert S. Klein, "The Integration of Italian Immigrants into the United States and Argentina: A Comparative Analysis," *American Historical Review* 88 (June 1983): 306–29; and Samuel L. Baily, "The Adjustment of Italian Immigrants in Buenos Aires and New York, 1870–1914," *American Historical Review* 88 (April 1983): 281–305.

Single-country research on immigrants in Latin America centers around the metropolitan areas of Argentina, Brazil, and Chile, where the largest numbers of Europeans went to settle during the age of mass immigration (circa 1880–1920). How does the process of creating an immigrant enclave in a Latin American city begin? This is the subject of Fernando J. Devoto, "The Origins of an Italian Neighborhood in Buenos Aires in the Mid-XIX Century," *Journal of European Economic History* 18 (Spring 1989): 37–64. The entrepreneurial model of immigrants' socialization is explored in Gerald M. Greenfield, "Privatism and Urban Development in Latin America: The Case of São Paulo, Brazil," *Journal of Urban History* 8 (August 1982): 397–426. Argentina, which contains the largest concentrations of European immigrants in Latin America, has received most of the attention of scholars. Ronald C. Newton, *German*

Buenos Aires, 1900–1933: Social Change and Cultural Crisis (Austin: University of Texas Press, 1977), explores the quiet development of an important group of European medium-sized and large-scale businesses. Another sophisticated study that focuses on a single immigrant group is Eugene F. Sofer, *From Pale to Pampa: A Social History of the Jews of Buenos Aires* (New York: Holmes & Meier, 1982). Immigrants settled in significant numbers in other urban centers, away from the capital city. The Argentine interior is the geographic venue for two important studies: Mark D. Szuchman, *Mobility and Integration in Urban Argentina: Córdoba in the Liberal Era* (Austin: University of Texas Press, 1980); and James R. Scobie, *Secondary Cities of Argentina: The Social History of Corrientes, Salta, and Mendoza, 1850–1910* (Stanford: Stanford University Press, 1988). The interior city of Rosario, Argentina, is the thrust of Michael Johns, "The Urbanisation of a Secondary City: The Case of Rosario, Argentina, 1870–1920," *Journal of Latin American Studies* 23 (October 1991): 489–514. Intranational comparisons of immigrant groups are not frequently found; one such study, comparing the immigrant experiences in the cities of Buenos Aires and Córdoba, is Eugene F. Sofer and Mark D. Szuchman, "Educating Immigrants: Voluntary Associations in the Acculturation Process," in *Educational Alternatives in Latin America: Social Change and Social Stratification*, ed. Thomas La Belle (Los Angeles: University of California Press, 1975), 334–59. Warren Dean, *The Industrialization of São Paulo, 1880–1945* (Austin: University of Texas Press, 1969), contains much material on the immigrants' role in the economic development of Brazil's largest city.

The economic, sociological, and psychological effects on migrants and cities became important subjects of interest early in the twentieth century among social critics who worried about the erosion of traditions and changes in culture as cities swelled with new entrants. These studies were characterized by a strong undercurrent of Social Darwinism prevalent in the "scientific" writings of the period. A prominent example was Agustín Alvarez's *South America: Ensayo de psicología política*, which was published in Buenos Aires by Editorial "La Cultura Argentina" in 1918 and raised concerns by linking the "antisocial" behavior of some immigrant groups with political instability. Modern social scientists, by contrast, evaluate the dynamic and effects on both the city and the migrant in very sophisticated and informative ways. Among these recent studies readers are guided to the following titles: Naomar de Almeida Filho, "The Psychosocial Costs of Development: Labor, Migration, and Stress in Bahia, Brazil," *Latin American Research Review* 17, no. 3 (1982): 91–118; Dennis Conway and Juanita Brown, "Intraurban Relocation and Structure: Low-Income Migrants in Latin America and the Caribbean,"

Latin American Research Review 15, no. 3 (1980): 95–125; Susan Lobo, *A House of My Own: Social Organization in the Squatter Settlements of Lima* (Tucson: University of Arizona Press, 1982); Larissa Lomnitz, "Horizontal and Vertical Relations and the Social Structure of Urban Mexico," *Latin American Research Review* 17, no. 2 (1982): 51–74; Philip Musgrove and Robert Ferber, "Identifying the Urban Poor: Characteristics of Poverty Households in Bogotá, Medellín, and Lima," *Latin American Research Review* 14, no. 2 (1979): 25–53; Alejandro Portes, "Housing Policy, Urban Poverty, and the State: The *Favelas* of Rio de Janeiro," *Latin American Research Review* 14, no. 2 (1979): 3–24, and "Latin American Urbanization during the Years of the Crisis," *Latin American Research Review* 24, no. 3 (Summer 1989): 7–38; and Henry A. Selby, Arthur D. Murphy, and Stephen A. Lorenzen, *The Mexican Urban Household: Organizing for Self-Defense* (Austin: University of Texas Press, 1990).

Family and Gender Relations

Research into the dynamics of families and family-making in Latin America opens up a wide area in which to examine social and economic relations in urban settings. In addition, the role of the family in cities offers unique opportunities to look into gender relations and women's history in an environment that both offered and hindered opportunities for different groups. Marriage and gender relations in colonial Mexico are examined in Patricia Seed, *To Love, Honor, and Obey in Colonial Mexico: Conflicts over Marriage Choice, 1574–1821* (Stanford: Stanford University Press, 1988); for nineteenth-century Mexico City, see Silvia M. Arrom, "Marriage Patterns in Mexico City, 1811," *Journal of Family History* 3 (Winter 1978): 376–91, and, on a larger scale, *The Women of Mexico City, 1790–1857* (Stanford: Stanford University Press, 1985). Samuel Baily studied marriage selection strategies in "Marriage Patterns and Immigrant Assimilation in Buenos Aires, 1882–1923," *Hispanic American Historical Review* 60 (February 1980): 32–48. A rare glimpse into the seventeenth-century family is provided by Thomas Calvo, "The Warmth of the Hearth: Seventeenth-Century Guadalajara Families," in *Sexuality and Marriage in Colonial Latin America*, ed. Asunción Lavrin (Lincoln: University of Nebraska Press, 1989), 287–312; for the nineteenth-century, see John E. Kicza, "The Role of the Family in Economic Development in Nineteenth-Century Latin America," *Journal of Family History* 10 (Fall 1985): 235–46. The relationship of household composition to the nature of production is explored in Elizabeth A. Kuznesof, "Household Composition and Headship as Related to Changes in Mode of Production: São Paulo, 1765 to 1836," *Comparative Studies in Society and His-*

tory 22 (January 1980): 78–108. The importance of racial characteristics in the calculations behind partners is featured in Robert McCaa, "*Calidad, Clase*, and Marriage in Colonial Mexico: The Case of Parral, 1788–1790," *Hispanic American Historical Review* 64 (August 1984): 477–502. The role of the authorities in the sometimes-stormy relations between husbands and wives is the focus of Kristin Ruggiero, "Wives on 'Deposit': Internment and the Preservation of Husbands' Honor in Late Nineteenth-Century Buenos Aires," *Journal of Family History* 17, no. 3 (1992): 253–70. The function of marriage in the socialization process of urban migrants is examined by Mark D. Szuchman, "The Limits of the Melting Pot in Urban Argentina: Marriage and Integration in Córdoba, 1869–1909," *Hispanic American Historical Review* 57 (February 1977): 24–50, while the intersection of national politics and urban households is explored in his "Household Structure and Political Crisis: Buenos Aires, 1810–1860," *Latin American Research Review* 21, no. 3 (1986): 55–93.

Social Control and Resistance

The history of social control is advanced by much recent work. The literature encompasses different elements of elites' thorniest problem—the maintenance of power on their own terms. Forms of dominance and strategies of resistance join together in multiple combinations in a diverse array of works. For a recent study of how some of these elements combine within the realm of criminal justice in Brazil, see Thomas H. Holloway, *Policing Rio de Janeiro: Repression and Resistance in a Nineteenth-Century City* (Stanford: Stanford University Press, 1993). Policing and criminality are also the subjects of Julia Kirk Blackwelder, "Urbanization, Crime, and Policing: Buenos Aires, 1880–1914," in *The Problem of Order in Changing Societies: Essays on Crime and Policing in Argentina and Uruguay, 1750–1940*, ed. Lyman L. Johnson (Albuquerque: University of New Mexico Press, 1990), 65–88. Johnson's collection of essays contains other titles of interest for urban historians, including Donna Guy, "Prostitution and Female Criminality in Buenos Aires, 1875–1937," 89–116. For matters of policing and criminal justice in nineteenth-century Mexico, see Pedro Santoni, "A Fear of the People: The Civic Militia of Mexico in 1845," *Hispanic American Historical Review* 68 (May 1988): 269–88. The concern for order and the role of police and the judicial system represent the focus of Mark D. Szuchman, "Disorder and Social Control in Buenos Aires, 1810–1860," *Journal of Interdisciplinary History* 15 (Summer 1984): 83–110. Finally, for an analysis of modern authoritarian control of the city, see Lauren Benton, "Reshaping the

Urban Core: The Politics of Housing in Authoritarian Uruguay," *Latin American Research Review* 21, no. 2 (1986): 33–52.
Social disturbances and riots are examined in several recent works. Riots in nineteenth-century Mexico City are analyzed in Silvia Arrom, "Popular Politics in Mexico City: The Parian Riot, 1828," *Hispanic American Historical Review* 68 (May 1988): 245–68. For a view of urban riots in Brazil, see Teresa Meade, " 'Living Worse and Costing More': Resistance and Riot in Rio de Janeiro, 1890–1917," *Journal of Latin American Studies* 21 (May 1989): 241–66, and Jeffrey D. Needell, "The Revolta contra Vacina of 1904: The Revolt against Modernization in Belle-Epoque Rio de Janeiro," *Hispanic American Historical Review* 67 (May 1987): 233–69. For turn-of-the-century Mexico, see Allen Wells and Gilbert M. Joseph, "Clientelism and the Political Baptism of Yucatán's Working Classes, 1880–1929," in *Political Culture in Mexico*, ed. Wil Pansters (forthcoming). Civil disorder in Colombia is not a product of the twentieth century, as can be seen in David Sowell, "The 1893 Bogotazo: Artisans and Public Violence in Late Nineteenth-Century Bogotá," *Journal of Latin American Studies* 21 (May 1989): 267–82.

Labor

The history of labor has had a prominent role in the scholarship of Latin American cities. Labor history represents part of the recent analyses of social control processes, an important component of social history. Among the more prominent titles, readers should consider Peter DeShazo, *Urban Workers and Labor Unions in Chile, 1902–1927* (Madison: University of Wisconsin Press, 1983); Kenneth P. Erickson, Patrick V. Peppe, and Hobart A. Spalding, Jr., "Research on the Urban Working Class and Organized Labor in Argentina, Brazil, and Chile: What Is Left to Be Done?" *Latin American Research Review* 9 (Summer 1974): 115–42; Emilia Viotti da Costa, "Structures versus Experience: New Tendencies in the History of Labor and the Working Class in Latin America—What Do We Gain? What Do We Lose?" *International Labor and Working Class History* 36 (Fall 1989): 3–24; John D. French and Mary Lynn Pederson, "Women and Working-Class Mobilization in Postwar São Paulo, 1945–1948," *Latin American Research Review* 24, no. 3 (1989): 99–126; and Deborah Levenson-Estrado, *Trade Unionists against Terror: Guatemala City, 1954–1985* (Chapel Hill: University of North Carolina Press, 1994). Racial considerations in the control of specific groups of urban artisans are analyzed in Lyman L. Johnson, "The Racial Limits of Guild Solidarity: An Example from Colonial Buenos Aires," *Revista de Historia de América* 99 (January-June 1985): 7–26. The role of urban workers in revolution is explored within the Mexican setting in Rodney Anderson, *Outcasts in Their Own Land: Mexican Industrial Workers, 1906–1911* (DeKalb: Northern Illinois Press, 1976); Alan Knight, "The Working Class and the Mexican Revolution, c. 1900–1920," *Journal of Latin American Studies* 16, no. 1 (1984): 51–79; and John Hart, *Anarchism and the Mexican Working Class, 1860–1931*, rev. ed. (Austin: University of Texas Press, 1987). For Allende's Chile, see Peter Winn, *Weavers of Revolution: The Yarur Workers and Chile's Road to Socialism* (New York: Oxford University Press, 1986). Comparative analyses of labor, especially within the urban domain, appear in Hobart A. Spalding, Jr., *Organized Labor in Latin America: Historical Case Studies of Workers in Dependent Societies* (New York: New York University Press, 1977), and, more recently, in Charles A. Bergquist, *Labor in Latin America: Comparative Essays on Chile, Argentina, Venezuela, and Colombia* (Stanford: Stanford University Press, 1986). Two important recent titles that address one of Latin America's most important labor movements, based largely in Argentine urban industrial settings, are Daniel James, *Resistance and Integration: Peronism and the Argentine Working Class, 1946–1976* (New York: Cambridge University Press, 1988); and James P. Brennan, *The Labor Wars in Córdoba, 1955–1976: Ideology, Work, and Labor Politics in an Argentine Industrial City* (Cambridge: Harvard University Press, 1994).

About the Editors

GILBERT M. JOSEPH is professor of history and the director of Latin American Studies at Yale University, where he received his doctoral training. A specialist in Mexican history, comparative social movements, and foreign involvement in Latin America, he is the author of *Revolution from Without: Yucatán, Mexico, and the United States, 1880–1924* (1982, rev. paperback, 1988); *Rediscovering the Past at Mexico's Periphery* (1986); and *Summer of Discontent, Seasons of Upheaval: Elite Politics and Rural Insurgency in Yucatán, 1876–1915* (with Allen Wells, forthcoming). In addition, he has coedited three collections, *Yucatán y la International Harvester* (with Allen Wells, 1986); *Land, Labor, and Capital in Modern Yucatán: Essays in Regional History and Political Economy* (with Jeffery Brannon, 1991); and *Everyday Forms of State Formation: Revolution and the Negotiation of Rule in Modern Mexico* (with Daniel Nugent, 1994); and he has published a variety of articles on export monoculture, rural crime, and peasant protest.

MARK D. SZUCHMAN is professor of history at Florida International University and managing editor of the *Hispanic American Historical Review*. He received his doctorate at The University of Texas at Austin and is a specialist on the social history of Argentina, the urban history of Latin America, and family history. His books include *Mobility and Integration in Urban Argentina: Córdoba in the Liberal Era* (1980); *Order, Family, and Community in Buenos Aires, 1810–1860* (1988); *The Middle Period in Latin American History: Beliefs and Attitudes, 17th–19th Centuries* (1989); and *Revolution and Restoration: The Rearrangement of Power in Argentina, 1776–1860* (with Jonathan C. Brown, 1994). In his articles, Professor Szuchman has analyzed the social conditions among internal and international migrants to Argentine cities in the nineteenth century, the relationships between nation-building and family structures, and the nature of shifting mentalities in Latin America's past.